The Life You Imagine

Derek Jeter

The Life You Imagine

Life Lessons for Achieving Your Dreams

with Jack Curry

Three Rivers Press • New York

The following photographs appear with permission: pages 134 and 223, Al Tielemans/ *Sports Illustrated.* All other photographs from the author's family collection.

Copyright © 2000 by Turn 2, Inc.

Published by Three Rivers Press, New York, New York. Member of the Crown Publishing Group.

Random House, Inc. New York, Toronto, London, Sydney, Auckland
www.randomhouse.com

THREE RIVERS PRESS is a registered trademark and the Three Rivers Press colophon is a trademark of Random House, Inc.

Originally published in hardcover by Crown Publishers in 2000.

Printed in the United States of America

Design by Cynthia Dunne

Library of Congress Cataloging-in-Publication Data
Jeter, Derek, 1974–
        The life you imagine: life lessons for achieving your dreams / by Derek Jeter.—
1st ed.   1. Jeter, Derek, 1974–.   2. Baseball players—United States—Biography.
3. New York Yankees (Baseball team).   I. Title.

ISBN 0-609-80718-8

10 9 8 7 6 5 4 3 2 1

First Paperback Edition

To my parents, who gave me the best of both worlds.
To my sister, whose complete honesty helps to keep me grounded.
To my grandmother, for taking me to my first Yankee game and much more.
To my friends, who have supported me.

In remembrance
To Grandfather Connors, who taught me the value of hard work.
To Grandmother Jeter, who through my father taught us the meaning of family.
—Derek Jeter

For Pamela, you are my inspiration and my infatuation.
For Mom and Dad, you are still with me every day.
—Jack Curry

Acknowledgments

This book would not have been possible without the assistance of several people:

I want to thank my father and my agent, Casey Close, for encouraging me to share some of my early life lessons that will be beneficial to children and young adults.

I want to thank Jack Curry, for helping me organize my words to share my lessons in a creative manner.

To my coaches, teammates, teachers, friends, and family, who took the time to participate in this project—thank you.

And thanks to my editor, Kristin Kiser, for her patience and guidance.

—Derek Jeter

I want to thank Pamela, my wife, for helping guide me through this project, as she does through my life; Rob, my brother, for introducing me to baseball and reading every word I write; Faith Hamlin, my agent, for a soothing, reassuring voice when progress came slowly; Kristin Kiser, the book's editor, for a blend of enthusiasm and realism; Mrs. O. and the rest of my family, for listening and caring; Ian, Kyle, and Shane, my nephews, for always making me smile, even on deadline.

I also want to thank the *New York Times* for granting me the opportunity to work on this book. Neil Amdur, Buster Olney, Bill Brink, Carl Nelson, Jay Schreiber, and Fred Bierman offered advice or assistance. And, finally, thanks to Derek and Mr. and Mrs. Jeter, for their class and cooperation.

—Jack Curry

Contents

Introduction

 had on a new, gray World Series T-shirt and a new, tan World Series cap and both were soaked as I tried wriggling through the tangle of sweaty bodies in our champagne-drenched clubhouse after the Yankees won another Championship in October of 1999. It was our second title in a row and our third in four years. Man, that night I felt like I was living in baseball nirvana. I didn't want that moment to end. I would have been content sleeping in our clubhouse.

It was steamy and crowded and loud, sort of like being in the sauna while waiting for the D train during rush hour. I couldn't dodge my teammates without getting doused with more champagne, more beer, and more hugs. Our lockers were encased with sheets of plastic to protect our street clothes from getting totally saturated. We should have wrapped ourselves in plastic, too. There were probably 200 reporters and dozens of photographers and TV camera operators moving around the clubhouse, so trudging even 30 feet without getting jostled took a lot of time and a lot of determination.

But I had the time and the determination because I was on a mission. I finally made it around the maze of bodies and bottles to the black clubhouse door, poked my head through it, and heard dozens of people hollering. They reached out for me and they hollered some more. I might have shaken some hands or slapped some high-fives—I don't remember. I know I was focused on something else. I looked left, I looked right, and then I saw them. I spotted my beaming parents patiently waiting with the other families and friends of players in the chilly hallway, minutes after their son had helped the Yankees win another World Series.

Everything was a blur and I'm not sure how I got to them, but I must have climbed over a few people and nudged aside a few others. My parents' eyes were moist when I reached them, still clutching a bottle of champagne. We never said anything about what had happened against the Atlanta Braves in Game 4 that night because we didn't have to. I didn't need to remind them about my childhood dream at that moment. We squeezed each other, knowing what this amazing journey meant for us, acknowledging where it had all started, without saying a word. Our hugs were real tight. They spoke for us.

I felt really lucky that night and I feel really lucky to be where I am today. I get to play the game I love in the most incredible city in the world. I'm young, I'm healthy, I have a terrific family, and I feel blessed that the Yankees have such great fans. New York is a great place to play baseball, maybe the best, and when I walk around Manhattan or get to the stadium in the Bronx I feel the amazing energy of this city.

I never thought about fans or endorsement deals or anything else like that when I dreamed of being a major leaguer as a kid. When I dreamed, it was only about playing on the field. The game-winning hits, the diving plays, the winning. That's what mattered to me then and that's still what matters to me the most today. I love to play and I love to win. The other niceties that

I wouldn't be a Yankee today if it weren't for the guidance I received from my parents. Here they are with me at age 11—you can't miss the Yankees cap!

come with being a Yankee are special, but they're window dressing compared to playing and winning. That's what my life is about and what I want it to be about. This is the life I've always imagined.

I'm not going to boast about being the shortstop on a team that has won three of the last four World Series Championships, but it does feel good. I'm not going to tell you that as a 26-year-old multimillionaire who still has all of his hair, all of his teeth, and can get dates I have a perfect life, but it's good. I'm not going to tell you that you should want to be like me, because everyone should want to be their own person, but I assure you that it's fun to be me.

What I do want to tell you is that I'm proud of where I am and how I got to this stage in my life, and I think there's a way for everyone to benefit from all that I have experienced while making it to my dream. I'm proud of the guidance my parents gave me in helping me determine the best ways to methodically move closer and closer to my dream, and I'm proud of how I've worked to reach that dream and to maintain it. For me, the dream of being a baseball player is a daily challenge—not only living that dream but ensuring that it stays alive.

Now my dream might not coincide with your dreams. You may dream about being a detective, a teacher, or the president of the United States. But I think what I've learned along the way to becoming shortstop for the Yankees are things that can be applied to achieving any goal. We're not just talking baseball here—we're talking about life, about realizing goals, and about living dreams, no matter what they are.

A lot of people have wondered about how I have achieved my goals. Did I have a game plan while I was growing up? The answer is yes and no. I've thought a lot about this and realized there were 10 guiding principles, 10 lessons that helped get me to where I am today. Of course I didn't realize while growing up that I was following these 10 lessons. I came up with the idea of these steps later in life. But though I wasn't conscious that I was following any master plan, I did take my direction from my parents, who really gave me guidance on how to live my life. I didn't have the luxury of having these steps all spelled out for me in the way I'm presenting them to you. My parents are pretty organized but they weren't *that* organized with me when I was growing up! But in reviewing my journey I talked to them and to my sister Sharlee, and what you'll read in this book are the principles we came up with.

I thought it was important to share my setbacks and successes because I've always wanted to help kids, even when I was still a kid. Not everyone is lucky enough to have parents or other people in their lives like I do, people who really worked hard with me to help me achieve my dreams. Everyone needs a little encouragement. I hope my story will help inspire you to chase your dreams. You know, I wasn't supposed to reach my dream of being a baseball player. If I had listened to all those people who muttered, "Good luck, kid," when they heard me say when I was young that I wanted to be a Yankee, I would have given up long ago.

Most people thought I really was foolishly dreaming to think that I could be a major leaguer, but my parents didn't. They encouraged me and that meant so much. I have to discuss my parents when I talk about my dream because there wouldn't be even one of these 10 steps if it weren't for them. Some people have love-hate relationships with their parents, some people don't want their parents to give them advice, and some people just don't like talking about their parents. Fortunately for me, I'm not one of those people.

I could talk about my parents for a year and still not be able to thank them enough for helping me fulfill my dreams. When I describe where I've been and how I've gotten to where I am today with the Yankees, I have to include a ton of information about my parents because they are as much a part of my story as I am. I always know where they're sitting at games and I always wink or nod to them because their guidance is the reason I'm even on the field.

My parents never read parenting books, and I never planned to write a book that discussed how they raised me, but I think the messages and the ideas that worked for me can work for anyone who is dedicated enough to set his or her goals and pursue them. Success is not about being lucky. There is a process that gets you from point A to point B in life, and you're never too young or too old to utilize some of the theories my parents used with me to pursue your dreams, regardless of what your goals are in life. The lessons I talk about here transcend baseball. These steps are about life and getting what you want in life, not simply about being a baseball player. Right now, I've got what I always wanted, and part of the reason why is because I had a plan for getting here.

I always wanted this to happen—every at bat, every inning, every amazing experience that I've had so far. I always wanted to play baseball in the major leagues, and I prayed that the Yankees would be the team that drafted me. I wanted to make it to the majors, win World Series Championships, and wake up every morning knowing that I loved my job. I wanted my office to be Yankee Stadium.

Have you ever wished so desperately for something that when it finally became reality instead of just another wish, you wondered if someone was bound to wake you up? As much as I chased this dream, that's how I feel about being a Yankee. This has been my dream job since I first pulled on a little pinstriped uniform and tiny cap two decades ago. I guess I never really took that uniform off. In some ways, I never woke up, and I know I don't want to. Give me another 10 or 15 years with this script. Let me continue being Derek Jeter of the Yankees and I'll be enthralled.

I was born in Pequannock, New Jersey. I lived in West Milford, New Jersey, until my family moved to Kalamazoo, Michigan, when I was four, and I spent the summers back in New Jersey with my grandparents until I was 13. So I was always close to the Yankees. From the time I was six years old and my grandmother first brought me to see the Yankees play in a place that looked bigger than anything I had ever seen, playing for the Yankees is something that I've thought about every day of my life. I'm serious. I can't remember a day where I didn't stop, allow my mind to drift during English class or while I was washing the dishes or flipping a tennis ball off my bedroom wall, and ponder what it would be like to play for the Yankees.

I was so obsessed with being a Yankee that I predicted it in my eighth-grade yearbook from St. Augustine's Elementary School. The cover is frayed and dirty now, but it has a cartoonish picture

Though it's a little hard to read our signatures on the cover of this yearbook from my elementary school, you can make out mine on the right. Doug Biro, one of my best buddies, signed at the bottom of the cover.

of our school and "Class of '88" on it. My signature is on the right-hand side of the autographed cover, along with the signatures of about three dozen other students. We wrote about a fictitious 10-year reunion, and the story includes these lines: "Derek Jeter, a professional ballplayer for the Yankees, is coming around. You've seen him in grocery stores, on the Wheaties boxes, of course." Actually, I guess this prediction is slightly incorrect, because my face is on my own box of cereal, called Jeter's. Seriously, I'm glad I have written proof for any cynics who don't believe I've longed to be a Yankee for as long as I've been able to dream.

I made it. I worked for years to make all of this happen, and I still feel tingly when I arrive at the stadium each day. There is no better place to be and no better place for me to play. There is an aura surrounding the stadium as it sits like a palace on 161st Street and River Avenue in the Bronx. I park my car across the street, look up and see YANKEE STADIUM in bold, blue letters, and I realize I'm home. I'm where I always hoped to be, doing exactly what I wanted to do.

When I get to the park four hours before a game, there are often hundreds of devoted fans waiting behind steel barricades for autographs, regardless of whether it's 90 degrees or 40 degrees. On some days I sign autographs, because I respect the passion of someone who would come to a game four hours before the first pitch. But there are some days where I'm in a hurry and I only have time to wave hello. Then I walk underneath the stadium, where the 77-year-old walls are blue and where a blue line directs visitors to the Yankee clubhouse. That white line became my yellow brick road. It still is.

I don't have a desk. I have a locker. I don't have a secretary. I don't have a staff. I've got 24 teammates. I don't wear a tie. I wear the most famous uniform in all of sports. I'm never tense before games. I've had friends ask me what I think about before World Series games. They're really careful as they ask it, not wanting to interrupt me or jinx me if they think I don't like to talk about my preparation. I know I disappoint their curiosity when I casually say, "I'm thinking about where I'm going to go for lunch." That's my short-term goal. My other short-term goal is to help the Yankees win our next game.

I think I have the best job in the world. I tell people that all the time, and I know I'm not the only Yankee who's ever felt that way because I've heard it and seen it from so many others. In the turf-covered runway that leads from our clubhouse to our first-base dugout, there is a blue metal sign hanging down from the ceiling with a famous quote from the Yankee Clipper, Joe

DiMaggio. It reads, "I want to thank the Good Lord for making me a Yankee," which is what Joe D. said on Joe DiMaggio Day on October 1, 1949, at the stadium.

A half hour before the game, I cruise down the runway to the dugout and always reach up and touch the white letters on that sign with my glove or with my hand. I guess I do it as a superstition, but also because I agree with those sentiments.

I never got the chance to have a lengthy conversation with Mr. DiMaggio before he passed away in 1999, which is something I regret. Mr. DiMaggio was an elegant man, and whenever he was around the stadium for Old Timers' Day or to toss out the first pitch, you took one peek at him and knew he wanted to be left alone. I respected that. I love that quote because it sums up how I feel, too. I say a prayer after the National Anthem, thanking God, too, and asking that we play to the best of our abilities and that no one gets hurt. Occasionally, if it's a critical game or we've lost a few in a row, I might lobby for a win. I know I probably shouldn't do that, but everyone prays for extra help once in a while.

Standing at shortstop and knowing that I am the shortstop for the Yankees is awesome. Someone once told my Dad that he is the only father in the world whose son is the starting shortstop for the Yankees. We know that, but when it was phrased that way, it resonated with us. The only father whose son starts at shortstop for the Yankees. In the world. That's pretty sweet.

I love digging my spikes into the brown clay, I love how the lights frame the field, and I even love the smell of hot dogs and hot pretzels that wafts down to us. Then there are the creative fans, who are the loudest I've ever heard and who make us feel special during every game. The raucous fans in the right-field bleachers began doing a roll call a couple of years ago in which they chant the names of the starting players in the first inning. They'll keep chanting your name until you wave toward them in right field. Do you know how cool it is to have thousands of people chanting, "Der-ek, Je-ter, Der-ek, Je-ter," over and over? It's too cool, man. Sometimes I feel like milking those chants a few extra seconds. If one of us doesn't wave, they'll keep chanting until we do.

Most of my life was spent working toward that elusive goal of becoming a major leaguer and most of my life now is spent keeping me here at a high level. My goal is simple: to keep getting better. I never begged anyone to believe that I could do this, other than my parents. I never cared if people told me that someone from Kalamazoo who weighed 156 pounds as a high school senior couldn't make it to the big time. That never mattered to me. In fact, it motivated me to hear the doubters. Tell me I can't do something and I'll work even harder to prove you wrong.

I dislike doubters and I dislike negative people. You know the kind I'm talking about. Every word they utter is about what someone can't do. What I cared about while I was growing up was doing everything I possibly could to develop myself into the best person and best baseball player I could be, and then I hoped and prayed that would be good enough to get me to the majors. I'm a positive person. I like to chase my dreams, and I advise everyone else to do the same. I didn't have total tunnel vision about baseball because I also cared about academics, and I would have considered attending medical school if baseball hadn't worked out.

Actually, my parents implored me to do well in athletics, in academics, in everything. Still, baseball drove me. It pushed me. I'm in my fifth full season with the Yankees and we're gunning for a fourth World Series ring, and baseball still does that to me. I work out 50 weeks a year because I want to keep getting better. Someone told me recently that only five players in major-league history had more hits in their first four full seasons than the 795 I had accumulated. They are Earle Combs, Joe Jackson, Paul

Waner, Ducky Medwick, and Harvey Kuenn. That's a flattering statistic, and it's unbelievable to think I have more hits at this point in my career than Pete Rose, Babe Ruth, Stan Musial, Hank Aaron, and Willie Mays, but it's not something I'll dwell on. It's only four years. It's not an entire career. I want us to continue winning, so I don't get excited about what I've already done. I focus on what I still want to do. No reason to reflect right now.

That attitude and that arrogance come from the inside. I think you have to have it to make it this far. You have to feel like you're the best player on the field, the player that thousands of people will stare at all game. They'll watch how you wiggle the bat high above your shoulders at the plate, how you position yourself with two strikes on a batter, how you're the first teammate to greet a player after a homer. Whenever someone tells my father how humble I seem, he'll chuckle and reveal a secret. He will tell them that I have more inner arrogance than anyone he has ever met. I believe I'm going to get a hit every time up and I'll let that arrogance drip through in my performance, not in what I say.

I believe you have to feel that way, but you don't have to flaunt your abilities. There's a difference between having a swagger and being so full of yourself that you're annoying to be around because every word out of your mouth is about how great you are. I don't like to talk much about myself, unless I'm answering questions to help someone, and I've got no use for players who talk about themselves all the time. If something I'll say can help kids, I'll talk forever. That's what this book is all about. Just don't ask me to elaborate too much on how good I might have been in a game, a series, or even a season. I'll leave that for fans, sportswriters, and my parents to say. Actually, my parents are also adept at keeping me grounded.

My father is a thoughtful man, with short black hair and a neat black beard surrounding his owlish face. He is a social worker with a Master's of Social Work and a doctorate from Western Michigan University, and his soothing voice reveals traces of his Alabama roots. My mother is feistier than my father (probably because she grew up in more bustling northern New Jersey), and her light brown hair frames soft, happy features. An accounting services manager, she has a bubbly smile and small, expressive eyes that bulge if she gets excited. Oh, by the way, my father is black and my mother is white, a biracial coupling that is a lot more interesting to other people, from the stares we used to get to the questions we still get, than it is to us. So you can add gutsy to the list of adjectives that describe my mom and dad—gutsy to make sure their love conquered all, including bouts with bigotry.

Without my parents, I probably wouldn't have written this book, because I probably wouldn't be playing in the majors. My mother and father are an amazing couple. Generous, intelligent, caring, supportive, proud, demanding, Charles and Dorothy Jeter are the two most incredible people I know. Obviously, I'm biased. But I can't recall ever witnessing a set of parents who have been more devoted and more supportive to their two children than my mom and dad have been to me and my sister, Sharlee. They wanted us to have options. They wanted us to have goals. No goals were considered outlandish. Everything was attainable. When you're only a kid and your parents make you feel that way about yourself, you can dream about doing anything. I hope reading this book will also convince *you* that you can accomplish anything.

The Life You Imagine

Set Your Goals High

I was about eight years old as I walked along our thick carpet, past the pictures of my grandparents on the hallway walls and into my parents' bedroom. I announced that I was going to play for the Yankees. They were already in their pajamas, but they patiently listened to what their skinny son with the wavy brown hair and green eyes had said, and then told me the type of thing I was aching to hear. They told me that I could do anything I wanted in life if I worked hard enough and stayed dedicated to it, which was like offering me season tickets. Forget about lounging in the box seats, because, in my mind, I was heading straight for the dugout. Before I was nine years old.

My parents could have gently put me off and told me to go to sleep that night, but instead were receptive to my dream and talked about what it would take to achieve such a difficult goal. They sat me on the edge of the bed and told me that if I was serious about being a professional baseball player, I had to realize I wouldn't just be competing against players from Kalamazoo or from Michigan, but against players from all over the world. Everyone in the Westwood Little League where I played wanted to be a major leaguer, my mother and father emphasized. The competition to be good enough to make it to the majors will be ferocious, they told me. But I didn't blink. I didn't focus on that right away. I had a dream and I was ecstatic, because they didn't say it couldn't be done—just that it would be tough to accomplish this goal.

I used to imitate announcers doing play-by-play, with me as the star, of course. "Deep to left," I'd bellow, "and that ball is gone! Jeter has done it again!" I probably weighed 70 pounds with two rolls of quarters in my pockets when I was eight, so the idea of me hitting a ball 420 feet someday was just a dream. When all of my questions about being a Yankee were exhausted that night, my parents told me it was time to go to sleep. I went

As a kid, I surrounded myself with anything from the Yankees. Here you can see how I hung a Yankees uniform and cap in my room for inspiration in seventh grade.

to bed, clinging to the blanket and to my dream. My dream remained with me, from the time I was eight until the time I was 18, and it stays with me now. It never left. It got stronger. It kept pushing me to get exactly where I am today.

I think we should all set goals in life and set them high. I did that, and my parents encouraged me to do it, which is one of the main reasons I am where I am today. I had a vision about playing baseball, and my parents used that positive vision to establish guidelines that would enable me to grow as a person while I pursued my dream. From setting high goals to dealing with growing pains, to surrounding myself with trustworthy friends, to understanding that the world can be an unfair place, to obeying and loving my parents, to thinking before I acted, I was learning about life while I was yearning to be a Yankee.

But it all starts with setting goals—we all need them. Whether your goal is to play for the Yankees or to win the pie-eating contest at summer camp, goals are what motivate us to do better. My ultimate dream was to play major-league baseball, but I had smaller goals along the way. No matter how elated I was on that night in my parents' bedroom, I wasn't going to be a major leaguer at the age of nine. I chased my dream through smaller goals. Making the Little League All-Star Team, starting on the high school varsity as a freshman, making all-district, making all-state, and so on, until I eventually wound up at shortstop for the Yankees. But, believe me, there were dozens, even hundreds, of small goals that led me to the point where I finally became a Yankee.

We all have to start somewhere. Think about it. What do you love to do? What are you good at? What is something you would like to do for the rest of your life? These are important and serious questions, questions that you might not feel like answering before you graduate from high school. Some people even get to college, or after, and still can't answer them. But you really should think about them as soon as possible, because when you find that interest, that goal that excites you like nothing else, you'll want to open your bedroom window and yell it to anyone with ears: Guess what I'm going to do with my life?

A feeling will envelop you and you'll treat that goal like it is the most important thing in the world, acting the same passionate way I used to act about baseball. No matter who asked me what I wanted to be when I grew up, I told them I was going to play baseball and I was going to play for the Yankees. I was so confident in my abilities and so consumed with my dream that I wanted to shout out my intentions.

If you don't set goals, you're not going to have dreams, either. The goals are the achievements along the way to get you to your dreams. Dreams don't just happen, and you're not going to make your pursuit easier by being lazy about it. The longer you wait to decide what you want to do, the more time you're wasting. It's up to you to want to do something so badly that your passion shows in your actions. Your actions, not your words, will do the shouting for you. People will see how devoted and prepared you are as the captain of the debate team, and they might say, "One day, that kid is going to be a great lawyer."

Once you've set goals and pondered what kind of dream you want those goals to lead to, it's extremely helpful to have someone who can support you. It might be your parents, a sibling, a teacher, or a friend, but we all need somebody who is going to be there to prop us up when things aren't going well and to keep us levelheaded when things are going very well. My parents provided this for me.

I think I could have told my parents that I wanted to be the first astronaut to play shortstop on the moon and they would have encouraged me to do that, too. My parents have always been supportive and available. I can't remember a sporting event or an academic meeting that at least one of them didn't attend. Most of the time, it was both of them.

They wanted to discuss tests before I took them, asking me questions to see if I was prepared. They treated parent-teacher meetings like sessions with the Internal Revenue Service, bringing evidence to support their opinions. They made me present oral reports to them the day before I was scheduled to read them in class. My knees still wobbled. They urged me to join different clubs, to shoot for first place with my science projects, to pick stable friends. After I injured my ankle as a freshman and a few other players also injured themselves because of our choppy field at Kalamazoo Central High School, my parents led a successful crusade to make improvements to our field. They were relentless about their involvement in their children's lives and in what we dreamed of doing with ourselves.

People thought I was crazy and I know they thought my parents were crazy for fostering this impossible dream for a kid from Kalamazoo. There were millions of kids who wanted to be professional athletes, and I'm sure there were millions of parents who wouldn't have urged them to do it. Why bother? You have no chance to do that. Pick a more sensible career. I know many parents who told their kids this or didn't say anything to their children about their goals. Some didn't know if their sons and daughters even had goals. That's even worse.

I really felt as though my parents thought I could do it. Whether they did or not at that time, I don't know. Looking back, I'm sure they had their doubts. I was skinny. I lived in a state that averaged about 70 inches of snow a year, which made it difficult to focus on baseball for more than a few months. If you wanted to really prepare for baseball in Kalamazoo, a lot of the work had to be done indoors. But I believed and I believed that they believed, and to me that was significant. The mental part of getting to this level is crucial and I'm not sure I would have been so optimistic if they hadn't encouraged me and helped lay the groundwork for me.

"Our feeling was to let you keep dreaming," my father later told me. "If you had two left feet and were uncoordinated, it would have been different. But we encouraged you. We made sure we looked at your interests and made sure that they jibed with what you said you wanted to do. We thought, if that is what you dreamed, why not?"

My parents were shrewd. They realized early on how I cared about baseball and they used my goal as motivation to keep me focused on academics. It didn't matter that I wanted to be a baseball player. If I had told my parents I wanted to be a doctor or a lawyer, they would have been just as supportive in guiding me to make the right decisions. They would have gotten me medical books or law books, instructed me about classes to take, and even told me to watch educational shows dealing with medicine or law. I quickly figured out what they were doing and I embraced it.

Being a baseball player is a positive goal, so my parents allowed me to chase after it while molding me in other areas. They told me that I couldn't just be a good baseball player. I had to work hard, take care of my body with proper diet and rest, and do well in everything. They told me that I had to have the mind-set that I wanted to be the best in everything. Don't just try to excel in baseball, they told me, try to excel in everything. Set your goals high.

I don't see how anyone can lose by setting his or her goals high. We all have to be realistic, of course. You can't climb one tree and decide you're ready to tackle Mount Everest. That would be idiotic. But you can and you should strive to do things that you've never done before. There are reasons why you haven't accom-

Dad always helped Sharlee and me set our goals, and then he worked with us to achieve them. It is never too early to set goals for yourself.

plished certain things in your life. But sometimes the reason is that you simply haven't tried them yet. By setting your goals high and trying to do what you've never done, you give yourself a cushion to fall back on if you don't make it. And if you do falter, you should try for that lofty goal again.

That was a natural approach for me, most of the time anyway. I had been so dominated by my father in checkers, pool, Scrabble, basketball, and anything else we did while I was growing up that I wanted to be the best at everything. I used to watch *The Price Is Right* with my father before I went to my afternoon kindergarten session as a five-year-old. If I guessed $400 for a basic toaster, he wouldn't say a word and would guess $20 and win. If I spelled out "gate" in Scrabble and felt proud, he would overwhelm me by stealing the word and coming up with "investigate." My father was soft yet stern as a dad, but he was tough when it was time to compete. No matter how young I was, he wanted me to be motivated to win legitimately, so that I could truly enjoy victories when they eventually came.

I knew my parents were serious about what I was doing so I knew I had to be serious, too. I saw Yankee Stadium every night, I saw myself in a pinstriped Yankee uniform every night, and I heard fans chanting my name every night. I know I'm one of around a billion kids who have envisioned themselves like this, have seen themselves playing for the same team as Babe Ruth, Lou Gehrig, Mickey Mantle, Joe DiMaggio, Yogi Berra, Whitey Ford, Reggie Jackson, Don Mattingly. And the list goes on and on. Walking into the stadium every day provides me with a history lesson because it's the same office that so many legendary players used.

Now I see kids wearing jerseys with my number 2 and JETER on the back and it makes me smile, like the first time I walked into the stadium. I know my father gets emotional whenever he talks about seeing a mother, a father, and a few kids all sporting Jeter jerseys. That really hits him because he thinks it makes a strong statement. Not only do the parents feel that I've behaved capably enough to be a role model for their kids, they're wearing the jerseys, too. My father likes seeing that because it means I'm more than a baseball player to them. He tells me it means that they approve of how I conduct myself off the field as well. I don't know if that's true with every fan wearing a Jeter jersey, but my dad thinks it is. Keeping those fans is another goal I've embraced.

Shoot for the Stars

You might not ever have to worry about fans, but you should be concerned with setting goals. All of my life, I have set lofty goals. One day when I was a freshman at Kalamazoo Central, I was sitting in our living room when I opened up *USA Today* and saw that they had picked Tyler Houston of Las Vegas, Nevada, as the High School Player of the Year. So I thought ahead three years. How great would it be to be the High School Player of the Year? To me, that was the biggest and best honor a high school player could get—so I made it a goal.

When was the last time you decided you wanted to be the best at something? It's an honor to be ranked in the top 10 in your class, but did you really try to be *first*? Or were you satisfied with being in the top 10? Striving to be the best is something that you should do all the time because, obviously, no one is going to do it for you. No one on my high school team could chase that Player of the Year goal for me. That was my goal, another small step toward the dream.

Tyler's picture in *USA Today* was made to look like a baseball card, and I was envious. I studied the paper and envisioned how I would look in my maroon-and-white uniform if there were a baseball card picture of me there in three years. I saved the paper and showed it to my mother. She nodded, admitted that it looked pretty nice. Then I told her that I planned to be the *USA Today* High School Player of the Year. I was 14 years old and looked 12 because of the twigs I had for arms and legs. But, responding as matter-of-factly as if I'd said I wanted another piece of chicken Parmesan, she told me that was an excellent goal.

That's one of the reasons I could have lofty goals. I knew that my parents would give me positive and honest feedback. I was lifting weights at high school with some other baseball players before my senior year and they were talking about how *USA Today* picks a Player of the Year. I had batted .557 with seven homers in my junior year and was already considered one of the finest high school players in the country. Now my goal was much more practical than when I had first mentioned it to my mother

Don't be fooled by me sitting at the piano at age 1—I have no talent in music. It's a good thing I can play baseball!

three years before, but I didn't say anything to my teammates between bench presses. I didn't want anyone to think that I was consumed with myself or that I was being egotistical. I'd received reassurance from my mother about my goal, so that was enough. I wound up winning it, too. And I still have that picture of myself.

When you set a grandiose goal like that and you accomplish it, you become a stronger, more confident person, and it fortifies how prescient you were to establish that goal. It's an effective approach, too. If I had just tried to be the best player in the state of Michigan that year, I would have shortchanged myself. If that had been my goal, who knows whether I would have won the *USA Today* award? That's why I think you should elevate those goals. Don't risk missing one because you never thought you could achieve it.

I think I stunned my mother even more two years later when I told her I planned to become the Minor League Player of the Year. This time she asked me if I was serious and if I really thought it was possible. I told her I thought so. We talked about how I would be competing against hundreds of minor leaguers and how the award was so subjective. I could have a superb season and the voters for the awards could like someone else. It wasn't like winning a batting title where you simply have to get the highest average. Still, I told my mom that because I loved to set my goals high. You have nothing to lose. She told me she'd help me by watching me and making sure I was doing everything I could to get there. If she thought I was slacking off, she'd call me on it.

I started the 1994 season at Class A Tampa in the Florida State League, but was quickly promoted to Class AA Albany and then to Class AAA Columbus. I combined to hit .344 with 5 homers, 68 runs batted in, and 50 stolen bases at three different levels in the organization. The Yankees, who had been very careful about promoting players through the system quickly, broke that routine with me. They kept challenging me and I kept succeeding, knocking aside goals as I moved from level to level.

Guess what? I was named the Minor League Player of the Year by *USA Today, Baseball America, The Sporting News,* and *Baseball Weekly,* which was more than I had been striving to achieve. I was hoping to be selected as Player of the Year by just one publication. If I hadn't won any of the awards, I wouldn't have been devastated. But since I did win several, it compelled me to continue to have massive goals.

Not everyone I've played with throughout my career is so dedicated—and that's too bad. I remember sitting in the clubhouse in the minor leagues and overhearing a teammate discussing how he was playing and saying, "I hope I can finish around .260." It was halfway through the season and this guy had already decided that he was trying to max out at .260. Why would you say that? Why would anyone be happy with .260? You might hit .260, but is that exactly where you *want* to be? What happens if you did hit .260? Shouldn't you have shot higher? Even worse, what happens if you fall short and hit .230? That would be awful.

The Bumpy Road to Success

I spent parts of four years in the minors before the Yankees recalled me for a brief stint in 1995, and then I became the starter in 1996. That four-year climb is something that a lot of people forget. I didn't just parachute in from Kalamazoo as an 18-year-old and reserve my spot at shortstop with George Steinbrenner as if I were making a reservation at a steakhouse. This has not always been a smooth ride, and while I felt and believed that I would make it to the Yankees, I never knew it for sure until I actually made it.

Some of what I experienced early in my career was humbling. Every major leaguer will tell you stories about the days when there were doubts. Almost everyone who makes it to the majors had grown up as the premier player in high school, but then things change in the pros. Then everyone else is an All-American, too.

Sometimes I wondered if I would ever make it. I batted .202 in my first minor-league season with the Class A Tampa Rookie League team in 1992. Imagine that? Two oh two? I was 18, all arms and legs, shaggy hair and a baby face, and I was pretty lost. Gary Denbo, my first minor-league manager, compared me to a new colt frantically trying to get its legs steady for the first time. I made 56 errors in my first full season at Class A Greensboro the next year. Fifty-six! Some of my teammates have teased me and told me I must have been trying to make 56 errors. I wasn't.

I *will* tell you this: I probably cried at least once about each error. Cried to my parents and cried myself to sleep. Man, that was difficult. But no one with the Yankees knew how much I was hurting. Only my parents. I don't like to show my emotions to anyone. Still don't. So I showed up at the park every day and stayed positive, hoping that I would eventually find my way. I must have done something right, because, despite making 56 errors, the South Atlantic League managers named me the Most Outstanding Prospect that season. I was told that Mantle had made 55 errors as a shortstop in his second minor-league year. Then I felt better, because Mantle is a Hall of Famer and one of the greatest Yankees ever. But, as dominating as Mickey was, they also shifted him from shortstop to center field. I didn't want that to happen to me, too.

We're all going to experience pitfalls when we try to reach our goals. We know that and we tell ourselves that, but it doesn't make it any easier to deal with when the setbacks occur. You have to try to learn from those experiences, though. What could you have done better? How can you improve yourself? What can you do to make sure this doesn't happen again? Ask yourself these

I have a lot to thank my parents for, but one of the most important things they did was make sure Sharlee and I would be friends. Here we are at ages 7 and 2.

George Steinbrenner

ON DEREK JETER

eorge Steinbrenner actually calls Derek Jeter a buddy. Steinbrenner has owned the Yankees since 1973 and has written paychecks for hundreds of players, but he rarely calls any of them buddies. Except Jeter, who has somehow figured out the tricky technique for how and when to tease the Boss.

"It's a buddy, buddy–type thing," Steinbrenner says. "You can have that. But, even in a buddy, buddy thing, there's a gray area. He understands there's a boss and there's a player. There's got to be respect and the respect is there."

Steinbrenner met Jeter after the Yankees drafted him in 1992 and watched him play in his first two minor-league seasons, but Steinbrenner most remembers Jeter soaring in 1994. That is when Steinbrenner's baseball advisers implored him to rush over to the University of South Florida to see the lanky kid named Jeter playing shortstop like he was already at Yankee Stadium.

So Steinbrenner attended several of Jeter's games in Tampa and noticed a player who was far superior to the other Class A players. Jeter was confident, smooth, and was no longer mired in the hitting and fielding slumps that plagued him for his first two years. Steinbrenner reminded himself how comfortable Jeter looked when the ultraconservative Yankees wound up elevating the shortstop from Class A to Class AA to Class AAA in a span of three months that summer.

questions and remain confident that in the end you will succeed. The path to your goal is not always going to be smooth. Obstacles will arise and problems will develop, but you have to remember what you're striving for and how you have to act to get

"I remember his composure. He moved swiftly through our system that year. I don't think we've had any other player go from Single A to Triple A in the same year. He just had that composure of a veteran then. Not a minor-league veteran, a major-league veteran."

When Jeter was only a 22-year-old rookie in 1996, Steinbrenner watched him handle being the shortstop on a team that would eventually grab the World Series Championship and boldly said, "There's not a better shortstop in the game today than Derek Jeter." It was probably a stretch to declare that four years ago, but Steinbrenner meant it and he still believes it today.

While Steinbrenner praised Alex Rodriguez, Nomar Garciaparra, and Jeter for forming the greatest threesome of shortstops that he has seen in almost 30 years in baseball, he still considers the player who has poured champagne on him twice and who calls him "Boss Man" as the best of a talented group.

"I don't know anyone I'd take ahead of him. He's as good as the others. If I had my choice of those three, I'd take Jeter."

Steinbrenner has heard how Jeter told his parents that he wanted to play shortstop for the Yankees when he was an eight-year-old and the owner admitted that Jeter's life has evolved like a fairy tale. But Steinbrenner asserted that Jeter, his buddy, worked diligently to achieve his goals and that work ethic is why his life can now seem so scripted.

"I can't think of any player who is more exceptional than Derek Jeter. All the things that you'd want a player to be, he is. He does it on the field and off the field. He uses his abilities and talents the right way."

there. Don't forget the big picture and don't let small mishaps or small failures stop you.

Michael Jordan was cut from his high school basketball team and came back to become one of the best basketball players of all time. You have to believe that you can rebound from setbacks. You shouldn't consider any setback so significant that you can't recover from it. If you fall into that trap, you're only hurting yourself. There wouldn't be any sneakers named after Michael if he had given up in high school.

One of the most rewarding parts of achieving any goal is in surmounting what you have to endure to get to that goal. If you spend a month working on an important school project, you should feel total satisfaction and relief when you are done. All of the problems that you encountered along the way, whether they are small setbacks like the library being closed when you needed a reference book or major setbacks like your little sister accidentally throwing away your notes for the project, slowly dissipate when the goal is met. That's an awesome feeling, and when it occurs nothing else matters. The goal has been reached. That's where you want to be.

Sometimes I think about what has happened to me and I shudder. I'm 26 years old and I have the dream job of all dream jobs. Who wouldn't want to play shortstop for the Yankees? Everyone from my father to Billy Crystal to Denzel Washington tells me how great this job is. I still feel weird when some of the people I'm fans of tell me they like me. I remember being in the on-deck circle at the stadium once and Jack Nicholson nodded to me. Come on . . . Jack Nicholson? I couldn't believe it.

The one thing I must admit about playing shortstop for the Yankees is that I've never been scared. I love playing games that really matter and I want to be out there when the games are the most important, when the calendar says October. To me, that's the reason we all play. Players always say that, but I really believe it. The Yankees have been in the postseason for the last five years, so I wouldn't know what to do if our season ended before

October. I just know that when we get there, whatever year it is, I won't be afraid of the challenge.

If you're frightened, you're probably going to prevent yourself from succeeding. It might not be today or tomorrow, but eventually a lack of confidence could keep you from doing something you're capable of doing. Don't act that way. Don't put yourself in a poor position before you even start pursuing a goal. If you prepare yourself, your dreams will be attainable. Conquer those fears with confidence.

World Series Dreams

I always tell people that if this is a dream, don't wake me. I don't know if people really believe me. I don't know if they think this is a cute line I've devised to answer questions about being successful, but I really do feel that way. I'm living in a dream world—playing baseball in New York, making millions of dollars to take care of my family and the next generations of Jeters, doing it on a team filled with players I admire, and doing it so well that I've garnered some fans. OK, I have many fans, and for that, I'm grateful. That was never one of my goals, but *keeping* the fans is.

Now, having the dream job is amazing enough, but I've also been on a team that has won three of the last four World Series. Some of the greatest players in history never played in a World Series. Ernie Banks, a Hall of Fame shortstop who clubbed 512 homers and who was a player my father adored, never made it. Don Mattingly, whom I watched in the 1995 postseason in the same way that a son watches a father, played 14 stellar years with the Yankees, and he never got a whiff of the World Series, either.

I wasn't officially on the roster when the Yankees played Seattle in the 1995 Division Series, but I traveled with the team as a learning experience and watched Donnie hit .417 in one of the most electrifying series in postseason history. If there were any purists who were against the Division Series, they disappeared after this series. The Mariners came back from a 2-0 hole, beat us in five games behind Randy Johnson, and sent everyone home. Donnie went home to Evansville, Indiana, for good and retired. You can learn a lot from doing nothing but watching. I know I did. I learned a lot by just watching how players like Mattingly and David Cone dealt with that loss. It made me hate losing even more.

We won the World Series the next year, something I think about whenever reporters ask me if I feel blessed. Sure I do. The Yankees made it to the World Series the year before Mattingly reached the major leagues and won it the year after he left. You know I feel blessed. I've gotten three chances to appear in the World Series and I think we can do it again in 2000. One of the silliest questions I hear during the postseason is when someone asks, "Does this get old?" Sometimes I feel like answering, "Would winning the lottery more than once get old?" Well, that's what the World Series feels like to us. Like you just hit the lottery.

"I don't know if Derek knows how good he's got it," Mattingly said during the 1999 World Series. But believe me, I do.

In 1996, I won the Rookie of the Year award and helped the Yankees win the Championship after we reached the postseason for the first time since 1981. It was a year that was filled with incredible stories and emotions. Joe Torre, who I feel is the perfect baseball manager because he knows what it's like to play the game and never gets too emotional, made it to the World Series after 4,272 games as a player and manager. It was a year in which his brother Rocco died of a heart attack in June and his other brother, Frank, had heart transplant surgery one day before we clinched the title. Cone, one of our best pitchers, came back from

Here I am signing my autograph for my cousin Nick during a visit to Yankee Stadium.

career-threatening aneurysm surgery to help us win the Championship for the first time since 1978.

Two years later, we might have outdone ourselves when we won an unprecedented 125 games to win another title. That was a magical year. Everyone wondered if we could keep winning at such an incredible pace and we did. Some people called us the greatest team of all time. I agree. Then, in 1999 we were supposed to win it all again, and that's when winning is the most difficult. We did it in another season filled with emotional stories. Mr. Torre had to overcome prostate cancer, and three of my teammates endured the deaths of their fathers. We soared through the playoffs by winning 11 of 12 games, a stylish conclusion and a better postseason spurt than in 1998 when we won 11 of 13.

I want to win it again and again and again. I remember the first time we won the title in 1996 and the emotions and euphoria we felt during the ticker-tape parade along the Canyon of

Heroes. I took the subway to lower Manhattan with Jim Leyritz that morning, and the parade started on the train. It was kind of scary because the train was packed with so many fans I wasn't sure if we were ever going to get off.

It is surreal to be on a float with three million people surrounding you and thousands of pieces of paper drifting by your eyes each second. They tossed ticker tape, toilet paper, newspapers, any kind of paper. So many young ladies held signs asking me to marry them that it turned into a joke with my teammates. "Nothing Is Sweeter than Derek Jeter" and "Marry Me, Derek" and "No. 2, Be My No. 1." It got embarrassing for me because my teammates teased me relentlessly. Still, I'll never forget how we felt that day. I wasn't dreaming about parades as a kid, but now I do. Every year.

I had wondered if anything could surpass 1996, a wondrous ending to my rookie year. Then we did it again in 1998 and again in 1999. What the heck? I'd like to see us win it again in 2000, and I think we can. That will give me more things to tell my parents the next time I burst into their bedroom to talk about chasing dreams. Yes, I wanted this to happen. More important, my parents were there to help lead me toward it, and I was determined enough to make it happen. You have to feel that way about your goals, too. Find someone who will support you, and lean on them. Believe in yourself and you'll be surprised at what else you can accomplish.

I set goals in baseball every year, very high goals. I don't tell anyone except my family because I don't want to seem too boastful and I don't want people asking me if I think I really can win a batting title or a Gold Glove or crush 35 homers. Are those my goals for 2000? Maybe they are. I won't say for sure. Remember, I said I like to shoot for the stars. I think everyone should act that way. I will admit our team goal is to win a third straight World

Series and become the first team in history to do it since the 1972–1974 Oakland Athletics. It would be time to christen another Yankee dynasty if we do that.

I believe in setting goals really high. Then, if you stumble, you still might be very good in the eyes of others. But, if you set them low, once you get there, you're going to be satisfied with what is probably not your best. You're never going to push yourself to achieve even more. That's what dreams are about, aren't they? I've been doing that since I was six. Dreams become realities when you love what you're doing. Hey, my office is at Yankee Stadium. Yes, dreams do come true.

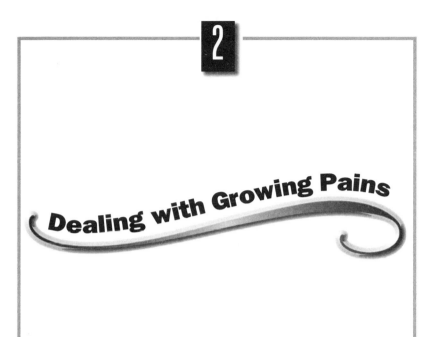

2

Dealing with Growing Pains

 remember sitting in my hotel room on a warm evening in July in Tampa, Florida, in 1992, feeling antsy. It was too warm to stay inside the room. Besides that, I had too many questions swimming through my mind about where I was and what I was doing. This hotel was a long way from my bedroom in Kalamazoo, the one with a poster of Dave Winfield on the wall and, more important, the one that was under the same roof as my parents and Sharlee.

So I ventured out onto the balcony at the Radisson Bay Harbor Inn—George Steinbrenner's hotel and the place where most of the minor leaguers who played in the Gulf Coast League stayed. I watched the cars buzzing by on the Courtney Campbell Causeway. I counted the cars, counted how long it took for the light to turn from green to red. I did anything to keep me from focusing on baseball. I don't know how long I was out there, but I didn't get any answers right away.

I couldn't escape from baseball. I felt like I had already failed. I had been playing with the Class A Tampa Rookie League team for about a week and it had been torturous since I failed to get a hit in my first 14 at bats. I stood on that balcony and questioned myself. Had I made the right decision in signing a professional contract at 18? Of course, everyone would say. You were the sixth pick of the draft and the first high school player selected, you were fortunate to go to the team you cherished, and you received a signing bonus worth $800,000. How could I possibly think of that as a mistake?

But the money wasn't helping me much as I stood there watching cars and doubting myself. I could have attended the University of Michigan on a baseball scholarship, and I would have spent my first year playing baseball and hanging out in a dormitory room with no pressure on me. My toughest decision probably would have been whether to get pepperoni or sausage on my pizza. Instead, I felt like I'd never felt before in my life. Lost.

I had imagined being in this hallowed position for over a decade, wearing a Yankee uniform, earning a paycheck from the Yankees, and playing baseball every day. Even though I was still in the minor leagues, this was a crucial part of my goals if I was going to eventually make it to my dream to be a major leaguer.

But you never really know what is lurking in front of you if you've never experienced something before. You never really know how difficult that next step is going to be. I knew it was going to be an adjustment from high school to pro baseball, but

I hadn't expected to feel as overwhelmed as I did. I hadn't imagined that I'd wind up crying in my hotel room night after night because I was playing so poorly.

As much as I struggled with being away from home and with playing against a higher caliber of players than I'd ever competed against before, I was smart enough to know that I had to continue thinking about reaching my goals. It wasn't easy. There will definitely be times when pursuing *your* goals won't be easy, either—where you'll feel like standing on a hotel balcony and ignoring the obvious.

You might coast through high school, telling everyone that you're going to own your own business and do your own accounting for it someday. Then you get to college and labor in the first accounting course you take. Debits? Credits? None of it makes sense to you. Or you've struggled to reach management level in your company, telling your bosses you can handle the pressure. But when you have to run your first meeting, you're uncertain about how to be a manager. These arduous experiences are the times when you have to remind yourself how important and how attain-

At 18, I was on my way to the Rookie Leagues after the Yankees selected me as a first-round draft pick. Here I am in Tampa, ready to play rookie ball in the Gulf Coast League.

able your goals still are. Don't quit because of one rocky experience. We all have to persevere to get something we desperately want. Our goals wouldn't be worth much if we didn't have to fight through some obstacles to get to them. If you don't have obstacles, it probably means you're not setting your goals high enough. Basically, you should know that once you set the goals, the obstacles are going to emerge at some point. Just be ready for them.

When I got to the Rookie League team in the Gulf Coast League in July, I was late. I didn't sign my contract until a month after the amateur draft, so I missed the first two weeks of the season. I was even late for my first game. The players took the 52-mile ride from Tampa to Sarasota on a crowded bus that day. I must have looked like a prima donna when I hopped out of the air-conditioned car of Bill Livesey, the vice president of player development and scouting, with a duffel bag over my shoulder. The Yankees didn't let me play on that first day, a day when the main thing I learned was to stop tilting my cap back on my head like I was a big man on campus. As a Yankee, you tugged the cap down tight over your brow to look neat and professional.

I just watched, said hello if someone said hello to me, and tried to get acclimated. The nightmare started the next day, July 2, when I went 0 for 7 and struck out five times in a doubleheader. I also made a throwing error on a grounder up the middle that caused us to lose one game, an error that Ricky Ledee still chides me about. I had struck out just once in 59 at bats during my senior year of high school, so you can imagine how I felt after that hardly auspicious debut in the pros. I felt like going home that very first day. Could someone erase this day from my life and let me start over?

Other than visiting my grandparents during the summers, I had never been away from Kalamazoo for any lengthy period. Now I was on my own in Tampa—the first-round pick trying to make it. I wasn't really on my own because my parents were a telephone call or an airplane flight away, and the Yankees had a classy manager in Gary Denbo, who still knows my swing better than anyone, and a great minor-league field coordinator in Mark Newman. Still, I was 18 and I needed to know I could do this and needed to feel like I belonged. I had to remind myself again and again why I was in Tampa and how much the Yankees valued me. I had to tell myself I was good enough to do this.

That positive reinforcement is sometimes the only friend you'll have. I know what it was like to feel like I didn't belong. Though I had done well playing in high school, this was a whole new challenge, and I would have to constantly push myself to make the right decisions. I knew I was picked in the first round for valid reasons, but we all need to remind ourselves why we have that great job or why we're in that special class, especially when we're having one of those bad days.

Even after I signed with the Yankees, I don't think the significance of what had happened really sunk in. I signed on June 28 and was so naïve that I actually asked the Yankees if I could stay home for an extra week. I wanted to be in Kalamazoo for the Fourth of July, one last chance to see my parents and Sharlee and to spend time with my girlfriend, Marisa Novara. The Yankees politely told me that I needed to report to Florida immediately. They had invested almost a million dollars in my future and naturally wanted me to begin working out.

As much as my family was prepared for me to leave, the finality of it still caught us by surprise. I don't think you could ever be totally ready for it. Sharlee was about to become a teenager, and she was mad at the Yankees for taking me away from her when she knew that she would need an older brother the most. She kept asking me why I couldn't wait a few more years. I know she didn't get over my absence for a while. My mother was concerned because I didn't know how to iron or how to cook and I had to live on my own. I was leaving, and if everything proceeded as planned, I would be gone for good.

My father drove me to the Kalamazoo airport the day I departed. Mom met us at the airport. We were probably better off that way because we would have needed two boxes of tissues if she had driven with us. As it was, my father and I had a quiet ride. He asked me if I'd packed everything and told me to call as soon as I got settled in Tampa. I didn't say too much. I don't say much if I'm feeling emotional, but he knew how I felt. This was everything I wanted, but this was also the beginning of a point in my life where I wouldn't see my parents or my sister every day anymore.

Leaving my family was one of the hardest parts about becoming a ballplayer. I had always relied on them for support, but when I got to Tampa they were only a phone call away (and I sure made a lot of calls home!). Here I am with Dad leaving for rookie camp in 1992.

I got on that plane with a lump the size of a golf ball in my throat, and the only thing that prevented me from crying was thinking I might see someone I knew. My father told me a few years later that when he got back to the car that day, he wept uncontrollably. Even after he reached his job as a substance abuse counselor at Adventist Hospital in Battle Creek 45 minutes away, he could not stop. He sobbed and explained how emotional the parting had been, and one of his female coworkers called him a "sissy," making him laugh and stemming the tears.

When I got to Tampa, it might as well have been another country. I didn't know anyone and I didn't have a roommate because everyone else was already paired up. I was the only first-round pick who got $800,000, the second-highest the Yankees had ever paid a player at that time, so I felt like everyone was scrutinizing me. The other players had already established a routine and they were a team. I showed up and it was hard not to feel like an intruder. I cried a lot.

That was the one time in my professional career, a career that had barely started, when I wondered if I was good enough to play at that level. Even though I had been voted the finest high school player in the country and was the first high school player drafted, I'd come from Kalamazoo, and the talent level there was not nearly as rich as it is in many of the warm-weather states. We only played about two dozen games a year, and we played lots of doubleheaders to take advantage of any decent weather we had. If a pitcher threw 85 miles per hour in Kalamazoo, he was considered untouchable. In rookie ball, everyone threw harder than that. The pitches looked like Tic Tacs. So I wondered if I was really as good as everyone had predicted, and that's what brought me out to the balcony on that warm night.

I had doubts. I felt like I was overmatched in everything. The whole game seemed like it was moving in fast-forward. The mound seemed like it was 80 feet away, instead of 60 feet 6 inches. The throw from shortstop to first base felt like I was throwing it from center field to home plate. It seemed like everyone else was on Rollerblades while I was slogging through quicksand. I was using a wooden bat, not aluminum, for the first time, and that was an adjustment. After I made an error in one game, I heard two Spanish-speaking teammates conversing and I figured they were saying, "This is the worst first-round pick I've ever seen."

That was probably paranoia seeping into my head, although I knew that I had to prove myself to the Yankees. I wanted to achieve my dream so badly that the rough moments I experienced just made me sadder. But, you know what? I know these struggles made me fight harder, too. There were times when I was so angry at myself for not hitting a pitch I felt I should have hit that I was driven to work that much harder on my swing the next day. You can't quit when something doesn't go your way the first or second time. Even if it takes 10 tries, you have to keep trying. If you think you're good enough and you stay persistent, you'll eventually get the task done.

I still think that the Rookie League is one of the toughest leagues any player ever has to conquer. The games in the Gulf Coast League were played in sweltering 90-degree heat throughout Florida, and there are very few spectators, just family members and friends who might be in town, and some scouts. If you're not doing well, and I wasn't, you can let those dreary elements get to you, too. I always liked to play in front of crowds as a kid. My mother used to say it was like I was on Broadway. I would try on my uniform the night before a game to see how I looked in it. I did that from Little League through high school, parading around my house like I was a model on the catwalk. Now, a few weeks after I had 40 scouts at some of my games, I was playing in the pros and there might be as few as a dozen people there.

Having no fans at a pro game was incongruous to me. It shouldn't have bothered me, but it did.

I could have really disintegrated in rookie ball. I could have crumbled and never recovered. But I kept getting positive reinforcement from the Yankees and from my parents. The Yankees have an organizational rule that they will not alter anything a player does in his throwing, hitting, fielding, or running until he has been with the team for at least 30 days. They don't want young players to show up and feel like everything they have ever done is incorrect. They do it to help build and maintain confidence. I think it's a smart approach, and I think it helped me work through my problems. Even though I was struggling, I didn't have coaches berating me for what I might have done wrong. When you're dealing with young people in new surroundings, I think that's a critical strategy. When I was trying to establish myself, I wanted to feel as though I was making progress and doing something worthwhile. My statistics stunk, but I didn't lose all of my confidence.

If you are not performing as well as you'd like to be doing in a certain class or in a certain sport, it helps if you get an understanding coach or teacher to critique you and help you see the big picture. Just because you only got a D on the first history test doesn't mean you'll get a D for the semester. If you can talk to someone about why you didn't get a higher grade, you can be prepared to do better the next time. It works the same way in sports. If you missed all nine shots you took in a basketball game, you should talk to your coach about whether you're forcing shots that aren't available or whether your shooting form is just inconsistent. In any instances where you're feeling uncomfortable, getting these questions answered will help you the next time around.

When I think back to being a nervous 18-year-old and think about the way the Yankees handled me, I have to give them credit for their strategy. They were teaching me about dozens of aspects of baseball, and, even if the results weren't always immediately positive, they continued to try to build my confidence. They worked hard to keep me focused on what I was doing well and explained why I was still pretty good at some of the things I hadn't mastered yet. I think that's a great approach for everyone, not just baseball players. If you can remember one or two positives from your pursuit of a certain goal, you'll begin each day with confidence. It's hard to overlook mistakes, and we shouldn't ignore them, because we can learn from them. But when you're really toiling, you need to find those shreds of optimism and cling to them. If you didn't get the score you wanted on the SATs, take solace in the fact that you've gained more experience at taking that kind of test for the next time you give it a try. The Yankees saw me as a long-term investment, the way a good teacher would notice a potentially stellar student during his freshman year. The teacher shouldn't worry if the kid has a little trouble in his freshman year because the goal is to equip him to make it to college by the time his four years are up.

I remember the Yankees didn't talk about my batting average much in that first year. They told me that I had a nice feel for the barrel of the bat, that I was being selective, and that I wasn't totally fooled by breaking pitches. They liked my habits and my approach and told me that no one would ever remember what I batted in my first year. Newman, who is enthusiastic and intelligent and who is Steinbrenner's vice president of baseball operations now, looks right into your eyes when he speaks. He was always encouraging and he sat down next to me in our clubhouse after another shabby game and said, "You're not going to be a good player, you're going to be a great player."

Those were reassuring words. I hung on to them, but I also knew that I had to go out and prove that to everyone. As reassuring as the Yankees were with me, I still burned up the telephone lines to Marisa and my parents, seeking even more assurances. My phone bill ranged from $300 to $400 a month because I called home several times a day. Sometimes I'd call my parents at midnight, awakening them and forcing them to have a quick debate about who was going to answer the call this time. I needed to hear their voices. I could tell my parents were worried about me, but they calmed me by talking about how I had to remain confident and to maintain the work ethic that had helped get me there. They visited me twice in the six weeks I played in the Rookie League. Marisa came to Florida, too. I needed to see them.

Keep Your Head Up

My mother never let me use the word "can't" when I was growing up. If I started to say I couldn't finish reading a book on time to write a report about it, my mother would cut me off before I finished. If I doubted my abilities to cover a tough player in a basketball game, my mother would stop me and tell me what I could do. I wasn't allowed to make excuses.

Whenever I wanted to complain, I'd sit on the stairs between our family room and the kitchen, with my back to my parents, who were in the kitchen. I'd talk about how an umpire made a bad call and my parents would respond, "That was one at bat; what did you do in your other three at bats?" If I complained about not hitting a fastball, they would say, "Let's take some extra batting practice tomorrow." They would always be honest with me and always figure out ways to get me focusing on what I could do better instead of allowing me to harp on things I couldn't control.

Those early discussions with my parents came in handy while I was in Tampa. Gently, my father reminded me there was no turning back and that this was the goal I had worked so hard to achieve. In a weak moment in those first couple of weeks, my mother told me I could come home if I wanted to. It seemed odd for her to say that. Could I really leave? Would the Yankees allow me to go home? What I didn't know was that my father was waving his arms wildly and saying, "Dot, he *can't* come home. He has to stay there. He's committed to staying there."

It helped that my father spoke to the Yankee officials like Brian Sabean, Mitch Lukevics, and Bill Livesey, and they told him that despite my sorry statistics they noticed progress. My father also reminded me how Chipper Jones, who was the first player selected by the Atlanta Braves in the 1990 draft, had struggled in his first minor-league season. Chipper batted .229 for Class A Bradenton in the Rookie League, the same league I was floundering in. Two years later Jones hit .346 at Class AA Greenville; four years later he was in the majors to stay; and in 1999 Chipper won the National League's Most Valuable Player award.

I was relieved when the Gulf Coast League season ended, and I didn't even want to go to Class A Greensboro. It was a promotion of sorts so that I could get more at bats, but I felt like heading home. Those six weeks in Tampa had felt like six months. Two more weeks at Greensboro were not what I wanted.

I took a break from baseball after hitting .202 at Tampa and .243 at Greensboro and spent the fall semester at the University of Michigan in Ann Arbor. It was good to be a regular student, living in a dorm and doing what regular students do. I got used to living on my own and taking care of myself, something my mother said I was never ready for before I left for Tampa. I went to basketball games, football games, and parties. College was fun, but I knew my immediate future was still in baseball. My parents insisted that the Yankees put a clause in my contract that they would pay my college tuition when I wanted to go to school, and I've promised my parents that I'll eventually get a degree. I'm 26

and I have one semester in the books, so at this rate it's probably going to take me about 20 years to graduate. Sharlee will earn her bachelor's degree first and I'm proud of her for that. Now I've got to catch up to her.

The Yankees started me at Class A Greensboro in the 1993 season, and that felt more like the big leagues to me because we'd have a few thousand people at every game. I was there at the start of the season and that made a difference, too. I did well offensively, hitting .295 with 5 homers and 71 RBIs.

But I just couldn't get comfortable on defense. By the third week, I was hoping that no one would ever hit another grounder to me. My footwork was lousy; I was bobbling balls before I could make plays; and I was trying to do too much with my arm. I had great range and I was going into the hole and up the middle to make highlight-reel plays, but then I would rush the throw to first and toss it away. I was the king of robbing a player of a potential hit and whipping it past first so that the hitter wound up on second. My father told me that people in Kalamazoo were asking him if the Yankees planned to move me to the outfield, which was a strong rumor. It sounds humorous now, but it wasn't funny then.

I still relied heavily on my parents and used to wait until I was alone in my room to call home. I know my parents could tell I was whimpering on the other end of the phone. They talked to me about taking extra grounders before games, about visualizing myself doing well, and about how much better a player I was when I was confident. My father mentioned Chipper again, and that resonated with me because he had been the first high school player selected and he climbed out of his hole. I knew I had to get through this. I just had to have the confidence to do it.

We were playing Charlotte, the Texas Rangers' Class A club, the previous year and I roped a base hit in one game. I was on second when Benji Gil, another shortstop who had been drafted in the first round in 1991, walked over and asked me how I was doing. I had never met Benji, but I knew who he was and I felt enough of a kinship to tell him that I wasn't doing well at all.

I told him I was struggling on defense and that hampered my confidence. Gil taught me a trick about how he took a positive out of every game. Even if you make two errors and botch a game, focus on that line-drive single you had; build on that hit. It was the same advice I'd been getting from my parents and the Yankees, but it had more of an impact coming from another young player who was trying to accomplish the same things that I was.

Why dwell on the mistakes? Even if the only thing I did in the game was rip a foul ball, I made sure that I took that to bed with me. That approach really applies in any occupation, not just baseball. If you're a salesman and it's been a horrible day, try to focus on the best sales call you made all day. Tomorrow, everything starts anew, and you want to have a good attitude going into it.

Even as my batting average hovered around the .300 mark, I know the Yankees were concerned about whether I could play shortstop at the major-league level. About midway through the season they sent Gene Michael, the former slick-fielding Yankee shortstop who also managed the Yankees twice and had been the general manager, to Greensboro. I already had 35 errors.

Stick (which is what everyone calls Michael because he was thinner than a credit card as a player) talks fast, and even faster when he's making a point. You can tell he's got the blood of a scout in his veins, because when he wants to describe something, he'll get down in an infielder's crouch or take a hitter's stance and use his actions to describe what he's talking about.

That's what Stick did with me. He watched me for a few days and told me that I was fielding every grounder differently. A grounder would be hit to me or would be a foot to my right or left, but I'd have two or three different ways of fielding it. I wasn't consistent. He explained how Cal Ripken, Jr., the Gold Glove shortstop for the Baltimore Orioles and a player I loved to watch, was a machine at shortstop. Ripken would take the same steps to catch the ball, would throw from the same arm angle, and would throw the ball the same way. Every time. It was almost mechanical, Stick said. You do it so often that it's habitual. I incorporated what Stick had said into my game by approaching grounders the same way and by trying to make the same throws to first each time, in workouts and in games. I trimmed my error total to 21 in the second half. Still, 56 errors over 126 games is awful. I knew I had to improve or I'd never make it to the Yankees—not as a shortstop anyway.

There are always going to be people like Stick who can help you—people who have done what you're trying to do and can offer sound advice. Don't ignore these people. If you're writing an essay for your college entrance form, one of the best things you can do is talk to college graduates who remember what they wrote to help them get admitted to a particular school. I was lucky. The Yankees had a lot invested in me so they sent Stick to help me, but I've always been the type of person to listen and try to learn from as many people as I possibly can. We aren't totally alone in pursuing our goals. There will always be people who want to help you in life. I should know. I have had the privilege of being assisted by these kinds of people, and now I'd like to think I'm one of them because I'm writing this book.

Attack Your Weaknesses

I wasn't even mildly surprised when the Yankees told me they wanted me to go to the Instructional League after the season. I had thought about going back to the University of Michigan for another semester, but they made the decision for me and I couldn't argue. I needed to work on my defense. I'd heard the speculation about switching me to another position, either the outfield or third base, and I was opposed to that. I was a shortstop. I had always been a shortstop. I planned to improve enough to stay at shortstop.

Unfortunately, a couple of days after I was told about the Instructional League, I got drilled in the left hand by a fastball. The hand was bruised and it hurt so badly that I couldn't squeeze a bat. I couldn't believe how unlucky I was. I was anxious for the Instructional League and now I couldn't participate. Or could I? The hand injury might have been a blessing in disguise because the Yankees still wanted me to work out every day but, so that my hand would heal properly, I couldn't touch a bat. I could only work on my defense, which wouldn't be a strain on my left hand, because I'd be wearing a glove. At first I thought that was like giving a 17-year-old a new Mercedes-Benz and telling him he could only drive it around the block. Everyone loves to hit. Eventually, I thought, I'll be able to hit. I never got to hit, but those were still five of the most important weeks of my career.

Every morning at 8 o'clock, I would trudge through the one-floor cinder-block building that is the Yankees' minor-league complex on North Himes Avenue in Tampa. There are parking spots in front of the building, but the minor-league players park their cars on a grassy field on the side of the building. There are all sorts of signs around the building, inspirational messages and listings of every year the Yankees have won the World Series. It's hard not to get motivated. There are cars rolling by the complex on four sides, and right behind the building there are four spacious fields. When I got dressed on these mornings, there would be a slight chill in the air and some gusty winds to remind you that it can be a little brisk in Tampa in October and even brisker in early November.

I was prepared for my intensive course in defense that fall. Instead of going back to Michigan again and studying finance, I was enrolled in Basics of Defense 101 with Professor Brian Butterfield. The classes met seven days a week for five straight weeks. There are no days off during the Instructional League, not even Sundays. As much baseball as possible gets crammed into that time. For me it was all defense all the time. That was my weakness. That was what I needed to conquer. What are *your* weaknesses? Whatever they are, you can help yourself become more complete by recognizing them and trying to overcome them. None of us are perfect, but we can all do something to make ourselves better.

Butterfield, who is Buck Showalter's third-base coach with the Arizona Diamondbacks now, had been a player, coach, and manager in the Yankees' minor-league system for 13 years when we spent 35 straight days together. He later coached the Yankees in the major leagues and left the organization after the 1995 season. Butter was coaching at Class AA Albany that season, but he had visited me in Greensboro, too, and had analyzed my sloppy defense. He told me that he liked my swagger. Even after I made an error, Butter told me that I still looked like I wanted the ball hit to me. I guess I was fooling some people because, as I've said, there were games where I didn't want the ball hit near me. I already knew Butter and already liked him before the Instructional League.

If you're a 19-year-old baseball player and you can't pick up a bat for five weeks, Butterfield is the kind of coach you want to be around. He's barrel-chested, with neat blond hair and an enthusiastic approach, and he could probably pass for a drill sergeant if he wasn't so chatty and so fond of one-liners.

We talked defense; we practiced defense; we watched videotapes of defense; and we ate defense. Butter liked to work hard and we did work hard, but he also made the workouts fun. He'd shout encouragement, he'd joke with me if I muffed a bad hop, and he'd challenge me to do a little more each day. When you're working out as a baseball player after the season, you'd better like what you're doing because it can get tedious. You could get tired of seeing hundreds of grounders trickling across the grass each day. Luckily, I've always enjoyed it.

Butterfield studied me and told me that I had a tendency to give with the ball. I would step back to field a ball and sort of let it play me. I hesitated. He worked with me on stepping forward and attacking the ball. Fielding is about repetition and making plays so often that they become second nature. So, every day I would field grounder after grounder after grounder in an aggressive manner and work on getting rid of the ball in a nice, smooth motion.

I had lots of trouble fielding the slow chopper in front of me. It's one of the tougher plays for a shortstop. You're running full speed forward and you have to be sure-handed enough to reach low and scoop up the ball and then still set yourself and throw back across your body to first. We worked step-by-step to master the subtleties of this dicey play. By the second week, I was pouncing on slow choppers in my sleep.

Each day on those four fields, I found out a little more about my defense and a lot more about how to improve. I learned that I was sliding my glove from right to left when I was fielding a ball, regardless of where the ball was hit. That's unnecessary movement.

Butter lectured me on setting my glove up in front of me and moving it in the direction of the ball, instead of haphazardly jerking it from right to left. That cut down on the amount of movement and made me a surer fielder. You field grounders by keeping your glove low to the ground, keeping your eyes focused on the ball, and following the ball into your glove. My glove sometimes moved more than a belly dancer's belly.

The Yankees took computer images of me fielding, slide-by-slide snapshots of what I did at shortstop, and these were amazing to peruse. I was doing things that I didn't even realize. In high school I had been athletic enough and had a strong enough arm to get away with extra movement. But now that the competition had increased dramatically, I could not be so erratic. Those images really opened my eyes to the work I needed to do. Sometimes I fielded a grounder and tapped the ball against my glove before throwing to first, losing valuable time. I didn't even realize I did that. I was like a seven-foot center who doesn't realize that he dribbles the ball after grabbing a rebound, instead of taking it right back up and dunking.

After we did three hours of drills in the morning, I would play in the Instructional League games. But of course I wouldn't get to hit. I was only there to play defense as a designated shortstop. I understood it was necessary, but I wouldn't have minded a few at bats. The Yankees told me that 515 at bats at Greensboro were plenty and they didn't want to make me weary. By the end of those days, though, I could have done a commercial for pain relievers. That's how much my back ached.

Still, I sensed improvement. I felt myself getting better. I finished that crash course feeling as confident as I had felt since high school. When I made only 9 errors in 149 games with the Yankees in 1998, believe me, I thought about the 56 errors in 1993 and what I did after the season to improve myself and keep myself at shortstop. I thought about the mornings in Tampa of defense, nothing but defense, when I was willing to work and turn myself into a much more complete shortstop.

It's obvious that my dogged approach to improving my defense is what made me a better player. Practice helps in anything you do, whether you're learning how to play the piano or how to parallel park. You can't be afraid to admit that you have some weaknesses. We all do. The best way to deal with this is to figure out what your weaknesses are, attack them, and work on getting rid of them. The Yankees sent me to Instructional League, but I already knew that I needed to be there. It was no shock figuring out what my problems were.

I'm sure you can figure out what your problems are, too. If you have some trouble spelling, you should keep a dictionary handy for help and you should try reading as many books, magazines, or newspapers as you can. The more familiar you become with words, the easier it will be for you to spell them. If you can't seem to concentrate in class and either daydream or act like a class clown, force yourself to listen to every word the teacher says for one day. Every time you're ready to zone out or speak out, stop yourself. Do that for one full day. Then, come back the next day and do it again. It'll get easier and easier.

This advice is not that different from the advice the Yankees gave me when I worked on my fielding day after day after day. You have to want to improve. We all know what we can and can't do, and it's up to us to try to eliminate whatever weaknesses we can. I had Newman, Butterfield, and Stick to help me, but we're not always going to have people to guide us. Sometimes, we have to just do it on our own. Be honest with yourself, tell yourself how you need to improve, and then work on making those improvements. Even if you have to do something 35 days in a row, like I did, it'll be worth it.

Don't Let Them Outwork You

I almost didn't go to Kalamazoo Central. My parents thought I should go to Hackett, a Catholic high school. Central had over 1,000 students packed inside three floors of a mammoth tan brick building. Since my parents knew I wanted to play baseball and basketball, they thought I might have trouble doing it at a school as large as Central. I think they thought I'd be fine in baseball, but I wasn't the greatest basketball player and that's what worried them. They didn't want to see me languish in my freshman year or quit playing both sports.

Still, I begged them to let me go to Central, so my mother made a deal with me. She told me that I could go there if I made the Kazoo Blues basketball team, an elite Amateur Athletic Union team that drew its players from all over western Michigan. That was an arduous assignment because I had played basketball at St. Augustine's, a tiny Catholic school with six or seven players on a below-average team, and the premier players in the area were all from the public schools.

When my mother called to inquire about tryouts and told the person on the phone that I was from St. Augustine's, he tried to dissuade me from attempting. "St. A's?" he said disparagingly. "You probably don't want your son to waste his time. These kids can really play."

I always loved baseball first, but basketball was my second sport. Here I am eyeing up the basket for a free throw.

That just made my mother boil, so she demanded to know about the tryouts. I remember feeling I had a shot to make the team. I was quick, even if I didn't play great defense, and I had a sweet outside shot—man, did I love to shoot. I don't know how anyone played basketball before there was a three-pointer. I lived behind the arc in high school.

Most of my friends told me I had no chance to make this team, and it's not like they were being mean. They were being realistic. But I was always positive and thought I could make it. I made sure I hustled in every practice. I wanted to be noticed. If my parents had said that I had no chance, I don't think I would have been as confident or as daring. Everyone needs someone to believe in them because the mental part of sports can be as important as the physical side.

Even though this goal might not have technically been part of my dream to play major-league baseball, I still think this was an important learning experience for me. You have to be willing to tackle several different goals in life. Even if the situation looks bleak and you're the fifth-best lacrosse goalie and they're only picking three on the team, it still makes sense to try to make the squad. You'll never know if you were better than those other goalies unless you try.

There were some really talented players on the Blues. Kenyon Murray went on to be named Mr. Basketball in Michigan and played at Iowa. David Hart played at Michigan State. I was a baseball player who played hoops for something to do and to stay in shape, but I wanted to make the Blues so I could assure myself of going to Central.

I will admit that it was intimidating playing against these kids from the public schools because they played a different brand of basketball, and, frankly, they were better than I was. They could jump higher, they could dribble better, and they had experience in playing the run-and-gun style. All I had was my jump shot and my willingness to hustle.

The coach was Walter Hall, who had a booming voice, almost the voice of a radio commentator, and used to glide up and down the sidelines shouting, "Don't let them outwork you. Don't ever let them outwork you." My parents loved hearing Coach Hall say that because he was reiterating what they had said to me so many times before.

I listened to Coach Hall. We ran suicide drills where you start at one baseline of the court and run to the first free-throw line and return. Then you run to half court and return to the baseline again. You're just getting started. Then you run all the way to the other free-throw line and return. Finally, you go from baseline to baseline, all 94 feet, and you're done. This is where I was unbeatable. I didn't lose one suicide drill during the tryouts. It was impossible for Coach Hall to ignore me. While everyone else was

Dick Groch watched the skinny high school sophomore firing baseballs from shortstop like he was shooting a rifle. Boom, boom, boom. Groch watched the kid sprint from home to first base like he was flying down a runway. Whoosh, whoosh, whoosh. Groch watched the solid line drives jump off the kid's bat like lasers. Bang, bang, bang.

Groch watched the kid play some more to make sure he wasn't hallucinating. He wasn't. Derek Jeter was that good.

"In this business, sometimes you'll see a player who takes your breath away," says Groch, the scout who signed Jeter in 1992. "It doesn't happen too often, but it happened to me when I saw Derek Jeter."

There was a college coach beside Groch at the Nine-Star baseball camp in Mount Morris, Michigan, that day a decade ago, and he noticed Jeter's brilliance, too. The coach began talking about what a superb college player Jeter would be. Groch politely interrupted him, speculating right then that Jeter would be drafted so high by a major-league team that he would never play an inning of college baseball.

"I'm going to give you a suggestion," Groch told the coach. "I think you should save your stamp. You're looking at something special."

Groch immediately contacted the Yankees with a report on Jeter and spent the next two years driving three and a half hours from his home in Marysville,

gasping and falling down, I was flying and waiting for him to blow his whistle for the next suicide.

Later, when I heard my name called for making the team, I was stunned. I couldn't believe it. I know the reason I made it was not talent, because I wasn't the most polished basketball player. It was hustle and determination. I had made an impression on Coach

Michigan, to Kalamazoo to scout Jeter. The Yankees were one of the first teams to home in on Jeter, so, to remain surreptitious, Groch recalls that nine different scouts took turns observing the shortstop. Still, even though the same scout wasn't at every game, Jeter knew who was there from the Yankees and every other team.

"Every time he'd do something well, he'd peek over to see if you had been looking. I tried looking the other way. I didn't want him to think he was that good. But it got to a point where you couldn't take your eyes off of him. You had to watch him."

Beyond Jeter's obvious skills, Groch searched for the intangibles when he scouted. Groch noticed how Jeter, a star, easily interacted with his teammates, Groch detected the respect Jeter had for his parents and his coaches, and he sensed the enthusiasm Jeter had for playing. It is the same joy he has today.

"Derek Jeter enjoys playing baseball. He's like a kid at a family picnic. To him, this isn't a job. He's never had a job in his life. He's just playing baseball."

When Groch filed his final free-agent report on Jeter, he gave him a raw score of 59 and a future score of 64. Those numbers meant that Groch predicted Jeter would be an above average to a very good major leaguer. There is a small section on the sheet for additional comments about the player and Groch offered his most revealing insight there: "Major-league shortstop. Blue Chip. A Yankee."

Hall by simply outrunning everyone on the court. I knew how important that was. My parents wanted to see if I could meet this challenge and I did.

After I had made the team, my mother walked into Coach Hall's cramped office to thank him and said, "Coach, I know my son's not the best player here so I want to—" and he cut her off and said, "What did you say?" She tried again, figuring he hadn't heard her. "I know Derek's not the best player out here—" and, once again, Coach Hall interrupted her and said, "What are you saying, Mrs. Jeter?" My mother got the point. He wanted her to know that I could play with these guys and that I was good enough to make this select team. She said she already knew that, but she was happy Coach Hall confirmed her faith in me.

That's why I never understand when someone comes back to the dugout after striking out or popping out against a difficult pitcher and says, "Man, I've got no chance against this guy." Why even go up there if you're going to think that way? You can't go to the plate with a defeatist attitude. It doesn't matter who you're facing or what the situation is. You have to feel like you're going to get a hit. That's half the battle in sports—and in life. If you have an important meeting with a new boss and you're worried that it won't go well before it ever even starts, you're hurting yourself. Have confidence that it'll go well.

My mother's plan had worked. Making that team gave me even more confidence going into high school. I was already a real confident kid, but playing with the Kazoo Blues and traveling to different parts of the country enhanced my attitude and made me feel like I could accomplish anything. We played teams from Detroit that were led by Chris Weber and Jalen Rose, two members of Michigan's Fab Five who are both stars in the NBA now. I've got a picture in my scrapbook of me covering Weber, a bit of a mismatch. Weber could easily dunk over me today and make me look silly—but I'd like to see *him* hit Pedro Martinez's fastball.

Seriously, making that basketball team really inspired me to believe that I could do almost anything. It's why I keep saying that it's important to do things even if you think your chances of being successful are remote. Do you know how easy it would have been for me to not try out for the Blues? I didn't have a dream of playing basketball. I could have blown it off and worked on baseball instead and gone to Hackett. But that experience with the Blues helped me because it gave me an emotional lift that I didn't expect. Once I made a team that some people told me I shouldn't have bothered trying out for, it was almost impossible to tell me I couldn't do something. It was impossible for me to say "can't"—and still is.

Learn to Be a Team Player

I would have been excited to start my freshman year in baseball even if I hadn't played for the Blues, but responding to that challenge in my second-best sport made me even more hyped up about playing baseball. We had our first indoor tryouts for Central while there was still snow on the ground. We worked out in the gym, which had a maroon-and-white-laced hardwood floor and posters that said "Giants Rock the House" and "We Believe" hanging on the yellow walls. There was a railing above one side of the gym that allowed fans to peer down at the court, and the cavernous ceilings made the gym feel like an airplane hangar. Give me a glove and a ball, though, and it felt like it was 80 degrees and sunny.

I was on the court throwing a baseball before the junior varsity tryouts when Marv Signeski, the varsity coach, leaned over the railing and said, "Son, varsity tryouts are in another two hours." I told him that I was trying out for the j.v. and he had a quizzical look on his face. I didn't know it then, but later he told me that he had noticed my arm strength and thought I was a junior or a senior. I used to long-toss with my dad to strengthen my arm, and my throws from shortstop to first were actually clocked at 93 miles an hour while I was in high school. My father refused to let me be a pitcher as I was growing up because he didn't want me to hurt my arm or put too much stress on it by throwing curveballs.

Later that night, Norm Copeland, our j.v. coach, was hitting us grounders. There were 35 of us in line and I wanted to make a good impression. Everyone was fielding a grounder and tossing it in, fielding a grounder and tossing it in. I fielded a hot shot off the hardwood, set myself and fired the ball to the first baseman across the gym. The ball hit him in the stomach and he doubled over. He was used to everyone flipping lollipops, so my hard throw surprised him. I wasn't trying to hurt him or get attention. I always tried to throw the ball hard.

"When I saw Derek do that," Coach Copeland has said, "I knew that he wasn't going to be on the j.v. for too long."

I actually played on the j.v. for about two-thirds of the season, and it was an interesting experience. Coach Copeland had a rule that every player had to start at least one game if we played a doubleheader, so there were times when I didn't even start games. I was the best player on the team, but I was also a team player so I never complained about Coach Copeland's rule.

I think that's a lesson you can learn from, too. It is logical to want to be the best at everything and to strive to achieve as much as possible, which is how I've always behaved. But there's a difference between being an achiever and being selfish. The other kids on the team worked hard at practice, just like me, and deserved to play. It was j.v. baseball. It wasn't the Yankees. Not yet.

There was an All-Conference shortstop on the varsity named Craig Humphrey, a great hitter, and that's one reason I remained on the j.v. so long. Signeski finally decided to promote me and told Humphrey that he was going to start me at shortstop. Craig was an upperclassman and he could have been perturbed, but he turned to Coach Sig and said, "As long as you keep batting me third, that's fine with me." It meant a lot to me that Humphrey went to second base and didn't moan about my being moved to the varsity. I know it was Signeski's decision, but it's easier for a blossoming freshman to break in when the player you're replacing is cool about it.

Something similar happened when I made the Kalamazoo Maroons, a traveling team that played about 55 to 75 games each summer. The Maroons have been around since 1930; they have a reputation for being a quality program; and they journey all over the midwestern and southern states for tournaments, sometimes playing seven games in one weekend, so I desperately wanted to be on the team. It meant more baseball, which meant I inched closer to my dream. Since our high school season is so short, playing in the summer is critical to getting better and getting noticed by college coaches and scouts.

I made the team after my sophomore year. I was only 15. I was the second-youngest player to ever make the Maroons, and my parents were worried that other players would resent me for that. Their concerns increased when Mike Hinga, the coach who taught me as much about baseball as any coach I ever had, decided to start me at shortstop and shift Ryan O'Toole, a college player, to second base.

O'Toole had been on the Maroons for three years. Who wants to be unseated by a high school sophomore when you're in college? But O'Toole was a classy guy and he knew the territory I was in because he had been the youngest player ever selected for the Maroons. Ryan had been in the same situation I was in, and he wound up treating me like another teammate, maybe better.

Since I was just 15, I couldn't drive. Ryan used to come by my house and pick me up for games. That shocked my parents. They had wondered if Ryan would shun me. Instead, he treated me superbly. When we went on road trips, the veterans got to pick their roommates first. Ryan picked me. That showed me a tremendous amount about his character and about how he cared for the team, not for himself. I know Coach Hinga has said, "Even kids could watch Derek play and say, 'Oh, my God,' this kid can do things other kids can't do. Kids aren't stupid."

Still, those acts of kindness come back to me when I see a young player in the majors who is trying to fit in. I know what it is like to feel like you're out of place. I remember how Gerald Williams, one of my closest friends now, made me feel at ease the first time I went to spring training with the Yankees in 1993. He took me to dinner and advised me about how to act and what not to do. But I also remember a few players who got a thrill out of harassing me earlier in my career. Why that was important to them, I'll never know. Maybe they were jealous or insecure, or maybe they had forgotten how it felt to be lost sometimes.

I try to treat our young players the same way I hoped to be treated when I was a rookie. I took Ed Yarnall, Alfonso Soriano, and D'Angelo Jimenez, three of the Yankees' best young players, out in Manhattan after Soriano slammed a game-winning homer for us in September of 1999. You can act this way with people whom you work with or go to school with, too. It's pretty easy to see who is having trouble fitting in. If it were you, you would want someone to throw you a life preserver, so you shouldn't hesitate to do it for someone else.

I do it because I want other young players to feel comfortable in their new surroundings and know that I consider them the same as the rest of us. We're all on the same team. Being a pro baseball player can be a lonely experience, and you don't want to miss out on your goals because you're puzzled. I felt that way in rookie ball and I don't want to feel like that again. No one wants to be standing on a hotel balcony totally confused about baseball when that is supposed to be your life. No one wants to feel lost.

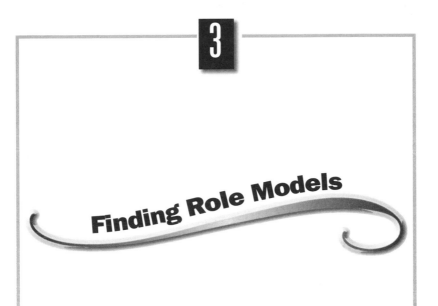

3

Finding Role Models

'm not sure the first time I heard the phrase *role model,* but I know that I was watching people, copying people, and learning from people before I even knew what the words meant. I didn't have to be told that a role model is a person you admire and respect and can model yourself after to know how to do that. My first role models were my parents and they still are my role models, but I didn't just limit myself to watching them. If I saw an attribute in any other person that I admired, I'd adopt it.

I was never bashful about selecting role models, even if I didn't know exactly what I was doing at the time. If I saw someone doing something that I really wanted to be able to do, I'd analyze him until I figured out the proper way to do it, too. It might be something as simple as diving into a swimming pool or as difficult as playing a musical instrument, but if I had a goal I'd follow what that role model did until I succeeded at it. I had lots of role models and some of them were only role models for one day because that might have been how long it took me to learn a particular skill. But, usually, I wouldn't have been able to catch on so quickly if I hadn't had someone to show me the way.

There are a lot of kids who consider athletes or entertainers their role models, and I take my responsibility in this area seriously. I did the same thing with Dave Winfield when I was growing up. He was my favorite Yankee player, and I thought he was a tremendous all-around athlete since he had been drafted professionally in baseball, basketball, and football. I also liked the fact that Winfield formed a foundation to help kids, something that's always been important to me. It makes sense to choose successful people as your role models, but, just remember, your role models don't have to be famous to be considered successful in what they do. I looked as closely at the person who might be at my house fixing my TV as at the athletes I saw on TV. There are worthwhile things you can learn from all kinds of people. Role models are really all around us.

You might know someone who visits a sick grandmother every week and you consider him a role model because of how dedicated he is to his family. You might have a teammate who wakes up at 6 A.M. to run three miles before school, and he could be a role model to you because he's so dedicated to his sport. You might have a friend who is working after school to save money for college or a friend who works two jobs to support her family, and these friends could be your role models in terms of working and saving. Hopefully, your parents are role models for you now

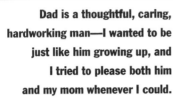

Dad is a thoughtful, caring, hardworking man—I wanted to be just like him growing up, and I tried to please both him and my mom whenever I could.

or were when you were growing up. I know that I was fortunate to not have to look too far for role models because I had two living under the same roof.

I always tell people that I don't like to boast and I don't like people who brag, but I break my own rules when it comes to my parents. I'll talk about my parents for days because I know how much they sacrificed to give me whatever I needed while I was growing up. More than anything, they gave me love, support, and security. They were always there for me, which is an advantage I know every kid doesn't have in life. Because of what my parents said and did, I knew that they cared.

The main thing that my father and mother gave me that every child wants and needs is time. Forget about the gloves, the bats, the sneakers. My parents were always there for me. If I needed a ride to a game at 7 A.M., one of them would take me. If I wanted to go to a movie with friends, one of them would drive me. If I asked for help with homework, one or both of them would stop doing whatever they were doing, sit down next to me, and encourage me until I figured it out.

I learned to value their trust so much that I would even call them from parties to let them know where I was, whom I was with, and what I was doing. At first, I did it because they required me to, and it seemed like a pain. Then it became a routine, and I *wanted* to do it. They showed me what it was like to sacrifice and be dedicated to a cause. It just so happens that Sharlee and I were their cause, and they never let us down.

I wanted to please my parents, but I also wanted to be like them, and that's why they were such great influences on me. There's an incredible amount of comfort in knowing that there is always someone there for you. Such assurance provides security and allows you to relax and try to do your best at everything, whether it's sports, studying, or dating. I've known many people who don't have close relationships with their families and I feel sorry for them. I've always believed that these relationships need to be nurtured, maintained, and mended, if necessary. I feel bad for people whose parents are not their role models, but, as I've said, you can find role models in many places. You should start

Mom has a great smile and a gutsy attitude—it's great that I can look up to both her and my dad as role models. Here she is with me in 1997, at a charity event for my foundation, Turn 2.

with your parents because they're usually going to be the closest to you and know you the best. But, even if your parents are wonderful role models, like mine, you shouldn't stop there.

Look around you, see which people are living the way you'd like to live, and pick them as role models. I liked having several role models. I'd pick out the parts of their different personalities that I admired the most and that had the most relevance for my life. This way, I didn't have to be enamored with everything one of my role models did. I might only be following one thing that I felt I could learn from them. I can find role models each time I watch a baseball game on television, or play a game with my teammates. If I like the way a teammate performs a fielding drill to get better, I'll adopt it and he'll be my role model until I perfect that approach.

I've always loved watching Luis Sojo play defense because I've never seen an infielder with softer hands. Luis just seemed to scoop up balls like a vacuum cleaner when he was with the Seattle Mariners. His glove was close to the ground and the ball would always find it, almost like he had a magnet hidden inside. He was smooth, very smooth.

I got the chance to play with Luis after the Yankees claimed him off waivers in 1996, and I got to personally witness how slick he was. He used to encourage me to try to make difficult plays during batting practice, like flipping the ball behind your back on a force play or shoveling it from your glove to second base without ever touching it. He told me to do this because you never know when you might have to make one of those types of acrobatic plays in a game.

Luis came up to me during the 1997 season and told me that he wanted to make a suggestion about the way I turned double plays. After I received the ball at second base, I liked to jump over the approaching runner and toward first as I threw back to first. I thought it was the best way to make the play.

But Sojo asked me what I was going to do when I couldn't jump as high as I could then. Luis reminded me that I was only 22 years old and that I was working my body and my legs unnecessarily. He taught me a trick about staying behind the base, which is the safest place for an infielder to be because no runners slide hard across the base. They slide hard leading up to the base.

Luis taught me to stay behind the base as I was prepared to make the throw to first. As I got the ball, I was to touch the back corner of the base with my right foot, then throw to first as I pushed away toward the outfield. I was amazed at how much easier it made the play, and for those few days that Luis worked on this with me, this fielding magician was my role model. That's what I mean about finding role models everywhere. I was the starting shortstop and Luis was a utility player. I could have ignored his advice if I had wanted to behave like a prima donna, but I'd never do that. Instead, I turned him into a role model.

The first thing I do every morning is check the box scores to see how Alex Rodriguez did for the Seattle Mariners the night before. The second person that I check is Nomar Garciaparra of the Boston Red Sox. They are immensely talented shortstops whom I admire. The three of us are constantly grouped together because observers have said that we are the new face of baseball. We've been called the future of baseball because we all play the same position; we all play with an infectious style; Alex is 25, I'm 26, and Nomar is 27; and we all have helped revolutionize the way a shortstop is viewed. It's not enough to hit .270 and play stingy defense anymore if you're a shortstop. Now I have to belt 30 homers, knock in 100 runs, hit .330, and make all the plays, or else I won't be able to keep up with Alex and Nomar.

I consider Alex and Nomar to be role models. I want to do what they're doing. If I see that Alex had a game-winning homer, I'm hoping my phone won't ring with a message from him until

I've done something new to match his accomplishment. Alex and I are best friends, and I've gotten to know Nomar better after talking to him at the All-Star Game last year and doing a photo shoot with him and Alex for a magazine cover earlier this year. I already knew that Alex is someone who shares the same vision that I do about constantly needing to improve and I think Nomar does, too. I know I can learn from these two hard-working players.

This is what I'm talking about with finding role models. I think Alex and Nomar might chuckle if I told them they have been my role models, since you don't always think of someone who is your own age as a role model. But in many ways and on many different days they are. We all have seen the enormous skills that both of them have on offense and defense. Alex has such a smooth swing, he is so powerful, and he's one of only three players to exceed 40 homers and 40 steals in the same season. Nomar is not as big, but he's an aggressive swinger with great bat speed who hits the ball equally well to all fields. Both of them play stellar defense, with Nomar being more daring and Alex having the stronger arm.

The thing that impresses me more than anything about them is the way they play the game. They play hard, they play to win, and they play that way whether it's a meaningless spring training game or a do-or-die postseason game. That's why I like watching Alex and Nomar and why I try to be just like them. I have always played hard, and if someone wants to compare me with Alex and Nomar, I hope one of the things that they'll talk about is the passion we share for playing.

If someone comes to watch me play a game for the first time and I go 0 for 4 and don't do anything notable on defense, I would still like that person to remember that I hustled. Did you see the way he ran out that grounder to the pitcher? Did you see him almost run into the stands chasing that foul ball? Those are the attributes that are important to me, and it's why I like comparing myself to guys like Alex and Nomar. They work at their craft and want to get better.

You can pick up on this sort of behavior, too. Even if you want to defeat your rival high school, you might learn something from the scrappy third baseman who is always diving for grounders. You might not even know the students on the opposing debate team, but you can learn something from how prepared they are for every argument. Or what about the woman in your office who has a great sales pitch—you can learn by listening to her when she makes her calls. So stop and look all around you. You can find teachers and role models everywhere.

A Man in the House

I found out at a young age that my father never knew his own father. Never even met him once. I was so young when I first discovered this that I couldn't understand what that really meant for my father when he was growing up. As I got older, though, I eventually grasped how growing up without a father had made my dad so much more determined to be an active parent. He wanted to be there for everything Sharlee and I did, offering the kind of male support that he hadn't received. I think my father tried to make up for what he didn't have by giving twice as much to his children.

I felt the security of a two-parent home all my life, which didn't exist for my Dad. As devoted as my grandmother Lugenia was to my father, she was only one person. She did so much to make him who he is today, a strong man who is generous, compassionate, loving, and ethical. She raised four daughters and one son in a small apartment in Montgomery, Alabama, and cleaned houses to pay the bills. She was a caring woman who was always supportive of her kids. *Caring.* That's the word that my father always uses to describe his mother, and, like my parents, her family was her passion. She was his role model, too.

"There was always love," my father has said. "There was no shortage of that."

But my father has told me that he suffered a little by not knowing his father. It was awkward when he was around kids who were doing something with their fathers at school or in sports. That's when my father would miss having that male presence. It wasn't because he felt like he wasn't loved, because he was. He had five women coddling him and there was endless love. But there was a void, something that couldn't be replaced. Kids can be cruel, and a kid with only one parent is an easy target. It wasn't something we discussed much as a family, but I could see it in how my father acted with us. I'd watch my classmates or my teammates to help make me a better student or a better player, but I also knew I had two role models at home. I knew that I was fortunate, especially whenever I compared my life to my father's as a boy.

My grandmother raised my father in a single-parent household in Montgomery, Alabama. Dad had four sisters, and there was a lot of love in their house. This is my grandma Lugenia, holding me as a baby.

When I wanted someone to pitch to me in baseball, I would throw the ball off the side of my house. If no one came out, I'd keep throwing it until I hit the aluminum siding. That would cause such a loud thump that one of my parents would usually come out to tell me to stop doing that and then they would play with me. My father really didn't have that luxury as a kid. His mother was busy supporting and raising five children and he didn't know his father, so he had to depend on other kids in the neighborhood to play. I know there are lots of kids who are sometimes in this predicament, either because their parents are working or because they come from a single-parent home. I can't identify with that because my parents were such an influence on me, but I hope that anyone who is in that type of situation has a sibling, an aunt or uncle, or a coach to provide some stability in their lives. The more competent role models you have, the better off you'll be.

Sometimes, I wonder how my father's life would have been different if he had had a father or a father figure, a true male role model. He thinks he would have been more disciplined and tougher. My father didn't have a curfew. He came home when it got dark. He was a very good baseball player, but he didn't really have anyone to guide him to the next level while he was in high school. His baseball career unfolded like a napkin blowing in the breeze instead of in the much more orderly fashion that mine progressed.

I listened to my parents, my role models, tell me how difficult it was going to be to become a pro baseball player. They didn't sugarcoat what I wanted to do and I'm glad they didn't. Your role models have to be candid with you, even if they're talking to you from a TV screen or if you're getting lectured to in an auditorium with 500 other kids. I'm always honest when I speak to kids. I don't tell them that playing for the Yankees came easily for me, because it didn't. Anyone who has reached his goals will tell you that. It's not easy, and that's one more reason why role models are necessary.

I knew what to expect when baseball scouts watched me play in high school because my parents had briefed me. But my father didn't have that same confidence while he was in high school because he didn't have a male role model to guide him. Even though Dad was scouted by a few teams, he was a good-field, no-hit shortstop and wound up receiving grant-in-aid to play at Fisk University in Nashville, Tennessee. He poked one homer in his college career, but he showed me the newspaper clipping so often you would have thought he had belted it in Game 7 of the World Series.

I know that my father has pondered whether he could have pursued a professional career if he'd had a father to push him harder and in the right direction. I'm sure that's another reason why he has been immersed in every aspect of my career and will continue to be for as long as I play. He wasn't going to let what happened to him happen to me, too. I've had a father and a mother at every turn. I've had two role models giving me daily advice, something they still do and something I still embrace.

Your role models should be honest with you, tough with you. My father has told me that his mother soothed him. She was a loving, gentle mother. If he came home with a problem, she'd tell him not to worry about it and almost always take his side. Not to sound chauvinistic, but most fathers are not going to always be so docile with their sons. Everyone needs discipline and needs to be taught when he has made a mistake and how not to make it the next time.

My dad said to me that, as he looks back now, he needed a kick in the behind once in a while. He needed to be told that he had done some things wrong. My grandmother was not like that with her kids. She showered them with love, and obviously it worked. Fortunately, my father picked up her caring qualities, but he also developed a strict side, probably because he knew that he had needed it in his development, and he used that in raising us.

My parents are my world. I talk to one or both of them at least once a day and they are still advising me. They ask me if I'm taking care of myself, if I'm getting enough sleep (which is never a problem for me), and if a gossip story in the newspaper about me being out somewhere or dating someone is true. Usually, I'll tell them it's not. That doesn't stop my mother from asking what percentage of the story might be factual.

My father has an easy yet stern way about him. I always loved to compete against him and we'd play checkers, board games, and basketball from the time I could talk. But my father was also very competitive and he'd never let me win unless I earned it. He wanted me to know that when I defeated him, I had beaten him fairly. Obviously, losing made me cry a few hundred times, but I think that's what a role model should do. He should help you get better. If I had beaten my father before I was legitimately ready, I probably wouldn't have worked as hard to get better and to be like him. He was my role model because he could do all of the things that I wanted to do in sports. He was bigger, stronger, and more experienced.

I'm sure there are people like this in your life. It doesn't just have to be a role model for sports. You might have an older brother who is in college and is getting excellent grades. You don't have to do everything exactly like him, but you can follow his lead by listening to what he says about doing well, and absorbing the information. Whether you're an English major or you're pre-law, there are different things you can learn from someone who is so close to you. That's why I don't think your role models have to be famous people. Your best role models can be the people you see and talk to every day.

I remember how my father's guidance finally helped me beat him. Dad had been working with me on my jump shot and I had gotten to the point where I was almost automatic from 15 feet out. If he left me open, I was going to sink the shot. I was 13. I thought I was ready to finally beat him in one-on-one. I was ready for an upset that I'd been waiting to pull off for about seven years.

So I challenged my father to play at Western Michigan one day and shocked him. As I was nailing jumpers and taking the lead, he kept saying his back hurt. I was much quicker than he was and I really hustled that day. I don't remember the final score, but I know how rewarding it felt to know that I had won. My father was right. All those years of losing to him didn't matter when I finally won. It made the wait worth it. I wanted to be like my father, and beating my father made me just like him—and on that day, even better. I had beaten my role model and I had done what a role model wants you to do: learn and improve. Dad had to clean the bathrooms for a month after that to pay off our bet. If I had lost, I would have been washing dishes for a month, so my jumper saved me on that day.

Sign on the Dotted Line

I tell people that growing up in my household was like growing up on *The Cosby Show.* Dad's not as funny as Bill Cosby, but we had those same kinds of hilarious experiences as a family. Bill Cosby's character on that show was a doctor who liked to dictate the rules. Just like my father. He's a social worker, and he and my mother were very particular about how they raised their family. There were enough rules to fill a notebook, which is what my parents literally did.

Two weeks before I started attending Kalamazoo Central High School, my parents called me into the family room on a Sunday night. They sent my sister Sharlee upstairs because they said they wanted to talk to me alone. My father had a yellow legal pad in one hand, a pen in the other, and he looked real serious. I was sitting on the couch, not sure what was about to happen. I felt like one of my father's patients, and I racked my brain trying to recall if I'd done anything wrong. They shut off the television, a sign that this meeting was going to be serious, and I waited.

My father put his pen down and told me that he and my mother wanted to discuss a one-year contract I had to sign before my freshman year. The contract would be explicit and would discuss the goals my parents expected me to achieve that year. It covered everything from grade-point average to how many telephone calls I could make each night. It covered everything except what color socks I should wear on Tuesdays. It was strict, it was comprehensive, it was a binding contract. They signed it and I had to sign it and abide by it.

Your role models should teach you, inspire you, criticize you, and give you structure. My parents did all of these things with their contracts. They tackled every subject. There was nothing we didn't discuss. I didn't love every aspect of it, but I was mature enough to understand that almost everything they talked about made sense.

As a social worker, my father had seen desperate parents use contracts to try to improve the behavior of kids who had made mistakes. The contracts were strict and were really a form of punishment since the children had violated some rules. But, instead of using contracts after a mistake, my parents felt it would be better to use the contracts as a guideline before I even had the chance to do anything wrong. Why make the contract a form of punishment when it could be used as an effective tool for helping me figure out my goals and letting me know ahead of time what was acceptable

Sharlee and I had to sign contracts with my parents that spelled out our behavior and goals for the year. If you can read my father's handwriting (not easy!), you can see some of the things I had to promise to do.

<u>Derek</u>

★ After School

1. Homework Time? | NO Events
- Take Phone messages unless done | work done

2. No Phone Calls after 10 in wen out.

3. Friends over after School / Easy on Food + Soda.

4. Expect 3 Times week at YMCA for weight Program - Regardless of what Ben does. / Use for Basketball.

5. No Arguing.

6. Trouble at school - we want to know about from you.

7. Rewards - 3.8 or above 4.0 - Extra Special.

8. Alcohol / Drugs. mono Res - Don't get caught up / Avoid.

9. Interaction with the opposite sex. Respect Girls / Same way you want to be respected.

10. Respect Students / Teachers / Coaches →
They are to respect you - if that doesn't happen let us know about it.

11. SEX time will be for study 3 nights and Review / no going out.

12. During the week ★ Bed Time ? 10:30

13. Cur Few / During week - by 10 night after sporting event.
/ Fri + Sat - 11:30 PM unless school / east / last longer.

14. House needs to be clean if some are spend the night or Bathrooms upstairs / downstairs

15. Allowance - Pay for lunch $12.00/day through October. Be able out mom's loan for ready money - $10 unless not fully mentioned - $10

16. Involvement in school activities / new. ★ 2 organizations

17. Clothes - ready the night before

18. Eat your lunch!

I agree [signature]

and unacceptable behavior? I now see how much sense this made, because it gave me structure. I knew the difference between right and wrong, but this put everything in writing. There were no gray areas and there could be no excuses if I strayed. I knew the rules.

The contract discussions were usually one-sided. I'm not confrontational, especially when it comes to negotiating with my parents, so I usually listened to what they had to say and just agreed. Sometimes, I'd make faces. Sometimes, I'd shake my head. Sometimes, I'd answer in an aggravated voice. But I really didn't debate the points. I knew my parents had spent hours formulating these contracts. If they felt it was best for me, I wasn't going to bicker. My father just kept reading more and more clauses and scribbling notes on his pad and my mother chimed in with her opinions to embellish certain points. I sat there for 90 minutes, listening to how my life was supposed to unravel for the next year, barely uttering a word because the outline actually sounded promising. I liked getting feedback, one more thing a role model can provide, and these discussions gave me feedback before I'd done one thing. I knew that if I failed a class, my baseball glove would get cobwebs on it while I waited to play again.

We'd talk about academic goals, the types of courses I expected to take, and the types of grades I was expected to get. My parents put a clause in the contract that said I had to do one hour of homework before anything else when I got home from school. No TV, no music, no phone calls. If I had practices or games, I still had to spend that first hour on homework. They preached about not talking or becoming a distraction in class, about not cutting classes, and about completing assignments on time. I had to respect all teachers, look them in the eye when I answered questions, and report my progress in each course to my mother and father.

My parents didn't overlook anything regarding academics. You needed a 2.0 out of 4.0 to be eligible to play sports at Kalamazoo

Central. My parents had their own standards and they demanded that I strive for a 4.0 because they knew that I was capable of doing that. You know what? I didn't have any problems with these clauses. I wanted to do well in school, especially since most of my friends were achievers. Sharlee was five years younger and more rebellious than I was, and she'd tease me for doing my homework expeditiously. Sometimes she'd watch TV when she first got home and basically challenge my parents to send her to her room to do the work, which they did.

"Derek was a wimp," Sharlee has lovingly said. "He never got grounded. I used to have fun getting grounded." But I knew that I wasn't being a wimp. These were the rules, and hopefully they would help me get to the goals I had. My parents were challenging me, and I liked that. If they thought these goals were attainable, I thought they were, too.

As we would discuss the contract, my father kept notes and acted like a banker who was considering whether or not to approve me for a loan. He would peer through his glasses and ask me questions. If I shrugged or didn't respond, he'd keep going. "You understand that, Derek, don't you?" he'd say. I nodded. "Does that make sense, Derek?" I'd nod again. My negotiating ability was lame. Sharlee knew my father had sloppy handwriting and she used to try to use that to her advantage. After she got to high school and had her own contracts, she would question whether she had actually agreed on a certain clause and thereby force my father to reread his illegible writing.

I enjoyed reviewing the athletic portion of the contracts because my parents were extremely supportive of my goals and they wanted me to participate in as many sports as possible. They wanted me to play two sports, not just one, and they reminded me of the importance of making it to all practices. When my father coached my Little League team, I once told him that I was

Alex Rodriguez
ON DEREK JETER

I t happens to Alex Rodriguez at least once a week. He never knows when to expect it and no matter how many times it happens, it still surprises him. But, Rodriguez, who plays for the Seattle Mariners and is one of the best players in baseball, is routinely mistaken for one of the other premier players in baseball when he is outside of Seattle. Is that Alex Rodriguez or is that Derek Jeter?

"I don't know if it's odd or if it's weird and I don't know if it happens to Derek, but I'll be walking down the street and someone will come up to me and say, 'Hey, Derek Jeter,' " says Rodriguez. "I'll hear them calling me Derek. It's really weird to be so parallel to someone else. It's almost like looking in the mirror when I see the way he looks and the way he acts. It's crazy."

It is crazy, but it is true. In addition to being best friends, Derek and Alex have as many similarities as twins. They are both All-Star shortstops and twenty-something millionaires. They are both 6 feet 3 inches, with dark hair, and with no wedding bands on their fingers. They are both former first-round draft picks with lifetime .300 averages, who stay in each other's homes whenever the Yankees play in Seattle or whenever the Mariners visit New York.

"At this point Derek has become like my brother."

going to miss practice because one of my teammates had asked me to go fishing. My father was incensed. He explained how I had a commitment to the team, and if I didn't come to practice, I wouldn't start. It made me angry at the time because I'd never been fishing, but, again, he had a point. It wasn't fair to the other kids for a player to miss practice and then start games. So I bagged fishing and went to practice. My friend went fishing and didn't start the next game. I don't think I've missed a practice

They talk on the phone frequently, gabbing and laughing like a couple of high school kids before the junior prom. But, between the joking and teasing, the conversations get deep, too. Rodriguez and Jeter have talked about remaining humble and about avoiding trouble, and have spent hours trying to "figure life out." While Alex and Derek have a deep bond, their relationship changes when the Yankees oppose the Mariners.

"We want to kill each other. I think we both drive each other and motivate each other. But, when we're off the field, we're like family. I think the nice thing about it is we became good friends before we even made it to the big leagues. That makes it more of a healthy relationship."

Jeter was the sixth selection in the first round of the 1992 amateur draft so Rodriguez, who wound up being chosen first overall in the 1993 draft, called Jeter for advice before the Mariners picked him. The two wound up becoming fast friends who are now two of the best players in baseball.

"We always talk about getting old, gray, and fat when our careers are over and just having a good time. He's like me. He wants to have a good time and be a good person. It's a weird situation for us. It's just like we're looking in the mirror. The only difference is I'm on the West Coast and he's on the East Coast."

since then, other than one or two optional workouts in which Mr. Torre has told me to take a day off. Even then I felt like I should be working out.

There's something satisfying about being there every day, working. I think I picked that up from my parents and my grandparents, too. My grandfather, Sonny Connors, used to get up at 4:30 A.M. to go to work. I'd hear him get up in the mornings when I stayed with my grandparents for the summer and I'd have trouble getting back to sleep again. I wanted to start my day, too. I'd usually get up a couple of hours later and drag my grandmother out of bed and force her to play baseball with me. I didn't care how early it was and neither did she. You used to have to hit the ball about 100 feet to get a homer in my grandparents' yard, but that meant the ball would sail into the highway and that could be dangerous. I blasted so many homers that we had to reverse the field so the homers sailed into the woods, which were about 75 feet away. It was a shorter homer, but it was a safer homer. When I think about my grandfather getting up and out before most people had even opened their eyes and about my grandmother ignoring her other responsibilities to play baseball with me, I realize they were important role models, too.

So I watched my parents and grandparents work all their lives, trying to make life better for their families, and it inspired me. I'm still inspired by hard workers, whether it's one of my teammates taking early batting practice or a hotel housekeeper scrubbing the tub until it shines. For me, there is no other way to do things. If you want to get the most out of your potential, you should work as hard as possible, too. Then you might go from searching for role models to being someone else's role model.

Academics and athletics were important to me and my parents, but we talked about important life issues on those Sunday nights, too. Like I said, everything was covered. I wasn't allowed to drink, smoke, or do drugs. My parents told me that they were opposed to premarital sex, but if I decided to have sex, I should use the proper birth control protection. They never quizzed me on that important issue, but they emphasized their feelings on the topic. If a child is ever born, you will be responsible, they said. Having a baby when you're only a teenager is one devastating way to derail your dreams, they said.

It's impossible to remember a time when I didn't love baseball.

I've got so many great memories growing up with my family. I'm sure I wasn't always the perfect older brother (really!), but Sharlee and I had a lot of fun. Here I am at 9, and she's 4, and it's easy to see what holiday we were celebrating.

Baseball and basketball were my true loves, but I even played soccer as a kid.

The family that plays together stays together—here we are on vacation when I was 10. Mom and Dad were always doing fun stuff with me and Sharlee.

Check out my batting stance when I played shortstop for the Maroons in high school.

Here I am with my first coach at Kalamazoo Central, Coach Signeski, who taught me a lot about the game of baseball. The guy next to me was another player and someone I tried to mentor throughout the season.

This picture is from a trip I took to Yankee Stadium in 1992, the year I was drafted out of high school. It's like home to me now, but when I was 18, I was still learning my way around.

Sharlee and I are watching other speakers at the Jeter Day Celebration my old high school had for me. It was great to go back and talk to other students about their dreams and goals.

My whole family turned out for the first Turn 2 Foundation dinner in New York City. I have a lot of fun helping my dad plan these events, and all the hard work is for a good cause.

From the author's family collection.

These are some of my best friends from high school. You can tell we're going to the prom. I am in the second row on the left, and Doug Biro is next to me. Shanti Lal is on the far right in the first row.

John Iacono/Sports Illustrated

I always try to be the first one out of the dugout whenever one of us Yankees hits well or crosses the plate. Here Ricky Ledee hit a home run to beat Cleveland in July 1999.

Chuck Solomon/*Sports Illustrated*

Here's another picture of my batting stance. I am always making little adjustments to my swing. I watched tapes while I was recovering from a pulled muscle in May 2000, and I noticed a small error in my swing that I was able to correct when I came off the disabled list—it really helped, and my batting average started to rise.

This is one of the hardest moves to make—I've got to stay out of the runner's way and still maintain control of the ball.

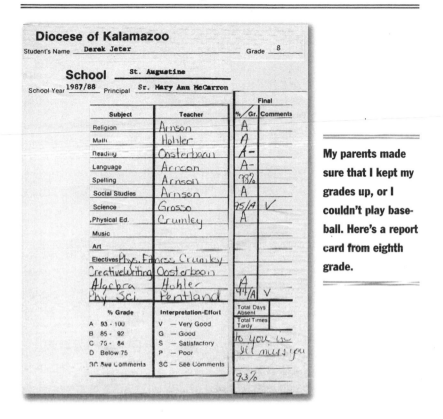

Diocese of Kalamazoo

Student's Name ___Derek Jeter___ Grade ___8___

School ___St. Augustine___

School Year ___1987/88___ Principal ___Sr. Mary Ann McCarron___

Subject	Teacher	% / Gr.	Comments
Religion	Arnson	A	
Math	Hohler	A	
Reading	Oosterbaan	A-	
Language	Arnson	A-	
Spelling	Arnson	98%	
Social Studies	Arnson	A	
Science	Grosso	95/A	V
Physical Ed.	Crumley	A	
Music			
Art			
Electives Phys. Fitness	Crumley		
Creative Writing	Oosterbaan		
Algebra	Hohler	A	
Phy. Sci.	Pentland	99/A	V

% Grade	Interpretation-Effort
A 93 - 100	V — Very Good
B 85 - 92	G — Good
C 75 - 84	S — Satisfactory
D Below 75	P — Poor
SC See Comments	SC — See Comments

Total Days Absent	
Total Times Tardy	
	to you in
	all miss you
	93%

My parents made sure that I kept my grades up, or I couldn't play base-ball. Here's a report card from eighth grade.

My parents had a very good rule when it came to drugs and alcohol. They told me if I was ever at a party or around a group of people who were "drinking or drugging," as my father used to say, I could call them, they would come and pick me up, and they would ask no questions. But if they found out I had been with people who used drugs and alcohol and had not left immediately, they would ask *lots* of questions. I never needed to call them once while I was in high school. Sometimes I would come home from a party and my parents would ask me why I left early and I'd just say, "Don't ask." That meant there was some unpleasant stuff going on so don't probe for details. Just be happy that I was smart enough to leave.

I don't think it's ever too early to start talking to your kids about the evils of drugs, and I don't think you can be too strong in what you say to them about drugs. Dad counseled people who had substance abuse problems, so he and Mom knew what to say to me and Sharlee about this. Since my father treated so many people who had struggled with drugs, he understood how powerful drug addictions could be, even for kids and teenagers.

When I was in the fifth grade, my parents heard rumors that drug dealers were trying to push stuff on kids near St. Augustine's. The school was located in downtown Kalamazoo, so we weren't isolated from the hustle and bustle of the city and my parents were naturally worried. I remember their reiterating to me that I shouldn't speak to anyone I didn't know or accept anything from anyone I didn't know once I left school grounds. I should just wait for the school bus and then get on it immediately. I heard this every day. I heard it so much that I could have repeated it in my sleep. I'd do the same now if I were a parent. Fortunately, no one ever tried offering me any drugs while I was in elementary school, or, for that matter, in high school. If anyone had, I'm confident I would have walked away.

Appreciate the Little Things

I'm not saying I was perfect. I had fun in high school. The key was not getting caught. Seriously, I didn't do anything that would shock my parents today. But, like lots of kids, maybe I stayed at a girlfriend's house after I said that I was going to be at a friend's house. Things like that. But I didn't drink, I didn't smoke, and I had a girlfriend they adored and I respected, so I was fine there. I was always scared to drink or try drugs. I thought that was going to mess me up. I didn't want to jeopardize all that I'd worked for to have fun for one night. Even as a teenager, that just didn't make sense to me. Why risk it? Why waste months, even years, of preparation in your life to drink six beers on your 17th birthday? I think that's silly. I knew my parents would have been devastated and I knew that wasn't the kind of behavior I'd find in someone I respected. I had a younger sister who looked up to me, too, so I didn't want to do anything like that and have her think it was cool to do.

The most glaring mistake I ever made started out as a visit to see a few girls, ended up with the cops being called in, and cost me the use of our family car for two months. When you're a senior in high school, losing car privileges is like walking around school with your zipper undone, with a "Kick Me" sign on your back, and with a permanent pimple on your forehead. All at the same time. But I did something silly, my parents were perturbed, and I paid for it.

Douglas Biro, whom I've known since I was in the fourth grade, Josh Ewbank, Andy Vorhees, and I were supposed to stay overnight at Doug's house. Andy's parents were away for the weekend, so we decided to go there. There were some girls having a slumber party down the street from Andy's house, so we got in my gray Datsun 310, which had 127,000 miles on it, and drove there. We weren't planning to do anything crazy. We just thought that it would be cool to stay at Andy's house while also seeing what these girls were doing.

I guess I should have known that this was not something I would have done if I'd followed the rules my parents had enforced. I was out too late. I wasn't where I was supposed to be. I was getting too close to danger, and unfortunately I found it.

We crept up to the house and Doug tossed rocks at the windows to get the girls' attention. Bad move. One of the girls' uncles came out of the house, shirtless, and yelling that he was going to teach us a lesson about bothering girls. Well, when someone without a shirt is running at you and yelling, your inclination is to bolt and that's what we did. We scampered into the woods, leaving the car behind, and I suddenly felt like I was in *Rambo*. We were hiding behind bushes and trees, we were running like there were bloodhounds chasing us, and we were scared. We heard the sirens of a police car and really got frightened. It was the first night my parents had ever let me use the Datsun and now I was running away from the car and from the police. The uncle sat on the hood of the car and told us, "Now I've got your car." I just stayed hidden, thinking, "Great move," and hoping my parents wouldn't hear about this. I knew I had to get back to the car so I switched sweatshirts with Doug, taking his black one and giving him my white one, thinking that would help camouflage me.

My parents got a call about 1 A.M. asking them if they knew where their car was that night. My father told the officer that his son had it at the Biro house. Wrong, the cop said. The car was abandoned and we need you to come and retrieve it. My parents were equally worried and angry as they drove to the scene because they didn't know where I was and didn't know what had happened.

We had left the car and avoided the police and were hanging near Josh's house, feeling like we were safe. But then I saw my parents' van, with all of its lights turned off, heading toward us. Sharlee was in the backseat and was as excited as if she were in an episode of *Cops*. She told my parents where they would probably find us and also told them to shut off the headlights so we wouldn't see them coming. My parents later told me they'd never seen her happier because she'd never seen me get in so much trouble.

Once I saw my parents, I knew I was doomed. I didn't say a word and hopped in the van with Doug. We drove home in silence. I didn't think it was a big deal because we were supposed to be at one place and went to another. It was late so I didn't call and I never told them that Andy's parents weren't home. I guess I really knew it was a big deal and I knew I'd get punished. I shouldn't have left Doug's house and I shouldn't have taken the car out after my midnight curfew. If I had been following what my role models taught me, I never would have done that.

We walked through the doors, with Sharlee still snickering, and my parents scolded me. My mother was crying. They could not believe how irresponsible I had been and they pelted me with questions: Why did I leave Doug's house? Why did we bother those girls? Why did we run away? What would have happened if someone had been hurt or if someone had stolen the car? I had no answers. I knew that none would suffice. I wanted people to be honest with me and so I had to be honest back to them. I had done something stupid.

They told me they were worried that I had lied to them. That was the major problem to them, because my parents had trusted me. They were more upset about my lying to them and about the police calling because they didn't know where I was. We've all heard that honesty is the best policy, but that night I was reminded of that saying again. One lie leads to another and, in my case, led to my mom crying and me winding up with no car to use.

When you're a senior, your car is your lifeline. I used to pick my girlfriend Marisa up for school and we'd arrive as a couple. Now she had to pick me up, or even worse, I had to walk. That stunk, but it taught me to think before I acted the next time. I knew what we had done was wrong, even if we were just trying to have fun. I had still participated. So I didn't see the car keys until two months later.

By my senior year, the most depressing clause in the contract was curfew. It was the only clause I ever zealously fought against.

Marisa had a later curfew than I did and that got embarrassing. There were times when she would leave a party or a dance to drive me home by midnight on a Friday or Saturday and then go back out again without me. I felt like I was a 15-year-old dating a 20-year-old.

Even if Marisa was over at my house, my father would wake up from a sound sleep at 12 o'clock and 30 seconds and announce very loudly and very clearly from upstairs, "Marisa, it's been nice seeing you. Time to go home." We'd be watching TV in the family room and I'd feel like climbing underneath the couch. To my parents, curfew meant that you were home and all activities had ended for the night. I argued that because Marisa and I were in our house, I had met my curfew. I lost that argument. They told me it was unfortunate for me that my girlfriend had a later curfew, but they weren't going to change their rules. For a guy who never had a curfew when he was growing up, my father was unrelenting.

"There's nothing good going on after 12 o'clock," my father used to say—sensible logic that a 17-year-old couldn't dispute.

Why did I abide by the contracts? Well, there were consequences. I didn't want to violate any of the clauses. If I did, I'd be grounded. And, if I was grounded, I wouldn't be able to play sports and that would destroy me. So my parents were shrewd. Even when I questioned the curfew, my father brought baseball into the equation by saying I should get to sleep by 10:30 whenever I had a game the next day because that extra sleep might give me an edge over the pitcher. I'm not sure if another hour in the sack helped me hit a curveball, but I listened and I don't think the extra sleep ever hurt me.

I think what made the contract easy to accept is that I understood it was my parents' way of showing how much they cared about us. They weren't making up rules just for the sake of making up rules. They were very interested in what we did and how we would develop as people. It wasn't about their trying to be strict because they thought that's what they had to do. It was about finding ways that Sharlee and I could stay safe and realize our potential.

So I've told you about how my parents had us sign contracts and had dozens of rules and were serious parents. But they were serious about recognizing what we had accomplished, too. They didn't just focus on what we shouldn't do. They gave us unconditional love and made us feel proud when we did well. They expected us to do well, but they also celebrated with us when we did. It wasn't like any of our achievements were taken for granted. We'd get hugs for good grades and good athletic performances, and my parents also created something called the Wall of Fame in our family room.

Two of the walls looked like a doctor's office that housed three dozen doctors because there were certificates scattered all over it.

This is the Wall of Fame in the Jeter house. Sharlee and I both looked forward to putting a new award on the wall.

My father wanted us to be proud of what we had achieved, so we displayed the honors we received for athletics and academics. You couldn't just toss any piece of paper on the Wall of Fame. We voted as a family on whether something belonged on the wall, making it even more exciting. Anytime I got a certificate at school for winning something or a letter for participation in sports, I hoped that it was worthy of making it up on the Wall of Fame.

When I look back now, that Wall of Fame was a worthwhile idea. Both Sharlee and I viewed our parents as role models, and getting on the Wall of Fame was an indication that we had pleased them. It was a simple idea. It didn't take much for my parents to put these certificates on the wall, but it made us feel a strong sense of accomplishment. It gave me something to strive for. I wanted my folks to recognize my achievements, so I tried to do things that would get me on the wall.

The Wall of Fame started in our first house, which we moved into when I was 10. It was a cozy yellow quad with a small front yard, a one-car garage, and a backyard that was about 60 × 60. But, to me, the best thing about our house on Cumberland Street was that it sat directly behind Kalamazoo Central. Forget the 60 × 60 yard. All I had to do to get to a playing area that was about the size of three football fields was jump over the five-foot fence in my backyard and onto Central's property. I turned Central into my personal backyard.

Central had a baseball field, a football field, and a soccer field, and was bigger than some colleges. Since my father and I shattered our picture window throwing a football on the very first day we moved in, my mother was thrilled whenever we scaled the fence to Central. She'd come with us a lot, too.

Sometimes my entire family would lumber the 60 feet out our back door, climb over the fence, and play baseball for hours. My father would pitch to me, and my mother and sister would play the outfield. Then we'd switch to a softball and my sister would hit. Or my father would hit me grounders and I'd throw to my mother at first. Those were some great times. I remember those days as fondly as I remember winning any World Series title because it was there that my family solidified our bond. We were doing something together, we were unselfish about it, and we were having a blast.

My father didn't have to be pitching to me. He could have been relaxing. My mother didn't have to catch my throws to first. She could have been reading. My sister didn't have to play the outfield. She could have been hanging out with her friends. But we all went. We made it a family outing, not just three hours of practice for me. That's what made it special. How could I not consider my Mom and Dad role models when they spent so much time doing what I loved?

When it was over, we would tease each other. I'd tell my father that he was moving a little slower and he'd tell me that he was better than me at this age and that he would have made the pros if there were more teams after he got out of college. My mother would tell both of us that we were slow, that we needed to wake up even earlier tomorrow, and that Sharlee was the best natural athlete in the family anyway. Actually, Sharlee was. She didn't have to practice the way I did and she was an excellent softball and volleyball player.

We'd cross the fields at Central, sweating and talking and laughing. No matter how dark it got, we always knew our way back home. Sometimes, I'm amazed when I think how fortunate I was to live behind those fields. I was motivated to be a good player, but even if I felt lazy one day, it didn't take much to walk 60 feet and hop over a five-foot fence.

My father grew up without his own home in Alabama, and he has always spoken about appreciating the little things in life. My mother was born in Jersey City, New Jersey, and was raised in West Milford, New Jersey. She was one of 14 children, so she learned to appreciate the little things, too. Neither one of their families was affluent. They couldn't have all of the things my parents worked hard to get for me. We weren't rich. Maybe we were middle class, but my parents provided for me in terms of the material things I needed, and more important, gave me the two most important role models I had.

Even as I have made millions of dollars playing baseball, my parents have reminded me to appreciate the little things. Don't forget to appreciate what is going on around you, they will tell me. Not everyone gets to play baseball every day. Soak up the sights, the sounds, and the scenes. Not everyone gets fan mail, they will say. Be sure to appreciate it when someone sends you a letter or says something nice to you. Be sure to remember that you had role models, and now you have to act like a role model, too.

My parents still appreciate the little things. A quiet dinner together, a movie, a phone call from one of their kids. Those types of little things, which are really big things, are still important to them. I try to emulate them in this way, too. I'll call my parents after every flight I take, just to let them know I'm doing OK. I still hug and kiss them whenever we part company. I still call them to seek advice. They are the two best role models I've ever found, but I haven't stopped looking for more. And I'm proud if I can turn around and be a role model for anyone else.

The World Is Not Always Fair

he stares often followed us into restaurants, during searches for apartments, and when my mother picked me up from an after-school program for black children. There were a lot of people who stared at my family and me when I was younger. Even more people stare at me now, but the majority of them are staring because they have seen me playing with the Yankees. That's fine. But I haven't always been noticed because I'm with the Yankees. I used to get noticed because my mother is white, my father is black, and my sister and I are in between with olive complexions.

I have strong memories of my parents telling me as a child that I would encounter people in the world who weren't fair. They told me that I would meet people who wouldn't like me and who would treat me unfairly because my mother and father were not the same color.

I was an innocent kid, so I couldn't understand why someone would dislike me because of my mom and my dad. How could they not like them? My parents are gracious people. I didn't really dwell on race unless someone else made it an issue because a white mother and a black father is the only family that I knew. To me, it was and still is normal. That's my family and my life.

But I soon learned there was something different about how some people treated us. I felt it when I'd go shopping with my mother and I'd drift off to look in the toy section and I'd have a salesman following me. I asked my mother why that happened (and it would become even more prevalent when I was with one of my darker-skinned cousins) and she told me that the salesman probably thought I was planning to steal something. I think it confused me more than it angered me. My mother told me not to give someone who was so ignorant the satisfaction of even acknowledging what I knew they were doing. So I didn't.

Sharlee had some white friends who used to think it was fun to shoplift, so she would stay away from them in certain stores, but the salesman would follow my sister instead. I've always tried to give people the benefit of the doubt and figured that most people are fair, but I didn't always get the same treatment in return. I've always felt that the best way to deal with this is by not turning it into a major deal. Don't let someone else's ignorance dominate you. My way of dealing with ignorance was usually by ignoring it, if that was possible.

Obviously, my parents noticed more things than I did. Parents see their kid not invited to a birthday party, maybe a birthday party where every other kid is from the same race, and it makes them suspicious. Parents see their kid omitted from an All-State baseball team, even though their kid had better statistics and wound up being named one of the top five high school players in the country a few months after the team was announced, and they wonder if it was related to race. My parents had more intuition about these incidents then I did, especially my father. He can still recall what it was like to be a young boy in Alabama who had to drink from separate water fountains and go to a movie theater for blacks only. I wanted to believe that people wouldn't judge me by the color of my skin. It's not always true, I know, but it would be a wonderful world if it were.

We're all going to have to deal with some kind of unfairness in our lives. We are going to be treated in ways we don't want to be treated and judged by people who don't even know us. This unfair treatment can happen because of race or religion or where we live or what we look like. It's a sad part of our society.

You might get called nasty names at school because of your color, because you come from a single-parent home, because of the clothes you wear, because you have acne, or because you're overweight. Obviously, no one deserves to be chastised for any of these things, but it still happens every day. You know it and I know it. We've all heard it and, unfortunately, we've all probably used some of these names, too. I used to routinely tease a girl in my elementary school until my parents scolded me for not treating her the way I expected to be treated. I was only 9 or 10, but the lesson stuck with me because I knew what it was like to be teased, too, and I wanted everyone to treat me fairly. I left her alone after that.

As aggravating as it is to be the target of abuse, it's vital to be able to get past it. How you respond to any kind of unfair treatment will eventually dictate how damaging that treatment will be. If you obsess over what someone has said or done to you, you give that person's actions more power. We always tried to avoid letting that happen in our family, which can be a strain.

You have to try to be strong enough as a person or as a family to prevent someone's ignorance from having that much of a grip on you. I'm not saying that you should forget things and act like they never happened. Sometimes you can do that and should do that. But it also helps to remember the inexcusable treatment you have received because it'll make you work harder and will remind you of how not to treat others. I don't think you can let someone who is trying to provoke you succeed. One of the best things you can do to any antagonist is offer no reaction. That will probably give him or her less incentive to treat someone unfairly the next time.

My parents enjoyed raising their family in Kalamazoo, a town of about 220,000 in southwest Michigan, about halfway between Detroit and Chicago. Because Western Michigan University is in Kalamazoo, professors and students from all over the world live there, and that helped make Kalamazoo and Kalamazoo Central High School culturally diverse. We moved there from New Jersey when I was four, and Sharlee was born a year later. I had lots of close friends, people like Douglas Biro, Shanti Lal, and Marisa Novara. My parents had dear friends, too, though I don't remember them going out with other couples for dinners or movies. I think Sharlee and I were their entertainment.

I liked growing up in Kalamazoo and have great memories, although I don't miss the cold weather. Man, it gets cold there. I live in Tampa during the off-season now and anytime I go back to Kalamazoo, I feel like I'm going to Alaska. My father always tells me that I've gotten soft and asks me how I lived in Kalamazoo for 14 years. So I tell him I didn't exactly have a choice. I couldn't just pack up my suitcase and bicycle to Hawaii when I was 13 years old.

This is me at 10 years old with a bunch of my cousins.

I'm proud of being from Kalamazoo, but, like anywhere in the world, there were some ignorant and insecure people who lived there, and in the 20 years my family was there, we encountered some of both. We didn't run into problems every day, but there were some isolated incidents that are hard to forget.

One of the first times that we hunted for an apartment in Kalamazoo was a disastrous experience. My parents twice visited apartments that were supposed to be vacant, but curiously were told the apartments were unavailable. The next time there was a vacancy my father went alone and was rebuffed. So my mother then tried for the apartment by herself and she got it. After she filled out the necessary papers to secure the agreement, she sent my father back to pick up the keys. That was a shock for the superintendent, I'm sure. I was a little kid so I didn't know what was going on, and at that point my parents tried to keep it that way.

I know it wasn't easy for my parents to be a biracial couple and then to be a biracial couple with two kids. They met almost 30 years ago, when the Civil Rights Acts of 1964 and the Voting Rights Act of 1965, which guarantee basic civil rights for all Americans regardless of race, were still fresh in people's minds. I know some people today who won't even date a person from another race because they don't want to deal with what other people might say or do. It isn't worth the possible ramifications to them, but it's too bad they feel that way.

My parents met in Frankfurt, Germany, in 1972 while both of them were in the army, and they met in an interesting way. My father had a white sergeant friend from Kentucky who wanted to date a black female soldier, who happened to be my mother's roommate. The sergeant thought the safest and easiest way to go on the interracial date was to bring my father along. My mother's roommate was not too enthused about the date so she asked my mom, who had been in Germany for just two days, to join her. The sergeant and the roomie barely lasted through that first date, but my mom and dad clicked.

Still, I can only imagine how some ignorant people felt about interracial dating in the 1970s. It's 2000 and there's a college in South Carolina that only recently began to allow interracial dating, and you have to have a note from your parents to the school saying it is acceptable, all of which is revolting. Yet my parents still fell in love and never let others dictate how they would act. Not even after my mother's dad expressed reservations, something that saddened my parents.

When my parents returned from serving in 1973, they decided to get married and they wound up doing it quietly in Tennessee. My father's mother and sisters were accepting of my mother and of the marriage, but my mother admitted that some people in her family took some time to come around.

Sonny Connors, my grandfather, was a deeply religious man who gave more than half a century of his life to working in churches. He had always taught my mother and his 13 other children that everyone was equal in the eyes of God. So my mother was surprised when her father sidled up to her after she told him she was going to get married and said, "Look at the problems it might bring. Have you thought about that?"

My mother had already made up her mind. She had found the man she loved. Ironically, part of the reason she fell in love with my father is because she thought he was so much like her father. They were both quiet men who were hard workers and were devoted to their families. I know my mother was disappointed. I know that she would have preferred that her father had never asked her that question, but she blamed it on the times.

All my grandfather was really trying to do was remind her about what she was getting into, but it unnerved her. My grandfather was not a racist. Maybe, at that time, he was being a realist and wanted to let my mother know she was about to traipse down a potentially rough road. My mother knew that. It didn't matter to her. What mattered to her is that she was in love. My mother wasn't going to let the world decide whom she could marry. That would be unfair.

"I wasn't accepted, I don't think, at first," my mother has said. "It was never stated or spoken, but there was that tension. We didn't grow up in a very nice neighborhood, but my father always said that everyone was created equal. I always thought that my dad would be the one to accept. He always used to say he wanted the best for his daughters. Look at the problems it might bring. That was it. That was the only time he ever said anything to me."

Out of respect for her father, Mom never made a big deal out of how upset she was with his initial reaction. She figured that she knew her father and that he would eventually realize how much she loved this man, no matter what color my father's skin was, and the tension would dissipate. She was right, although it took some time. That's one of the reasons my parents used to just send Sharlee and me to my grandparents' house for the summer on our own. Besides, my mother has told me, my grandparents could offer us so much more since they lived on a lake and since my grandmother was home all the time. My parents didn't travel too often to New Jersey because there was little communication at times between my grandfather and father, but no matter what they felt, they never kept us away from our grandparents.

My grandfather grew to be extremely fond of my father, and my mother thinks that by doting on me and Sharlee my grandfather tried to make up for ever questioning the marriage. He loved both of us dearly. Later on in life, after one of my aunts married a Mexican and another aunt married a Colombian, he joked about the melding of the family. When everyone gathered at his house for Christmas, Grandpa would smile proudly and talk about how his house and his family were now part of the United Nations. Everyone laughed.

This is Grandma Connors with me at the Triple-A All-Star Banquet in 1995.

"It took him a while, but he grew into it," my mother said. "He never ever shunned the kids. It was a society type thing that made him ask that. I think he tried to compensate for that in other ways. I think he tried to give my kids a little more love."

This story illustrates what I meant about overcoming unfair treatment. All my grandfather was doing was trying to look out for his daughter, but even back then my parents were resolute about what they felt was right and didn't let anyone's opinions stop them. And, in the end, everything worked out for them. My grandmother, another Dorothy who happily calls my father "Jeter," said he is the best thing that ever happened to her daughter.

If my parents had not reacted in the quiet, respectful way they did to my grandfather's question, I never would have been as close with him as I was. If they had reacted angrily, there could have been some friction and it might not have ever dissipated. But they did not let this issue mushroom into a problem that wouldn't go away. They were bigger than the problem and they wouldn't let it stop them from living the way that they wanted to live or from staying close to the people they loved.

Love What You Do and Do What You Love

My grandfather was a quiet, strict man, just shy of six feet tall, with a full, worn face and thin, light brown hair. All you had to do to know he was a blue-collar worker was look at him. From my grandfather's work boots to his work pants to his plaid shirt to his callused hands, he was obviously a man who knew what it was like to work hard for a dollar. Grandpa passed that work ethic on to his children and his grandchildren, including me.

When I stayed with my grandparents in the summer, I didn't really bother him. But I wanted to be around him. He was a custodian at Queen of Peace Church in North Arlington, New Jersey, and he also painted churches as a second job. He would come home from work, obviously tired after another 12-hour day, eat dinner, stay home with his family, go to bed, and start all over again the next morning. He always tapped me on the head whenever I rushed past him, and I was always running somewhere, or he'd ask my grandmother, "So where is Wonder Boy today?"

Even after I made it to the major leagues, he rarely made the 45-minute trip to Yankee Stadium because he had to get up at 4:30 A.M. to go to work. That showed me something. As much as I would have liked to have my grandfather in the stands watching me, he had a job and he was dedicated to it. That made a lot of sense to me because I've always been dedicated to what I'm doing, too.

There was one day where my grandfather taught me a lesson about hard work, the type of lesson I never forgot. Grandpa asked me if I wanted to go to work with him the next morning. None of the grandkids ever got to do that because he was so serious about what he did. I was so excited I couldn't sleep that night. I loved Grandpa, looked up to him in the same way I looked up to my father. Like my mother, I saw my father and grandfather as similar men.

When we got to Queen of Peace, I was already sweating. It was a muggy day in July and I knew that I could have stayed home and swum in the lake. But I was with Grandpa. For me, this beat anything that any 10-year-old would do that day. Grandpa took me over to the football field and I'd never seen anything like it. The field looked like a jungle. The grass reached my knees, and I felt sorry for the players who needed the field, and even worse for my grandfather.

My grandfather didn't say anything as we retrieved the lawn mower, a push mower with a bag. Poor Grandpa, I thought, how's he going to stop and empty that bag over and over? That is when my lesson started. My grandfather had me wheel the mower over to the field; he set me up in one end zone; and he told me that I had one job for the day—mow the football field. He told me that he would check back with me when I was finished. Then he left to do other chores.

I didn't say a word because I couldn't say a word. I never even dreamed of talking back to Grandpa, but I probably should have asked for some instructions. Instead, I started pushing the mower through the deep grass. My sneakers quickly turned green, I was wearing shorts, so the mosquitoes attacked my bare legs, and I could have drunk a gallon of water before I had walked 20 feet. It was bad enough that I had to use every ounce of strength to push the mower along, but as soon as I made minor progress, I had to stop, remove the bag, and empty the grass. The bag was almost as big as I was.

Grandma and Grandpa Connors and some of my aunts, uncles, and cousins attended one of my Triple-A games in Albany.

That felt like the longest day of my life. My T-shirt was soaked, my arms were hanging like branches falling off a tree, and I felt like quitting. It must have taken me, I don't know, six hours to finish mowing the field, but I did it. I got it done. It wasn't the most well-manicured field in the state, but it was a lot neater than the jungle we had encountered in the morning. My grandfather, with half a smile and half a smirk on his face, came to get me and I kept shaking my head. It was the only response I could really manage. I was too exasperated to do anything else.

"Now that you finally finished," my grandfather jokingly told me, "you're going to have to start all over because the grass has started growing again, it took you so long to finish!"

I never asked to go to work with my grandfather again. Though it had been a draining and annoying day, I took something valuable out of that experience. It helped me understand the importance of hard work and it helped me realize that I didn't want to do the difficult blue-collar job that my grandfather did so well. When I spoke to my mother on the telephone that night, she asked about my experience as an assistant. I didn't think it was funny, but I could tell by the tone of her voice that she was trying to suppress laughter.

"I don't ever want to have to do anything like that again," I told her. "I'm going to work even harder to make sure I'm a baseball player."

My grandfather obviously knew what he was doing. I was only 10, but I'd shown promise as a baseball player and as a student and my grandfather's plan was to vividly show me the sort of arduous work I could avoid. Not that he was embarrassed by what he did, no way. Grandpa was extremely proud of what he did and how he cared for two different churches for over 50 years. If you wanted to design a person who was talented enough and who cared enough about being inside God's house to be its caretaker, my grandfather was the perfect person.

But, in some way, Grandpa might have been showing me the kinds of things I'm trying to tell you in these 10 steps. There is a way to achieve your goals and do everything you've ever dreamed about. You shouldn't ever limit yourself and think that you can't do something. If I had wanted to take care of a church, I'm sure my grandfather would have encouraged me to do it. I think he wanted me to see what his 12-hour days were like and find out early on what I did and didn't want to do in life. I saw his world and I respected him even more for excelling in it because it was hard work.

There was nothing he wouldn't do for the people of the parishes he worked for. If that meant giving someone's car a jump start or getting to work at three in the morning to snowplow the driveway before the priests awoke or just being available to change a lightbulb for one of the nuns, my grandfather did it and loved doing it. I always tell people that my grandfather influenced more people in his occupation than I'll ever influence while playing for the Yankees. I know that because I saw it.

It was a gloomy January day in 1999 when we laid Grandpa Sonny to rest after he died of a heart attack. He was 68 years old. My grandpa was an icon in North Arlington. On the day of his funeral, Queen of Peace closed its elementary school and its high school as a memorial. Over 800 people attended the funeral. He probably knew each person by name and had probably done something for each of them in the 38 years that he had worked there. I was sad, so sad then and now, but it's comforting to know that so many people loved him and missed him.

About six weeks later I was in spring training, talking to some reporters about the upcoming season, when someone asked me if

I ever had a bad day. I was the shortstop on the Yankees and we had just won the World Series. I must never have an awful day, right? Wrong. I didn't have to think before describing how I had experienced one of the worst days of my life when my grandfather died. The reporters peppered me with questions about Grandpa and who he was and what he did, and I was happy to talk about him. My grandfather had seen so many stories about me in the newspaper and now I could honor his memory by talking about him for as long as anyone wanted.

The Yankees gave me copies of the articles the next day, and I remember reading a quote from Monsignor Thomas Madden of Queen of Peace that said, "It will be a long time before we see the likes of Sonny again. I've seen the way Derek carries himself, and in the long run, hopefully, he'll be the man his grandfather was. If he is, he'll really be accomplishing something in life."

You know what? He's right.

The World Isn't Color-Blind

Believe it or not, race wasn't discussed often in our house. I remember my parents explaining to me that racism would be a part of my life. They told me to always be aware of who was in front of me or in back of me and to always remain prepared. These lessons even extended into school. My parents talked to me about being better than everyone else. Don't just be as good as someone, because then there's a tie and you don't have any argument if that person gets selected ahead of you. You have to be better to make sure you are picked first, they told me. I think that's the right approach, no matter what color you are and whether you think you're going to be treated fairly or unfairly. I always try to be better than everyone at anything I do.

Usually, race became an issue in our house because of others.

Skin color has never been a big deal in my family—my aunts and uncles and cousins all look different, but we all are family. Here I am at age 11 with my little cousin Kerry.

Sharlee was athletic and personable and more of her friends were boys than girls. Some were black and some were white. It didn't matter to her. But it mattered to others. Sharlee had some white girlfriends who could only hang out with the black boys when they were at our house. Their parents didn't want them hanging out with black boys, so they'd do it by hanging out at the Jeters'. Where better to do that than in a house where the parents were biracial?

Sometimes, Sharlee wondered why these girls were allowed to hang out with her if their parents forbade them from befriending black boys. After all, *she* was half-black. I've encountered this type of behavior with acquaintances as well. There are some people who might be comfortable hanging out with me because they know me, but that doesn't mean they are equally comfortable with people from all different races.

I heard the silly names in school. Kids called me Zebra, or Oreo Cookie, or Black-and-White. When someone asked me what color I was, I always answered black-and-white. I still do. So that didn't bother me. The names didn't bother me much, either. I just listened to what my parents told me about race. They told me that I had the best of both worlds. I had a black father who loved me and I had a white mother who loved me. How many kids have two parents who love them? Not enough.

Sharlee used to be feistier, more like my mother when she was asked about her race. Sometimes, it wouldn't be enough for people to know that she had a white mother and a black father. So some people would ask her, "Who do you claim?" They wanted to know if she claimed to be white or black. Sharlee would sharply answer, "I don't claim anything. I claim both of my parents."

There are always going to be people who are ignorant or insecure or both and who don't know how to act around someone they've never seen. I got mad when an older kid called Sharlee an Oreo while we were riding home on the school bus. I was in the seventh grade, and I was perturbed that he was picking on my sister, a second-grader. I'm not big on fights, and my mother has said I wouldn't raise a finger to a fly, but I moved real close to this kid's face and told him, "Don't ever say another word to my sister again."

I was exasperated and Sharlee was crying when we burst through our door and told my mother what had happened on the bus. My mother had a soothing way about her and she did her best to turn the incident into something positive. She asked us if we liked Oreos. We said that we did. She reminded us that it was one of our favorite cookies and told us that everyone loved Oreos and we should not be upset about the comment. This boy had called Sharlee something that everyone loved anyway. It might sound trite, but it worked that day. All kids want to be liked.

Racism is such an ugly emotion. I know my kids will be asked someday if they are black or white, and the color of their skin will depend on whom I marry. But I know that they will be fine because they'll see me interacting with people of different races. I'm not worried about that. I think that parents should help their kids understand that it's what's inside, not what's outside, that counts in people.

Some people don't get it, never will, and don't want to try to understand why we're all the same. I discovered that on one of my first nights home after my first minor-league season. As soon as I finished up at Class A Greensboro in 1992, I returned to Kalamazoo and wheeled my 1992 red Mitsubishi 3000 GT around town. It was the one luxury I purchased for myself with my $800,000, and I was proud of it and proud of the fact that my baseball ability had allowed me to get it. I bought my parents a car, too, as a way of thanking them for everything they had done for me in helping me make it into pro baseball.

One night, I decided to drive a mile or so to the Taco Bell to grab some dinner. I parked in front of the restaurant and began walking toward the door when a group of kids in another car screamed, "Take that car back to your daddy, you n————."

I just stopped and stared at their car as it zoomed away. I had no idea who these guys were. To this day and for the rest of my life, I won't be able to figure out why anyone would ever be so hurtful and yell such a disgusting word at someone. That incident bothered me. I know I've talked about being able to let things go, but that stayed with me. As much as I'm a firm believer in not letting ignorant people invade your life, I also think we have to be honest with ourselves and be aware of what's going on in front of us.

I remember thinking that I was in my own hometown and I couldn't even go to pick up a taco without getting harassed. I know that most of the people I knew in Kalamazoo weren't racist, but all it took was one aggravating incident to anger me. I figured people would be proud of me for making it to the Yankees, and instead I had to listen to that nonsense.

You realize there are people out there who are insecure. If you have to sit there and dog someone out, then you're insecure. If it makes you feel good to talk bad about another person, there's something wrong with you. Not with me, but with you. We all need to learn not to internalize other people's insecurities and not let them get in the way of our goals. People will say stupid things, as I've witnessed, but it doesn't mean that you should let them adversely impact you. I know it's easier said than done, especially when it's particularly nasty and it really bothers you, but it's the best approach.

Don't forget that you can learn from unfair situations, too. If you see someone treating others rudely, he or she might unknowingly be teaching you more than one of your best friends could. By watching that person's disdainful actions and negative influence, you can remind yourself to never act like him or her.

I think a lot of times people feel threatened by things they don't know enough about. If there is something they're not familiar with, they don't know how to react. I think that goes back to education, and I'm not talking about the classes you take in school. I'm talking about being educated about different races and nationalities. To me, it's never been an issue. Quite often I'd play on all-black basketball teams and on all-white baseball teams. I was used to being around different races and used to being the one guy who didn't exactly fit in.

I've talked to other people who are the products of biracial parents and who have identity problems. They don't know who they are, what they are, or how they should act. I never had those problems and still don't. I think my parents prepared me for that. I was and still am proud of who I am. I have friends who are black, white, Spanish, Asian—you name it. I've had people ask me if I was Italian, Puerto Rican, Indian, white, black . . . and I'm probably forgetting some of the other guesses. It doesn't bother me. Why would it bother me? I have respect for every race and every nationality. If someone mistakes me for being something that I am not, I don't consider that a slight because I can identify with these people. I've been exposed to so many different people through athletic teams and through being in a melting-pot high school that I feel comfortable with anyone.

I had a visitor in my house in Tampa during spring training and we were talking about race. I was describing how I've never judged people by their race and that my friends are my friends because of who they are inside, not because of their skin color. He nodded and understood. Well, I couldn't have scripted what happened next any better in proving my point. In the next 10 minutes that night I received phone calls from Doug Biro, Gerald Williams, and Jorge Posada, probably three of my best friends in the world, to make plans for dinner. Doug is white, Gerald is black, and Jorge is Puerto Rican. Enough said.

Actions Speak as Loudly as Words

My father has told me that counseling Sharlee and me about being biracial was one more responsibility he and my mother had as parents. All parents have different responsibilities, and to my parents this was simply one more aspect of their jobs. After I got a little older and understood that there was usually going to be someone who would treat me differently because of the color of my skin, I think my parents used my biracial status as a character builder.

Since there are unfair people who would look for reasons not to take me seriously or accept who I am because of the color of my skin, my parents would constantly encourage me to outwork

My mom called this picture my "new family," and she's right. I've been playing with the Yankees since I was 18, and in the majors for five years. Some of the guys change every year, but I've made a lot of friends.

everyone and thus make sure that they couldn't ignore the quality of my performances. I've always been motivated to show people who I am by what I can do. I let my actions speak for me. But I'm not oblivious to the way that I'm being treated. If I ever felt that someone was trying to deprive me of something strictly because I was biracial, I'd want even more to get that something, whether it was a spot on a baseball team or an academic award.

Directly or indirectly, I think my parents prepared me very well for the life that I'm leading now. No matter how many dozens of times I said it, they couldn't have known that I was definitely going to play major-league baseball, that it was going to be with the Yankees, and that I was going to become so well known in New York. So recognizable that I have to be cautious in everything I do. But, by lecturing me about being aware, by the time I was 15 they pretty much made me the person I am now. They used to tell me that some people would judge me before I even opened my mouth or did one thing—so I shouldn't give them any reason to think their negative judgments were correct.

Basically, I've been cautious ever since I was a teenager. I'm like that even more now. When you play for the Yankees and you receive the attention that I have on and off the field through media coverage and endorsements, you always have to be "on." I can't saunter into a bar and act immaturely—or it'll be in the gossip pages. I can't scream at a cab driver or admonish a waiter, or it'll be in those same papers. I even have to be careful how I act walking down the street. People are going to judge me. Fair or unfair, it comes with the profession I've chosen and it's part of being a celebrity. I always have to be on and I'm used to it. My guard is always up. It stays up.

I think that's a shrewd strategy for anyone, no matter how anonymous or how famous you are. I'm not saying you should be distrustful of people, but I think you should always be wary of what you're saying and doing. This shouldn't prevent you from having a good time, and I'm not saying you should wear a muzzle. But a little caution should help you think situations through more clearly.

Even when I'm dealing with reporters, I keep that protective shield around me. I have a lot of respect for most of the writers who cover the Yankees, but I know there could be a writer who is not as honest as the others and who will take a part of my quote and use it in a way it wasn't intended. I always make sure to give complete answers when I respond to questions so that I don't leave any room for doubt. I don't want anything I say to get

Dorothy "Grandma" Connors
ON DEREK JETER

When Derek and Sharlee stayed with their grandparents in New Jersey for the summers as children, Derek turned his grandmother, Dorothy Connors, into his baseball buddy. They watched baseball games on TV, they went to baseball games, and they even played baseball together. Grandma would play baseball with the energetic Derek, even if it was 6 A.M. and even if he eventually threw so hard that her palm hurt.

"That's all he ever wanted to do," Grandma Connors has said. "You could see how good he was."

Grandma Connors took Derek to his first Yankee game when he was only six years old. Neither Derek nor his grandmother can remember who the Yankees played that day, but she insists that they won. She remembers Derek, who was always excitable and who was wearing a Yankee jacket, being in awe when he saw Yankee Stadium. Billy, Derek's uncle, bought him a Yankee cap and he wore it all summer.

"I was proud that he wanted to be a Yankee. I knew that he could do it."

She has admitted that when she sees Derek now, she sometimes gets flustered. He has gotten so big and everyone shouts out his name, so she wonders if she can still treat him the way she always has. But then Derek will give her

twisted. I've followed sports since I was young, I've seen athletes whose comments got them in trouble, and I just feel it doesn't make sense to let your words create controversies. I don't try to be boring, but I'm cautious about everything I discuss.

I learned that from watching other players. When I was called up to the Yankees in September of 1995, I didn't play much, so I watched a lot to try and learn. One of the players I studied was a hug and massage her shoulders and she'll quickly imagine he's back in her kitchen doing the moonwalk.

"When he was young, he loved Michael Jackson's dancing. When I see him racing after those balls and catching them, I think back to that dancing and I think it helped."

Derek was so sensitive to his grandmother's feelings that he almost didn't stay in Michigan to play in a summer baseball league as a 14-year-old because he was worried how she would react to not seeing him. But Grandma Connors knew the talented teenager should be playing every day and told him, "Follow your dreams. I'll be fine."

She is a huge Yankees fan, always has been. She used to eat crackers and listen to the Yankees on a radio with her father. Grandma Connors's favorite player of all time is Babe Ruth, and she speaks about him in the same reverential way that some kids talk about her grandson. She waited in a line for several hours on a muggy August day in 1948 and was one of the 100,000 people who paid their respects as Ruth's body lay in state at Yankee Stadium after he died from throat cancer.

"You know how they say Babe Ruth passed the mantle to Joe DiMaggio and to Mickey Mantle and then the other great Yankees?" she says. "I've heard people say that Derek is the next great Yankee. He's headed there. I have no doubt."

Don Mattingly. He was the team captain and a spokesman of sorts because the reporters wanted to ask him about various topics every day. We were in a mad sprint for the wild card, and Mattingly had never appeared in the postseason so he was in demand. If I had been a reporter, I would have been hounding Donnie, too. I liked the way Mattingly dealt with the news media. He was cooperative and engaging, but there was also a distance he imposed in the relationship. I try to be available to the media whenever I'm needed and you will never see me ducking into the trainer's room if I've made a play that cost a game. If you're going to talk after you've hit a homer, you'd better talk after an error.

For the most part, reporters in New York have been very fair to me. The gossip pages—well, that's another story. At first, it used to bother me when I'd read that I was at this club with some model or actress (and I really hadn't), but now I chuckle about it. My parents still ask me about items that they read in the newspaper because they're just being concerned parents, but my mother stopped believing everything that she read when someone wrote I was out in New York on a night when she knew I was in Puerto Rico with Jorge.

Don't get me wrong, I do go out, so some of the stories about my being in a club after a game are true. I'm 26 years old, I'm single, and I like having fun. I go out more in New York than I do when I'm home in Florida after the season. But I get amused by some of the things that have been written about me because they're not always true. I don't take any of it seriously anymore.

My mother got a taste of the gossip pages once when it was reported that she went to a club in Manhattan to meet a hockey player. She was appalled. Not only is she happily married, she doesn't know any hockey players. That's OK, though. That helped me. It told my parents that not everything is true and it gave my father enough ammunition to tease my mother for a lifetime.

I don't go out by myself and I rarely go out with just one other person. I like being around a lot of people, and for me and in my situation, it makes sense to have as many people around as possible. If something sticky happens, it's nice to have my friends with me to help get me through it.

Once in 1996 I was out in Manhattan with Gerald Williams, the former Yankee who is playing for the Tampa Bay Devil Rays this year, and Sean Twitty, a close friend and one of my former minor-league teammates. We were in a club that was about a block from my apartment and we were standing by ourselves in the corner after a game. I'd been in this place before and figured it was fine to be there on this night, hanging out with Twitt and Gerald.

But then the owner, someone I'd met before, stumbled up to Gerald in a drunken stupor and said, "You're black and you're in my club." The guy was loud and obnoxious and put extra emphasis on the word "black." I don't know if he was trying to start a fight, which would have been pretty dumb in his own club, but Gerald could have construed it as a threat if he'd really wanted. That's how belligerent this guy acted while pointing his finger in Gerald's face.

Gerald is as solid as a brick building and could probably bench press a taxi, so I don't know what this guy was thinking. But we all understood the right thing to do. There was nothing for us to gain from that situation, but there was so much to lose. This person wanted to incite us. He wanted a reaction. Instead, our reaction was to leave, never bothering to see who might be staring and never dreaming of returning to this club ever again.

5

Don't Be Afraid to Fail

 had made this shot so many times before. Tossing a piece of paper into the garbage can, throwing my socks into the hamper, or shooting a 20-footer in the schoolyard until it swished. Every time I did any of these things, I imagined that I had just buried a shot at the buzzer to win the game. It always had to fall at the buzzer, it always had to be a tough shot, and the ball always came to me. If I ever missed with the paper, the socks, or the ball, I'd do it again until the ending to my script was perfect.

Then, in my sophomore year at Kalamazoo Central, I got the chance to try what I had been acting out for so long in a game that counted. We were behind, 67–65, to Portage Central, one of our main rivals, and there were three lonely ticks on the clock. The game was at Zuidema Gymnasium, our home court, and our fans were loud and anxious. No one knew what to expect in those few seconds.

We felt that the referees had given Portage most of the calls, but we got a lucky break when Anthony Harkness, one of our players, dribbled the ball off his leg and out of bounds. No one from Portage was within five feet of him. Everyone in the gym saw it, but, inexplicably, neither referee did. We got the ball back with three seconds left and a chance to steal the game. I wanted to be the one to steal it for us.

Thankfully, our coach felt the same way. Don Jackson knew a potential gift when it was waved in front of him. Coach Jackson was going for the win. He didn't want the game to go into over-time, because one of our best players had already fouled out.

So Coach Jackson diagrammed a play that was designed to get me open for a three-pointer. I heard the crowd howling as we sat in our huddle, but as soon as Coach Jackson talked about going for three, I blocked out every other sound and heard only his halting voice. "We're going to win this game," he said. "We can do it." I was one of our best three-point shooters, and though I hadn't scored a point until the fourth quarter, I prayed the play would come to me.

Harkness inbounded the ball about 10 feet from halfcourt on the left side of the gym. I was supposed to run my man toward a pick near the top of the key, keep going when he got screened by Rashaan Hawkins, receive the pass, and then turn and shoot from beyond the three-point arc. I was told to go for the three, go for the win, and send us home smiling. I felt confident that I could drain the shot and even more confident after Coach Jackson planned for me to take it.

The next time you ask someone to complete an important task, remind him beforehand about how confident you are that he can do it. I'll bet you that he will perform that assignment even better than usual because he will know you feel secure in his doing it. It has to help someone's state of mind. I know it helped mine in that game. The play worked beautifully. I shook free of Rashaan's pick, I took the pass, I dribbled once, and I calmly and smoothly nailed the three-pointer, giving us a 68–67 victory. I got knocked down afterward and tumbled to the hardwood, but it didn't matter. I'll never forget the feeling of seeing the ball drop through the net. It happened 10 years ago, but I can still feel that ball in my hands and I can still remember the emotion I felt after it went in. It was magical. There's no better feeling than that for an athlete. None.

I'd take that kind of situation, a chance to be the hero or the goat, in every game I play for the rest of my life. Those moments are what make playing sports so exhilarating, whether it's a last-second shot, a field goal as time expires, or a 3–2 count with two outs and the winning run on base in the ninth inning. I love being in those situations with the Yankees, those tense moments in the postseason as we chase another title. To me, that's fun. Shouldn't it be fun to do what you love? If you find something you love doing and you can find a way to make a living at it, seize the chance. You'll go to work happy every day.

Ever since that three-pointer against Portage, I always wanted to take the final shot, and of course I always wanted to be the batter in the most crucial spots in baseball. Whenever I was in those situations in basketball and whenever I've been in them with the Yankees, I've always believed that I'm going to sink the jumper or that I'm going to get the hit. You have to feel that way. I think you should feel that way in life, too. If you don't believe in yourself, why should anyone else believe in you? We can be our own best friends or our own worst enemies. I have always vowed to be my own best friend by exhibiting a positive attitude.

I think that once you get the feeling of being successful and of winning, those feelings outweigh the possibility that you might not succeed. That's the chance we have to take in life. I like that danger. I like the thrill of competition. I love dangling off that cliff, not knowing whether I'm going to fail or succeed. I would rather have the chance to succeed at some endeavor and eventually falter than to never even have the chance to succeed at all.

Why? Because I never think I'm going to fail. I want a chance to be that 15-year-old from Kalamazoo Central again and again because I truly believe I can do it. Obviously, I don't succeed every time. But I can honestly tell you that I go into every game thinking I'm going to be the hero that night. I have to, or I wouldn't enjoy it so much. It's really a great approach. Believe that you're going to get an A on a test, believe that you're going to get accepted to your first college choice, believe that you're going to get that dream job. Believe in yourself and you'll be closer to actually succeeding.

My approach in life is often similar to my approach to that three-pointer back in high school. I want to go for it and I like being in control of whatever decisions I make in critical situations. Even if, deep down, I know I'm not in total control of the outcome, I can control my actions. I've never hidden from a challenge. The more difficult something is, the more interested I get.

My mother has said that I've had an inner drive from the time I first picked up a ball. I've wanted to be the best at everything. A lot of people might have that drive, but she told me that I knew how to use it. I knew how to channel it. You know what? Even if I'd missed that three-pointer against Portage Central, I would have been hoping and expecting Coach Jackson to call the play for me the next time, too. Failure is part of success, and until you understand that, accept it, and learn to deal with it, you probably won't have as much success as you could and should enjoy.

If I ever do something unusual or extraordinary and people say it was a fluke, I'll vehemently disagree. I believe it's a fluke when I'm unsuccessful. Whenever anyone asks me about the home run I poked against the Baltimore Orioles in the 1996 American League Championship, the one where Jeffrey Maier reached across the Yankee Stadium right-field wall and interfered with the ball, I don't apologize. People have asked me if I thought the homer was tainted and if I felt bad about it, and I always tell them to ask the Orioles if they felt bad. To me, that was ruled a homer, so it was no fluke. You see what I mean? I got up expecting to get a hit. I didn't plan to have an overzealous 12-year-old lurking behind Tony Tarasco, but I did have to hit the ball 315 feet. Didn't I? When you go into a situation expecting to succeed, whatever good happens shouldn't surprise you.

I don't think I'm being cocky when I act that way. It's just the mentality that I have. You should always think that you're going to be successful and you should always want to be successful. If it doesn't work out for you and you strike out with the winning run on third or you fail your driver's test, you have to acknowledge that something went wrong, and adjust your actions and go after it again the next time. The next time you try that task, don't think about the time you faltered. Think about all of the times in which you have excelled. That's a path back to success.

One of the more disappointing things you can do to yourself is not even try to do something because you're afraid of failing. Maybe you want to design clothes or run marathons or work in Europe for a year. Don't shy away from it, because 10 years from now you will be asking yourself if you could have done it. That's why I work so hard now—because I don't want to question whether I could have done more with my career when it ends. I'm never going to put myself in a position where I wish I could have done more. We control what we do with our lives. Don't be afraid to use that control to make things happen.

Become the Big-Game Player

I used to love watching Michael Jordan play basketball. I loved how hard he worked, the way he took command of games, the way he seemed to glide around everyone or float over everyone else on the court. Michael is the best athlete I've ever seen, and he wasn't as bad a baseball player as some people liked to claim he was. He just hadn't played the game for so long. Sometimes, like every other fan, I wish Michael were still playing hoops.

My first meeting with Michael occurred during the Arizona Fall League in 1994 when he was playing minor-league baseball with the Chicago White Sox. He made it to second base, grinned,

I was number 23 on my elementary school team—maybe I wasn't as good as another number 23, Michael Jordan, but I sure played my heart out.

and turned to me and said, "What's up, D.J.?" I was stunned and I think I mumbled, "What's up?" but I stopped short of calling him M.J. or, thankfully, Mr. Jordan. I was blown away that Michael even knew who I was, never mind that he knew enough about me to use a nickname.

I bumped into him a few times in Arizona that fall and I was impressed with the way he handled himself. Michael always tried to make other people feel comfortable. I never had dinner with him, but I watched him and learned. I don't even know if he knows this or if he cares, but I have tried to emulate him on and off the field. He carries himself in a classy, dignified manner, and I think a lot of athletes could learn from his examples as a player and an entrepreneur.

There is a Nike commercial that I think says a lot about Michael Jordan and a lot about the way you have to act as a professional athlete and as a person who is trying to make the most of his life. The commercial shows Jordan getting out of a sport utility vehicle as he arrives for another game. This is what he says to himself as he walks toward the locker room: "I've missed more than 9,000 shots in my career. I've lost almost 300 games. Twenty-six times, I've been trusted to take the game-winning shot. And missed. I've failed over and over and over again in my life." Then Jordan vanishes into the locker room, but his voice is getting stronger as he concludes, "And that is why I succeed."

I agree with the philosophy of those 30 seconds, the idea that failure is part of success. There are going to be failures as you pursue your goals, some minor and some major, but the important thing is to always believe that you can succeed. I know that it's easier to say that than it is to do it, and I've told you how I struggled with my confidence in my first two years in the minors. But, even as I struggled, there was a part of me that believed I could succeed. Sometimes, it was a small part of me. But I wouldn't have made it this far if some part of me hadn't felt that way. You've got to find that confidence, even if it's only a sliver of confidence on some days, and cling to it. Some people are motivated by fear and that's what inspires them. That's fine, too. But there's got to be some semblance of confidence in your life, too, so you can move forward.

When I think about Jordan, I think about how talented he was during his playing career. Maybe the best player ever. But I also think about how confident he was. When Jordan had the ball with a few seconds left and the Bulls were down by one, his opponents knew that he was going to take the shot and knew that he believed he was going to nail the shot. It's kind of the same with Tiger Woods in golf now. When Tiger is in the hunt on the last day of a tournament, you know that the other golfers are staring at the leaderboard and wondering, "OK. Where the heck is Tiger?"

Everyone wants to be known as a big-game player in professional sports. When I come to bat in a pivotal spot, I want people to say, "Uh oh, here he comes." That's the way it was with Michael Jordan and that's the way it is with Tiger Woods. If you plant that seed in someone's head, it's one more thing for them to think about while they're trying to beat you. I'm always confident because I know I've done well before so I expect to do it again. If a pitcher senses that I'm confident, it works to my advantage.

This strategy can help you in any walk of life. If your boss notices that you are confident about completing a project and believe you will succeed at it, he's more likely to give you a more challenging project the next time. If your competitors see how confident you are about selling your product, they might be intimidated by you. At the very least, they'll respect you. You have to want to show everyone that you're good, even great, at what you do, that you've achieved a certain level of competency in your career. For me, the important things in my life are base-ball and trying to remain the same person I've always been. For you, it can be anything. Just have a passion for what you're doing.

Obviously, we all can't be Michael Jordan or Tiger Woods, but we can be very good and very passionate about what we do. I'm sure there's someone who considers himself the Michael Jordan of firemen. I'm sure there's someone else who considers himself the Tiger Woods of mailmen. I hope there's someone else who considers himself the Derek Jeter of waiters. You should take pride in what you do, no matter what it is, and strive to improve.

Thrive on Challenge

My passion has always been exactly what I'm doing today. When Joe Torre presented me with the Joe DiMaggio Toast of the Town award from the New York chapter of the Baseball Writers Association of America last February, he talked about the twinkle that I have in my eyes when I play. That was nice to hear. I do feel a special spark when I play baseball, and I get effervescent when the games are important. I've got a .326 average in 45 games in the postseason and I've gotten a hit in my last 17 post-season games, which ties me with Hank Bauer of the Yankees for the all-time record. I think part of the reason for this is because I'm so comfortable in pressure-packed games. I don't fear them. Those are the games we should all want to play in.

The more intense the game, the more I want that first pitch to be thrown so the fans can make noise and we can finally get going. Pedro Martinez pitched an unbelievable one-hitter and struck out 17 Yankees in Boston's 3–1 win on September 10, 1999, at Yankee Stadium. It might have been the most dominant game ever by an opposing pitcher at the stadium, and if Chili Davis hadn't knocked a ball over the right-field fence, Martinez might have pitched a no-hitter. Who knows how that might have further impacted the American League East race or even the postseason? As it was, the Red Sox gave us our only loss in the playoffs.

But do you know what I remember most vividly about that game? I remember that I was on deck when the final out was recorded in the ninth. As phenomenal as Martinez had been that night, firing 97-mile-per-hour fastballs and awesome changeups and making us look silly, I wanted to hit against him one more time. I was hoping Chuck Knoblauch would get on base so I'd have that chance, one more chance. But Pedro struck out Chuck with a 96-mile-per-hour bullet and preserved his gem.

These are the challenges I thrive on, even though it sounds perverse to want to face Pedro in the ninth. But I'll remember that game, that missed opportunity, more than some 11–3 win from May because I could have changed the outcome. Going up against Pedro and the Red Sox already has a playoff-like intensity, and getting one more opportunity to hit against him would have made my night. Like I said, I'll take intense situations like that seven days a week for the rest of my career.

The first time I had a critical at bat in the major leagues was an at bat that most fans probably don't even remember. When the rosters expanded to 40 players in September 1995, the Yankees recalled me from Class AAA Columbus. I was going to get the opportunity to experience the wild-card race and perhaps contribute as a pinch-runner or pinch-hitter, if that.

Manager Buck Showalter called me into his office when I arrived at the stadium. Billy Martin's uniform with the numeral 1 was in a frame on the wall behind him, and Showalter also had the lineup card from his first victory as a manager in 1992 on display. He told me that I was with the team because the Yankees thought I might be able to help them get into the postseason. But Showalter was adamant about what the Yankees were trying to do in getting there for the first time since 1981 and told me if I didn't act responsibly, he didn't want me around. I know he had to say that and I also knew I wouldn't be a problem.

Buck had purple bags drooping below his eyes and his couch looked slept in, two signs of a serious manager. He was in the last year of his contract, and the team had stumbled earlier in the year and wound up needing to win 26 of the last 33 games to win that wild-card spot. I remember Buck telling me to study players like Don Mattingly, Wade Boggs, Randy Velarde, Mike Stanley, Jimmy Key, and John Wetteland because they probably had superior work habits to anyone I had ever seen. I planned to do a lot of studying.

"I do remember that Derek wasn't wide-eyed," Showalter has said. "He was very respectful, but he wasn't overwhelmed by the situation. You could tell he had his feet on the ground."

I barely played. I didn't expect to play. I was there to watch, observe, soak up some insights. That's it. I got a break on September 26th when Bernie Williams was delayed returning from Puerto Rico to Milwaukee after he visited his newborn daughter, Bianca. Bernie was supposed to get on a 10:05 A.M. flight out of San Juan, but he missed the flight and Showalter had to scramble to make out a starting lineup without Williams that night.

There were a lot of questions before the game about how Showalter would replace Bernie. There were five games left and the Yankees had a one-game lead over the Angels for the wild card, so the timing was sticky. Buck waited as long as possible for Bernie, but, eventually, he submitted a lineup that had Gerald Williams in center field, Randy Velarde, our regular shortstop, in left field, and me at shortstop and batting eighth. Showalter's hope was that Bernie would get to County Stadium in time to be inserted into the eighth spot in the order, meaning I wouldn't have to bat.

I knew how critical this game was for the Yankees, but I tried to focus on doing my job and not focus on the magnitude of the game. I was 21 years old. If I started to think about the postseason and how my starting in this game could impact that, it would have been the wrong thing to do. As much as I've preached about confidence, there are different levels of confidence, too. Obviously, I was a bit nervous. I had confidence, but new experiences bring new challenges and this was new for me. I was playing in a game that would help determine whether the Yankees would advance into October, but I knew I had to just think about it being another baseball game. This wasn't the time to ponder the big picture.

The first and only time I batted in the game was in the second inning. I was loose as I went to the plate against Scott Karl with two outs and Gerald on first. I'm not sure what kind of scouting report the Brewers had on me, but I've always been able to hit the ball to the opposite field. I lashed one of Karl's pitches to right center field for a double that scored Gerald with the first run of the game. Even though I had gotten a hit in my second major-league game in May, this felt as if I had done something that really mattered.

I trotted out to shortstop for the third inning and I was probably puffing my chest out a little more than usual. I had gotten a big hit during a critical game in September, and I felt great. In fact, I felt more and more like I belonged.

When I got to my position, I thought I heard someone calling me. I turned and saw Velarde jogging toward me. Bernie had arrived, so Buck quickly put him in center (Bernie was still tucking in his uniform jersey as he took the field). He moved Gerald to left, and he put Velarde at shortstop. No one had told me that Bernie was at County Stadium, so I had to lope back to the dugout like a kid who was leaving the game because he had to go

I played in the Westwood Little League as a kid, here at age 14 for the All-Stars. I've loved playing baseball my whole life. There's nothing like putting on a fresh uniform or sliding into second base, whether you're 14 or 34!

to his prom. I wish I could have continued playing, but at least I had that timely hit. We won, 5–4, and my contribution was significant since we didn't clinch the wild card until the final day of the regular season.

There are times when I still reflect on that at bat because I look at it as a defining moment of sorts for me. I think we all have moments or events in our lives where we gained more confidence in ourselves. I was more secure after that game. It was only one at bat, one measly at bat. But I milked that moment for everything I could during the off-season. I ran harder, I lifted more, and I

Don Zimmer
ON DEREK JETER

Don Zimmer has been in professional baseball for 52 years. He is honest, affable, and not easily impressed. Zimmer played shortstop in the major leagues for 12 years, playing with Hall of Fame shortstops Pee Wee Reese on the Dodgers and Ernie Banks on the Cubs and against Phil Rizzuto of the Yankees. So Zimmer knows what a Hall of Fame shortstop should look like.

"That's the hardest thing for any player to do," says Zimmer. "Get into the Hall of Fame."

But, as Zimmer watched Derek Jeter field another grounder flawlessly, he made a case for Jeter, Alex Rodriguez, and Nomar Garciaparra as three shortstops playing right now who are gradually working toward becoming Hall of Famers. There have never been three shortstops like Derek, like Seattle's Rodriguez, and like Boston's Garciaparra performing simultaneously, not in Zimmer's or anyone else's lifetime.

"What did Pee Wee and Phil hit? In the 270s, right? You look at what these guys have done and what they have going on for them and you have to think that all three of them can make the Hall of Fame. I know that it's early and you don't want to put that tag on someone, but look at the numbers. I don't see how you can argue against them."

took more batting practice because I was juiced by the feeling that hit gave me. That's something we all can do.

If you accomplish something that you are proud of, whether it's in a high school class, in a Little League game, or at your first job, you should use that experience to help inspire you the next time you face a similar situation. I'm not saying that you should

Of course, Zimmer, the Yankees' bench coach, is partial to Jeter. Zimmer adores Jeter the way a grandfather adores his grandson. The 69-year-old Zimmer, who never knew what seven-figure salaries were during his playing career, said that Jeter deserves to make $10 million or more a year because he is the player that most fans want to see and because he keeps improving.

"This is the fifth year I've seen him play and he's gotten better as a player, but he hasn't changed as a person. If he does this for another 10 years, I don't think he'll change."

Jeter loves to tease Zimmer, whether it is about his mostly bald head or his gimpy knees or some advice that Zimmer has offered him. Zimmer has urged Jeter to steal more bases, and whenever Jeter does something Zimmer has advised him to, he peeks into the dugout as a way of saying, "I told you so."

"You knew in a minute that the guy could play," says Zimmer. "He's got a lot of talent and he's so coachable it's unbelievable. He doesn't go to sleep on you when you tell him something. He listens and then he does it."

"What have we heard all our life?" asked Zimmer. "This is a kid's game. That's the way he treats it. He's having more fun out there than anyone. We're having fun because we get to watch him play."

rest on your laurels. You shouldn't do that because circumstances change and you don't want to be caught clinging to the past. But there is nothing wrong with taking those positive moments, remembering why they were positive, and letting them work for you. Whether it's a physical or mental boost, it can help you overcome the next hurdle.

I think that whole experience helped set me up for a terrific 1996 season. I had witnessed what it was like to be involved in a race for the postseason and it was about what I expected. Exciting, exhilarating, and intoxicating. I'd been playing baseball ever since tee ball and I'd always played against older kids, so playing in the majors with more experienced players, some guys I had idolized, rarely made me tense. Besides, I loved the spectacle surrounding games. Wearing a new uniform, getting your name announced, and standing along the foul line, cheering for your teammates, getting hits, sliding. I quickly learned I was no different with the Yankees than I was as a 12-year-old dreamer.

When I played in the Westwood Little League in Kalamazoo, my favorite day was Opening Day, because all the teams would march to the gleaming fields and the park would be packed with hundreds of fans. I used to imagine that all of these people were there to see me, and if I ever felt nervous, that dissipated when I remembered that I was just there to play baseball. The same game I played in my backyard.

There used to be two dozen or more scouts watching me in high school and by the second inning I could tell you who was there and which team he represented. Coaches told me not to look around so much because scouts don't like that and think it shows a lack of concentration. I didn't listen. I still look around all the time. It's like I was on stage and I wanted to see who was in the audience. That's just my personality. I wasn't doing it for attention. I'm curious and I wanted to see who was in the house.

Even today, I have a habit that baffles my teammates and coaches. Before I bat, I will talk to the kids in the rows beside our dugout. We're not discussing nuclear fission or Middle Eastern politics. I'll ask them if I should bunt or if I should swing at the first pitch or if they think I'm going to get a hit. I like talking to kids, so I'll initiate the discussions as I'm waiting. If a kid asks me a question, I'll answer it.

This drives Willie Randolph, our third-base coach, batty. He told me that I shouldn't be chatting with fans during games because I need to concentrate on what is happening. But I do concentrate. I look for clues as to how the pitcher might be working us. Is he throwing fastballs early in the count to set up his breaking balls? Does he have a great slider that day? Is he trying to get us to chase bad pitches? I watch from the dugout, and even though I talk while I'm in the on-deck circle, I'll analyze the pitchers from there, if it's necessary.

I have tremendous respect for Willie. He was a superb second baseman for 18 years in the major leagues and started for the Yankees in 1976 when he was only 21 years old. He knows what it's like to be young and trying to succeed as a Yankee in New York. Heck, Willie grew up in Brooklyn, so he was waiting to play for the Yankees as long as I was as a kid. I call him Willow and I love to tweak him, but I lean on him for advice, too. He's honest with me. He doesn't say something just because he thinks I want to hear it. He'll tell me if I was soft coming across the bag on a double play, instead of powering through and making a solid throw to first. I take his advice all the time, but on this issue I disagree with him and I'm not going to change. I'll always talk to the kids.

Unlike Paul O'Neill or Bernie Williams and several other players, I don't need to get "locked in" while I'm waiting to hit. I get locked in when I amble to the plate, kicking my bat with my toes as I walk, and then digging my cleats into the batter's box. I can turn that switch on quickly. So, if a kid just told me he wants me to autograph his program, I'll smile and erase that discussion from my mind by the time I'm wiggling the bat above my shoulders. Seconds after I've heard that question, I'm focused on the pitcher and I'm locked in.

You see, baseball is fun for me. I don't overanalyze it and I don't sit around and think about every detail so much that I can mess myself up. I'm not saying I'm not prepared, because I am. But I don't let myself become crazed and obsessed in anticipation of what might happen. I just let it happen. I embrace the moment and let the moment come to me. I don't have a concentration problem. Talking to the fans is part of the game for me. Basically, I have fun out there, and one of the reasons I enjoy myself is because I'm not afraid to fail.

I have made errors that caused us to lose games, I have struck out with the bases loaded, and I've been caught stealing to terminate rallies. Everyone who plays is going to make these kinds of mistakes sometime. Maybe all of them in the same day, if you're really unfortunate. We all know that we're going to fail. No one is going to hit 1.000, and no one is going to catch every grounder. Baseball forces you to deal with failure. I entered this season with a .318 lifetime average, which is solid, but that means I've failed to get a hit slightly less than 7 times in every 10 at bats. If you look at those statistics, it's obvious that even the best players are going to fail more than they succeed.

That's why you have to be able to learn from your mistakes and why you can't be afraid to fail. If I foul off a pitch that I know I should have drilled to right center field, I'll cringe, but I'll remember that the next time up, so I've learned. If I fail at something, I don't dwell on it. I made a crucial error in the 10th inning of a game against the White Sox in August of 1996 that led to five unearned runs and caused us to lose, 8–3. One of the back-page headlines the next morning was "SHORTSLOP."

Now I didn't love the headline, but I can honestly tell you that I came to work the next day just as confident and just as determined that I would make every play. That one error and the attention it got didn't depress me and make me feel like a loser. I know I'm human and I refused to get down on myself over one miscue. If anything, I was inspired to do even better. The best thing you can do after a mistake like that is look forward to the next day.

I can't tell you how many times I come back to the dugout berating myself because I've felt like I just gave away an at bat. Maybe I thought I could have rapped a ball to the right side to advance a runner. Maybe I felt like I should have pulled an inside pitch, but my bat was too slow. I'll mumble, "I stink," and one of my teammates will tell me to relax, forget about it, and get him the next time. Even though that sounds trite and we've all heard our coaches say it since Little League, it's true. It's smart advice for anyone who sees an opportunity in failure. If you can learn from your mistakes and don't let the negativity fester, then you really haven't failed at all.

Stay Humble

There were 42,289 fans at Jacobs Field on April 2, 1996, and about 42,000 of them were howling for the Cleveland Indians. I knew my mother was sitting in the stands somewhere. I always need to know where my parents are sitting during games and I like to make eye contact with them before I start playing. I've done this for as long as I can remember. If my mother was late to a game, she used to tell me there would be a look of relief on my face when she finally got there. It was as if I needed one of my parents there to relax me. OK, my actions said, they're here and now I can play.

Actually, my mother and father had both been in Cleveland the day before because that is when we were scheduled to begin

Fielding is such an important part of the game. My parents took this picture of me getting ready to throw, playing for the Kalamazoo Central Maroons in high school. I am still constantly trying to improve my fielding skills.

the season against the Indians. But the game was snowed out on April Fools' Day, so my debut as the new shortstop had to wait 24 hours. Sharlee had a softball game for Kalamazoo Central the next day, so my parents left to watch her play and my mother came back to Cleveland the next day with a friend.

I remember reporters quizzing me about my parents' decision. Some of them seemed incredulous about why only one parent was at the game and asked how they could equate a major-league game with a high school softball game. But that wasn't the point. What they needed to equate was two parents, two children. My parents made sure they always supported both of us, so they did what came naturally and split up. It was not the first time my parents did that and it won't be the last.

To me, that sends a terrific message because it is extremely important to treat your children equally. That's something my parents worked hard at doing. Even in their home in New Jersey, they have a miniature World Series trophy, an autographed bat, and pictures of me as a Yankee in their living room. But, right above their fireplace and in the most prominent position in the room is a huge picture of Sharlee surrounded by the accolades she has earned in high school and in college. I like seeing that. They are just as proud of Sharlee as they are of me.

Anyway, my mother saw a terrific show on that memorable day. The Indians had won the American League pennant in 1995 and everyone was calling our first series with them a possible preview of the ALCS. I didn't pay attention to that because it was so early in the season. I remember telling myself to treat the game like it was another game I had played in high school or in the minors. It's just a game, the same game I'd been playing forever.

So when I scampered back into left center field and made a gorgeous over-the-shoulder catch, it was the type of play I could have made in my backyard, the big backyard known as Kalamazoo Central. And when I launched one of Dennis Martinez's pitches deep over the left-field fence, it was the kind of blast I used to hit every day when I played games at the Mount Royal Townhouse Complex where I lived as a kid. That's how comfortable I felt out there.

David Cone called that game my "coming-out party," and I think he was right because things seemed a bit easier after that. If you're a salesman and you have a great week to start the month, the rest of the month flows for you. That's the way I felt about getting off to a good start and getting that first game out of the way.

Still, I was subdued, probably even boring, when reporters questioned me in the clubhouse. I constantly deferred to Cone, who had allowed only two hits over seven innings in a 7–1 win. I didn't want the credit. It was a team win. I had contributed and the team had won so I wanted to talk about the team.

The Mets' Rey Ordóñez had made a snazzy defensive play the day before in which he nabbed a runner at home while throwing from his knees in shallow left field, so a lot of reporters wanted to compare us. I have a lot of respect for Ordóñez, but I didn't do an extensive comparison. To me, the proper thing to do was to talk about the team, not about me. Sure, I was happy about what I had just done. But it was one game. I wasn't going to start talking in the third person and say, "Derek Jeter is in the house, boys." That's not my style. Never has been. Never will be.

I don't think that ever gains you anything. The people who are constantly talking about themselves are probably trying to convince everyone else about how good they are. I've always felt that whether you're a professional athlete or a bus driver, it's better to be humble. If you constantly chirp about how terrific you are, people might put up with it while you back it up. But, if you struggle, you're going to be a lonely soul and no one is going to care, because they won't have to listen to you anymore.

That doesn't mean you should be dishonest or hesitant to voice opinions. I'm not. When the Yankees signed Tony Fernandez to a two-year contract before the 1995 season and there was speculation about what it meant to my future, I spoke up. Tony was a premium shortstop, so a reporter asked me if I thought that his new contract would delay me in making it to the Yankees. "You mean, like two years?" I asked. "I don't think so."

That's how I felt. I wanted to play regularly in the majors by 1996. I would be 21 then and I would have had three and a half years in the minors. I don't think there was anything wrong in saying that I had expectations. Just because I was confident didn't mean that I was undermining a colleague. I respected Fernandez. I focused on myself rather than whom I was competing against.

When Mr. Torre said before the 1996 season that I, not Fernandez, would be the starting shortstop, I didn't run with those remarks. I said my perception was that Mr. Torre meant that I'd be given the opportunity to win the spot. Mr. Torre appreciated that response, and I've heard him say, "The kid said it better than I did. But that told me that he was confident he was going to win the job anyway."

There's no way the Yankees, a team that was supposed to qualify for the World Series and did eventually win it, could just give the shortstop job to a rookie if I flopped. In New York, that doesn't happen. I knew I would have to earn the position or I'd be back in Columbus so swiftly I wouldn't have time for a roast beef sandwich at a Manhattan deli.

I had a mediocre spring and the team had an organizational meeting a week before the season in which one of George Steinbrenner's advisers didn't feel I was ready to jump to the major leagues. But Mr. Torre was emphatic about leaving me alone. He said it was too late to change after the Yankees had committed to me. Mr. Torre hoped that I would hit .250 and play solid defense. I didn't hear about these doubts until later in the season when I could laugh at them, but even if I had heard them, I think they would have motivated me. Doubters have always stirred my emotions and made me want to succeed even more.

I still treat every spring training like it's my first ever and like I'm trying to make the Yankees all over again. Every December or January, my father will remind me to do that. He doesn't really have to. I don't take anything for granted. I know, I know. People tell me I could go 2 for 40 next spring and Mr. Torre would still start me at shortstop. I've earned that with my play for the last four years. But I like to push myself and feel as if I'm an underdog.

Showalter once said that he couldn't detect if I was a first-round pick or a 40th-round pick by the way I worked, and that's a nice compliment. I worked out one day in January with a

Rookie League catcher named Troy Norrell. If someone who knew nothing about baseball had stumbled into our session and simply studied how hard we worked, I would've wanted him to have trouble guessing who was the major league All-Star and who was the Rookie League player.

I think it behooves everyone to strive to set him- or herself apart by working toward a new, higher goal, and not to settle for what they've done already. I know there are some businesses where the chief executive has a superior work ethic to the person working in the mailroom, and some businesses where the opposite is true. If someone watched you work when you thought no one was looking, would you be proud of your work ethic? Consider that the next time you're frustrated or feel like quitting.

Life Is a Game, So Have Fun

For me, the path to success includes a couple of one-liners. As much as baseball is a business—a billion-dollar business—it is still a game. I know there are people who don't and won't view it that way. I do, and I've promised myself that I will always view it that way. The game is serious, but I still have fun. If you can't have fun playing the game, then there's something wrong with you.

I learned a lot from Tim Raines about having fun in baseball. I have loved joking around ever since I shuffled home from St. Augustine's with a report card that said my conduct in class was unsatisfactory. My parents used to remind me to keep my mouth under control, so I had to bite my tongue a lot. But Raines showed me how to have a good time and still be serious when it mattered. Rock is my favorite teammate of all time because, in the three years I played with him, I never saw him in a bad mood. Not once. I can't say that about anyone else.

Rock was always joking, and he has this high-pitched cackle that you can hear for about a half-mile, and that makes you laugh even if he's not saying anything. I loved having my locker next to Rock's locker at the stadium because he would always have a humorous gripe. He would complain that my mail was taking up some of his locker space, that I had taken his cap, or that I needed to learn to respect my elders. Whatever he'd say, I'd respond with my own verbal volley. When we won 125 games and the World Series in 1998, Rock batted .290 in 321 at bats and was one of the most influential players in our clubhouse. We won it all again in 1999, but we missed him at the outset of the season. Missed his cackle, his wit, and his presence. He definitely has a presence.

Now Raines is a funny guy, but I also think he is a Hall of Famer. Rock was diagnosed with lupus in 1999, and he retired before the 2000 season with 2,561 hits, 807 stolen bases, and a .295 average. So if Raines found a way to balance joking with being serious and not being afraid to fail, so could I. So can you. There's a time to have fun and a time to work and you have to realize when it's OK to do one or the other. At work, at school, at home. I think that's a refreshing attitude, and it rubs off on everyone—teammates, coworkers, classmates, and bosses.

We lost our first six games of spring training in 2000, and the reporters were asking George Steinbrenner about it because he has a reputation for taking losing in the spring rather seriously. After we notched our first victory in the seventh game, I noticed that Joe Torre didn't take the team bus from Tampa to Clearwater, Florida, when we drove to play the Phillies the next morning.

Mr. Torre stayed behind in Tampa because Ed Yarnall was pitching after a back injury, so it was an important session. When Mr. Torre got to Clearwater an hour before the game, I still teas-

Joe Torre is such a professional—he knows how to motivate us and can be tough, but he has a great sense of humor.

ingly said, "Skip, you're late. What, were you out celebrating last night? Celebrating a big win?"

Mr. Torre laughed and mentioned Yarnall's workout, but I shook my head and walked away, accepting no explanation. A couple of days later, I was warming up at Legends Field and I heard someone hollering, "Jeet." It was Mr. Torre and he waved me toward him. I put the ball on the dirt, skipped down the dugout steps, and sat beside him and bench coach Don Zimmer. Mr. Torre spoke in a very solemn tone and said, "I wanted to let you know that we're going to have to make some changes here." He stopped for a second. "But you're safe. For now, that is. I'll let you know by next week if we're going to be able to keep you."

I cracked up and so did Zim and Mr. Torre. That's what makes Mr. Torre a terrific manager. He keeps it light when it needs to be light, lets us play when we need to play, and gets inside our heads when we need someone inside our heads. I didn't waste a second, though, and told Mr. Torre, "Keep me around, but you better get rid of Zim." Then I ran back onto the field like a first-time batboy before either one of them could respond.

I always feel that way about playing for the Yankees, like I'm out there playing for the first time. We were trying to finish off a four-game sweep of the Atlanta Braves last October 27, which would give us our second consecutive title and the 25th in club history. That would cap off the century symmetrically and styl-ishly. Even though we had a 3–0 lead in the series, there was still some anxiety. You don't want to give a team, especially a good team like Atlanta, an ounce of breathing room. We wanted to end the series that night.

Despite the pressure, I was having a blast. Some friends have told me that a television camera zoomed in on me during the game and I was smiling. I looked like a teenager who had been allowed to hang out with the Yankees for a night. That's how happy and unfazed they said I looked. That's because I felt that way, too. I don't specifically remember why I was smiling, but I can assure you that I was having a wonderful time playing in the World Series at the Stadium.

Watch me if we make it to the World Series again and the cam-era zooms in on me. I guarantee you I'll smile at some point. Getting into the World Series and having the chance to be the last team still standing are the moments that I savor. I work hard to try to help the Yankees get to that precious stage, and I always believe I'm going to succeed once we get there. You can be the hero or the goat. I always feel I'm going to be the hero. I'm not afraid to fail.

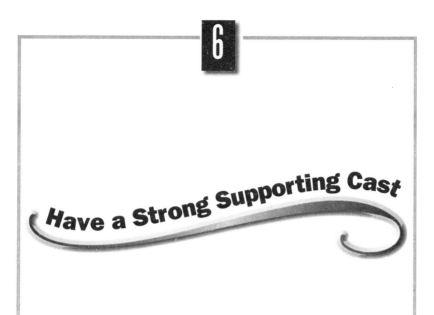

Have a Strong Supporting Cast

've always enjoyed being around people who are achievers. I gravitate toward people who have goals and who are serious about attaining them, because that helps motivate me. If one of my friends got a 98 on a test in high school, I wanted to get a 99. If one of my Yankee teammates gets two hits, I want to get three. A competitive approach helps make you better, and improving is a desire I always want to have.

Surrounding yourself with good, goal-oriented people is inspiring. If you have friends who are more interested in hanging out on the corner than studying for a test, you'll probably be more apt to hang out and blow off studying, too.

There's nothing wrong with hanging out with friends. I do it all the time and I love being around friends. But I don't like wasting time, particularly when I've got responsibilities. Good friends will help steer you in the proper direction and help you make the most out of your talents. There are some people you might consider as friends who wittingly or unwittingly could prevent you from succeeding. That's a problem you should correct by being smarter with your time and smarter with picking your friends.

What I've tried to do in choosing my friends is look for people who are serious about their goals, but who are fun, too. It's a delicate balance, one I think I've been able to master and one I think many of my friends have mastered, too. I know that when I'm around these friends I feel like I'm around people who care about life, theirs and mine, and about improving themselves. But they also know that you can have a good time in addition to being diligent about reaching goals.

Just like everyone, I've spent time in school and on teams with scores of people who didn't share the same goals or visions as I did and didn't have the same ethics or morals. Maybe they partied too much. Maybe they didn't respect people from all races. Maybe they were just nuisances. I don't want to be too close to people like that, but I don't totally shun them. I've managed to be an acquaintance of many people without following their examples. I think that is an important trait to develop in life. You don't have to like everyone; you don't have to loathe everyone; but you should be choosy about who you spend your time with. I've known what I wanted to achieve in life for a long time, and having friends with similar visions has been significant for me because we can push each other to greater heights.

That's why when I'm playing shortstop for the Yankees I know that I've got parts of many different people out there on the field with me. I didn't make it alone. I had my parents steering me to be successful, but I've also had friends imploring me to do well so that we could share our mutual dreams. If you want to better yourself, start by having people around you who are bettering themselves. You can find them. They'll be the ones studying that extra hour in the library, taking some extra grounders when practice is done, or working at a part-time job in addition to going to school. Those are some of the signs of achievers. Those are the people who impressed me, the people I wanted to be like and wanted to be around.

Driving Each Other to the Top

I met Douglas Biro when we were in the fourth grade at St. Augustine's Elementary School in Kalamazoo. He was a happy kid, full of zest and verve, and the kind of nine-year-old I wanted to hang out with. All Doug needs to do is act like himself and he'll eventually make me chuckle at something. He knows me as well as anyone because he knew me long before I ever put on a Yankees uniform. Well, make that before I ever put on a real Yankees uniform. I used to wear so many Yankees uniforms, jackets, and caps that George Steinbrenner should have given me a salary back then for all the free advertising I provided throughout Michigan.

Doug used to ride his bike a few blocks from his house to play baseball with me at the Mount Royal Townhouse Complex, where my family lived. The sprawling array of individual apartments, parking spots, and carports also included jungle gym equipment and a small grassy area where we played our games.

Doug Biro is one of my oldest friends. We're always around for each other and have been since we were kids. Here we are at high school graduation—I was 17 years old.

When I drive past Mount Royal now during visits back to Kalamazoo, it looks modest. But I know that place was nirvana for me. That patch of grass across from our townhouse No. 1183 was my field of dreams long before Kevin Costner made the phrase famous in a movie.

I ate, slept, went to school, and played baseball on this hilly slope about 150 feet from our townhouse. My parents always knew where to find me, so they didn't worry. They didn't even have to open the door to know I would be playing baseball on the hill. I was the Pied Piper of the development, and it didn't matter to me who wanted to play. I didn't care if it was kids who were younger, kids who were older, or kids who were just visiting relatives for a few hours. I wanted to play.

As long as I had one other kid there, I could play catch. As long as there were two others, we could have a pitcher, a batter, and a fielder. And, if we had three others plus me, we could actually play a game. I counted every one of my homers and I think

I almost passed Hank Aaron in one year. I must have had about 700 bombs. I played out there so often that the kids called the patch of grass Derek Jeter's Hill. I got in the habit of playing sports every day and talking about sports every day, which is, fortunately, what I do now, and Doug was a part of that early ritual.

Doug knew that I wanted to be a baseball player and I knew he wanted to be a golfer on the professional tour, so we shared each other's dreams and we pushed each other the way Burgess Meredith pushed Sylvester Stallone in *Rocky*. We had a way of looking out for each other that was all about friendship and achievement.

I was driving Doug in my car during our senior year in high school when we made a pact in which we promised each other that we were both going to fulfill our dreams.

"Doug, you better make it because I'm going to make it," I said, slamming my palms on the steering wheel. "I'm definitely going to make it."

I used to pepper Doug with questions about his golf game while we were at Kalamazoo Central. How did he think the team was going to do? How was he driving the ball? Was he going to play golf in college? The more we talked, the more it motivated us.

We were looking through the newspaper one afternoon and talking about how Nick Price had won a golf tournament with a particular score. Let's say it was a 72-hole total of 267. Doug scanned to the bottom of the players who were listed in the newspaper, maybe to some guy who shot 288, and told me that's all he had to be able to shoot consistently to be a tour professional. If he could shoot a 288 every day, he could compete on the tour.

I quickly jumped all over Doug. I told him that his goal should be to beat Nick Price, not beat what the guy at the bottom of the list shot. You've got to want to be the best, not be someone who is just hanging on. I grabbed the paper off the table, pointed to Nick Price's 267, and said, "This is where you want to be. This is what you should be trying to do."

He nodded his head and told me I was right. I know he appreciated the advice and I know that he agreed with me. I wanted my friends to say the same thing to me then and I want them to do that now, too. Let me know if I'm selling myself short. Let me know if I'm not chasing the highest goal. If I'm underachieving, I'd want the people in my life who are closest to me to let me know. We should all want that sort of guidance. That's the beauty of having an honest supporting cast. You get feedback, both good and bad.

Doug and I still do this for each other. We used to be roommates in Tampa and now, though we live in separate houses, we still talk all the time. I still ask him questions about each step he's taking to become a tour professional and he still asks me about my goals with the Yankees. I've made it to precisely where I want to be and I know Doug is about to make it, too. We made a pact. He has to do it. He will because he won't stop trying.

"I'd rather be a poor tour professional," Doug has said, "than a wealthy office worker."

The Boss Knows Best

I'll always pick a quiet moment once or twice a month to seek feedback about my game from Joe Torre. I might approach him while he's puffing on a cigar in his office before a game or it might be while he's sitting by himself in the dugout. I'll ease up to Mr. Torre, whose dark eyes and stoic expression reveal nothing about how he's feeling, and I'll ask him how he thinks I'm playing.

I guess my need to be critiqued goes back to signing those contracts for my parents in high school. I like to hear what the person in authority thinks about my performance. Hey, this is my job. We all want to know what our boss thinks about our efforts. At least we should want to know. Regardless of whether you like or dislike your boss, you have to respect him and you have to respect his opinion. If you don't, you might be in the wrong job.

Mr. Torre is my boss and I have tremendous respect for his insights, so that's why I'll pick his brain for answers and advice. I respect his opinions, and though he's the only manager I've ever had for a full season, I think he's the best manager in the majors. He's perfect for our team. He knows what's it's like to be a player who soars and who struggles. He's often told us how he hit .363 one year and .247 four years later and tried equally hard in both years. Players trust him because he's been where we are and because he shows trust in us.

The good thing about Mr. Torre is that he understands what I'm doing when I ask him for an appraisal. He might start out with a joke about how I probably won't be released anytime soon, but he doesn't tell me, "You're hitting .330 and you're making all the plays at shortstop. Keep it up." That's the last thing I want to hear. I don't care if I'm hitting .370. I would still want Mr. Torre to tell me where he sees the possibility for improvement.

He might tell me that I should have tried to steal second base with us down two runs a few games ago. He might tell me that he loves my aggressiveness, but not to overswing when I get two strikes. He might tell me to think about a bunt every once in a while to keep the third baseman from playing too deep. These might sound like minor flaws, but the key to getting better is improving minor flaws. Mr. Torre is straight with me whenever I seek one of these quickie report cards, which is why I repeatedly go to him. If you find someone who gives you good advice, you should use that person's knowledge like it's a free credit card. You should treat that person like you can't get enough of him.

That's how you'll improve, so you should immerse yourself in the information.

I've always loved to range to my right, snare a grounder in the shortstop hole, then jump and whip it to first base. I've got frame-by-frame pictures hanging in my house of my making a gorgeous play like that. But Mr. Torre has never liked my making that play in such a splashy fashion and he has never hesitated to tell me how I'm hurting my chances to get the runner at first.

Both Mr. Torre and Don Zimmer, our bench coach and a shortstop back in the 1920s, told me that as pretty as that play looks, I am much better off getting to the ball, planting my right foot, and then gunning the ball to first. I'll get much more on the throw and have a much better chance of throwing the runner out, they said. I tried it, realized they were right, and have incorporated that change into my game.

By the way, Zim wasn't a shortstop in the 1920s. It was the 1950s and 1960s, but I like tweaking him so I put that in there. I'm fond of Zim, whom I call "Hollywood" because we did a video game commercial together last year. I rub his mostly bald head for good luck before games and I always tell him that he needs a haircut. "Tighten it up, Zim," I'll say, sneaking up from behind and getting him to laugh dozens of times each season. Once, he wound up getting a haircut shortly after I jokingly demanded it. I think it took the barber about 45 seconds to complete the snipping.

I love talking to Zim because he's been in this game for 52 years. He's seen every situation and every scenario in baseball. There isn't anything that has happened that he hasn't seen. You can learn so much just by listening to him. He won't really coach me the way Willie Randolph will coach me, but Zim will tell me things about different situations. Why I should have cheated toward the left on a certain hitter or tried to steal a base in a certain game. I love listening because there's no equaling over half a century of experience, which includes managing four major-league teams.

Zim is a playful guy. I think you have to have that attitude to do the same thing for so long. Our relationship really started in my rookie year, when he would hit me ground balls before games. He'd hit them as hard as he could to the left and as hard as he could to the right. He would laugh at me if I missed them and they scooted into the outfield and he would continue challenging me, like a hockey player challenging a goalie with slap shots. We'd laugh. It was fun, but it was also important work. There's that mix of fun and seriousness that I was talking about that's so important when you're choosing your friends.

When we were playing on AstroTurf, I'd get Zim back by purposely throwing the ball so it would bounce several feet in front of him off the turf and then almost sail over his head. Zim's got bad knees so he would have to jump for it. He'd grumble at me if it went over his head or he couldn't jump high enough to retrieve it. Then he'd reach into his back pocket to pull out another ball and take his frustration out on me. You have to have that kind of demeanor, mixing work and fun, or you won't last long in any job. This is applicable for more than just baseball. You have to go to work each day knowing you are going to work hard, but also knowing you're going to enjoy yourself. That way you'll look forward to working, instead of dreading it. Too many people hate their jobs—and that makes the work a lot harder to do and almost impossible to enjoy.

Although I tease Zim a lot, I also listen very carefully to his advice. He was instrumental, for example, in helping me increase my range on balls hit to my left and up the middle. I had a tendency to get close to grounders and then lunge for them with both hands instead of just reaching down with my glove hand. It makes perfect sense to reach with one hand, because I gained about a foot and a half with my reach.

Go ahead and try it. Stand up and reach to the ground on your left side with both hands cupped together. You're constricted and you can only reach so far, probably barely touching the ground. But if you just reach with your left hand, you have a lot more flexibility and should reach the ground and beyond. That's a major difference if you're trying to cut a ball off with a runner on second base in a tie game.

You'll probably come across someone like Zim in your life, whether it's your boss, your grandfather, or the elderly person living next door. Don't dismiss their advice—embrace it. I've learned so much by being around Zim. I hope I can give that type of advice to young players someday. But, I'm sorry, Zim, I hope I've got a lot more hair when I'm doing it at your age.

There are always going to be people who are willing to tell you what you are good at. You probably don't need to hear from them because most of us know what we're good at. But the important thing is to find out the areas in life in which you can improve. Find the people who'll let you know when the project you turned in was inferior, the people who will tell you that you did a poor job cutting the grass, and the people who will tell you that you're not saving enough of the money you earn. Sometimes it's your parents or a brother or sister. Sometimes it's a close friend. Those are the people who'll help you improve. Those are the people you should listen to.

A High-Profile Friendship

Whenever I go out, I like having a large group of people with me. I've always been that way. I used to invite the entire team to go to the movies when I was in the minor leagues. I've always been the kind of person who wants to get everyone involved and have a lot of people around to make me feel comfortable. Believe it or not, I'm actually pretty shy. People see me playing on television and see me being interviewed and figure that I must love the attention. I'm not always as secure as you might think. Approaching an attractive woman is a challenge for me. I don't care who you are or how much money you make, that can be a difficult walk. There's always that fear of rejection, even though, just like in baseball, you have to be confident it'll be a successful venture. Even if it's a lot more complicated than trying to hit a 1–2 curveball.

I'll go out with Sean Twitty and Chuck Knoblauch, Jorge Posada, and Tino Martinez, three of my closest friends on the Yankees, in Manhattan. I know that they'll look out for me, and vice versa. They'll warn me if they think I'm doing something stupid or someone is doing something foolish around me. Your friends should do that for you, too. It's a wonderful world we live in, but it can be a dangerous world. All it takes is one person who doesn't like you or one person who is having an awful day to make trouble for you. That particularly applies to me because more people know who I am, but I think that logic of being cautious should apply to everyone. There's nothing wrong with being cautious.

Jorge has reminded me that I have to be especially careful around women I don't know well. He told me that I could bring a woman back to my apartment and nothing could happen. We could watch a movie. We could talk. We could hang out. But then Jorge said, "What's to stop her from leaving there and telling someone that this or that happened with Derek Jeter?" I've long realized that I have to be cautious in these situations, but hearing him say it made me think about it some more. It might seem a little self-serving to be thinking that way, but, if one of my friends felt strongly enough to mention it to me, it's important.

That advice might seem strong, but that's what a loyal friend will give you. If you don't have friends who will tell you when you're making a glaring mistake, then they're not great friends. If you let your friends do silly things that could be damaging to them without offering your opinion, you're not helping them, either. Sometimes the truth is difficult. But a real friend will always recognize what needs to be said and will also recognize when advice from someone else needs to be heeded.

I know I learned a lot from my relationship with Mariah Carey. I learned that it would be very difficult for me to seriously date a high-profile person. I'm used to getting a lot of attention for playing for the Yankees, but I wasn't used to getting a lot of attention because I went out to dinner with someone. It just so happened that someone was Mariah Carey, one of the top-selling female pop singers ever, and that turned my life into a more chaotic existence than I wanted.

I met Mariah at a charity function for the Fresh Air Fund in November of 1996, a month after we won the World Series. I know some people have written and want to believe that our romance started that day, but that's not true. I barely even talked with her that first day. I saw her out in the city a few more times after that and we became friends before we had our first date. We actually only dated for about six months and we were never close to getting engaged, though that's what a few newspapers wrote. A reporter asked my mother if those stories about me supposedly preparing to get engaged to Mariah were true and my mother looked like her eyes were going to pop out of their sockets. Don't you think my parents would have known that if it were close to being true?

I was intrigued with Mariah because we had a lot of similarities. Like me, she is from a mixed heritage. She has a white, Irish mother and an African-American, Venezuelan father. Like me, she had a dream in life that she zealously pursued. She knew that she wanted to be a singer and she made that her mission in life. Like me, she still works extremely hard at her profession. She's a beautiful woman, on the inside and the outside, and I had a deep respect for her and the way she handled herself.

I admired the way she went about her career because she started out with nothing but a dream that she would be a big star, and, to this day, she still works hard at fulfilling that dream. She's constantly writing, she's constantly in the studio, she's constantly trying to get better. She's someone a lot of people can learn from. I know I did. Whether you like her music or you think it's terrible, you could learn a lot from the way she has had a goal and pursued it.

That doesn't mean anyone who picks up a hairbrush and sings into it for a few minutes can become a Mariah Carey. But I think it shows you that there can be a reward for hard work and that dreams really can come true if you're willing to sacrifice for your goal.

Like I said earlier, don't ever let anyone tell you that you can't do what you want. I never did. I know Mariah never did, either. It doesn't mean you will end up with a recording contract or playing for the Yankees, but it does mean that you won't have any regrets about whether you should have tried to go for it. Try your best to be successful at whatever it is you want to do and then the questions will be answered for you. Even if your goal is not realized, you will know you tried hard to make it come to fruition— and you can't ask any more of yourself than that.

I'm not in the music business, but I don't have to be to realize what a superb accomplishment it is for someone to have 14 number-one hits. Mariah had as many number-one hits as anyone except Elvis Presley and the Beatles. That would be like getting compared to Babe Ruth and Hank Aaron in my business, so that's incredible. You see a lot of people and a lot of bands who have one hit song and whose popularity lingers for a year or two before they disappear, but Mariah is not like that. She is a star with staying power and she is someone I learned a lot from, someone I still consider a friend.

The one thing I couldn't adjust to was the endless attention we received. I'm used to being in the spotlight when I'm playing baseball because the games are televised, our pictures are in newspapers and magazines, and fans recognize us when we go to and from games. But I wasn't used to the attention that we got for simply dating each other. I don't know when two orders of rigatoni suddenly became so newsworthy, but I didn't like being hounded that way. For on-the-field stuff, I expect the attention. But off-the-field stuff is different. I don't want to be bothered all the time.

It's tough for two very high-profile people to have a relationship because there is no privacy. Though it seems like every other person in New York City knows who I am, I can still go a lot of places in the United States and not be recognized, and I can be even more anonymous when I'm outside this country. But Mariah is on another level in terms of attention. She can't go anywhere in the world where people don't recognize her. Someone in every country has probably seen her on MTV or seen her compact discs in stores. So she was used to this attention and it didn't bother her the way it bothered me.

I know there are people who have said that I should have known that any relationship between the Yankee shortstop and a pop superstar would naturally cause the tabloid newspapers and television shows to go ballistic. Of course, this was a big story. It was Derek and Mariah. Right? Wrong. I'm not saying I didn't expect some attention. That would be ignorant. I'm just saying I didn't like having my personal life so scrutinized and I didn't want to have to deal with it.

When she visited me in Tampa, Florida, during spring training in 1998, it was ridiculous for us to try and do anything. We'd go out to dinner and people would gawk at us and ask us for autographs, and the next morning I would hear disc jockeys on the radio talking about our evening. They would dissect the reasons we went to a certain restaurant. Once a waiter said that I had left a huge tip to impress Mariah. How silly is that? Why would I have to impress her? Every time I go out, I leave a good tip. I'm fortunate enough to be making a great salary, and I appreciate good service. Leaving a big tip? How would that impress her? Yet, that's what was on the radio.

Then I would get to Legends Field to play baseball and there would be interview requests from entertainment shows and tabloid shows. Come on. I'll talk to anyone from any news media outlet about baseball. I realize it's part of our job and it's important to help promote the game, but I didn't want to do interviews about my personal life with anyone. I don't see how two people like Mariah and me could have made it work. It would have been very tough.

I think the media scrutiny that we got had a lot to do with why we're not dating anymore. She might have been used to it, but I wasn't and didn't think I'd ever be comfortable with that kind of attention. I'm used to going to Yankee Stadium, and if I make an error, I talk about it after the game and it's over with. The next day is a new day.

But, when I was with Mariah, almost every day someone was coming up to me with a different story that I'd be asked to confirm or deny. It was too much. My personal favorite was someone writing that I took Mariah to a strip club on one of our dates and she seemed to enjoy it. A strip club? Where do people concoct this stuff? Obviously, the attention made things uncomfortable for me and it contributed to the end of our relationship. I still consider Mariah a friend, though we don't talk too much anymore. She did leave my parents tickets for one of her concerts at Madison Square Garden last April, and I'm sure she would have left one for me, too. I like her music, but I didn't go with them because we had a game the next day, and because I didn't want to get the rumors fired up all over again. She's a friend. That's it.

Make Each Day Count

The longest relationship I've ever had with a woman was with Marisa Novara, my high school sweetheart, who was a wonderful girlfriend for four years and is still a great friend. When the Yankees go to Chicago to play the White Sox, we try to hook up for lunch. It's refreshing to be around her because we can discuss everything except baseball. She's in graduate school to become a social worker and wants to spend her life helping families who usually don't know where their next meal is coming from. She looks like Elisabeth Shue with slightly darker hair. She's a genuine person and a nice person, someone who I know will be one of my friends for life.

Marisa understood me and understood my goals. The first time I met her we were in the eighth grade and I was, fittingly enough, wearing a Yankees jacket. We only lived about a half mile away from each other in Kalamazoo, which was convenient when we started dating as high school juniors. I am thankful for the support that I always got from Marisa, something I tried to give back to her and still try to give to all of my friends. Friendships

I am still friends with Marisa Novara, my girlfriend in high school. Here she is with me and Sharlee when I was 18 and had just been drafted.

can be like jigsaw puzzles. They can be rewarding, but only when you constantly work on them to make them complete.

I remember a beautiful, sunny summer day in Kalamazoo when all of our friends were going to the beach and Marisa was thrilled that we could go as a couple. She was bursting with excitement. But I told her that I couldn't go because I had a game with the Kalamazoo Maroons that night and I couldn't risk getting back late or tiring myself with a two-hour roundtrip drive. Baseball, not the beach, was my priority. There aren't too many high school girls who would understand or accept that explanation, but Marisa did. She knew me, knew what mattered to me, and didn't moan or call me a nerd. She went on her own and respected my decision. That's the sign of a friend, and those are the kind of people I've always tried to hang on to in life.

When I was in the Rookie League in Tampa, wondering if I'd ever fit in or ever get a hit, I used to call Marisa constantly. She offered a soothing voice at a time when I was depressed. The important thing for me was to know that my future in baseball would get brighter and I just had to get through this first perilous summer. I talked about just getting the season over with like I was an eighth-grader languishing in summer school.

In one conversation, I mapped out the entire summer and told Marisa, "I'm going to see you in two weeks, then the team goes on the road for a week, then I'll see you in another two weeks after that and the season will be over in one week." Marisa knew how much I loved baseball and knew that I should be trying to get better and enjoying myself, not counting the days on the calendar, so she told me a story that really resonated with me.

Marisa was 10 years old and was pining for her presents about a week before Christmas. Her grandfather was very ill at the time and the family didn't think he would survive much longer. She told her father how much she wanted her gifts and said that she wished the seven days would disappear so she could wake up on Christmas morning and scurry to see what was under the tree.

Mr. Novara listened to what Marisa had said and used the opportunity to teach her, and eventually me, a lesson. He reminded her of her grandfather's condition and told her that her grandfather would give anything if he could live the next week, the week after that, and so on. Marisa's dad told her that her grandfather would never dare wish away even one minute of his life.

So when Marisa told me that story and said, "Don't wish your life away, Derek, it's too precious," I knew that she was right. I still look forward to events: birthdays, parties, the World Series. But I savor every day. I think we all should. Tomorrow is never guaranteed. I've heard that line before and that's something I think about every day. Take something out of today because you might not have that chance tomorrow. You might not even have a tomorrow. All you have to do is be influenced by someone's death, especially if it's a young person's death, to fully realize that you can't take tomorrow for granted. I know because that happened to my friends and me.

Shanti Lal was a smart, generous, dedicated kid and one of my best friends. Like Doug, I had known Shanti since I was in the fourth grade. If there ever was a person who I was confident would reach his goals in life, that person was Shanti. He wanted to be a doctor, and it was amazing how dedicated he was in school. Shanti was a dreamer, just like me. He motivated me to be better in academics, which is what friends should do. I thought that if I kept up with Shanti, that was an accomplishment.

My phone rang on May 4, 1997, and it was my sister calling. Sharlee didn't sound right and she said, "Shanti didn't make it." She seemed distraught, like she had been crying, and I had no idea what she was talking about. "Didn't make it," I said. "Where was he going?"

She paused and that is when I got that queasy feeling in my stomach, the feeling that told me the next sentence out of her mouth was going to be awful. I clutched the phone tighter and heard what I didn't want to hear. "Shanti was in a car accident. He died," Sharlee told me.

He died. Those words shocked me, scared me, made me cry. Shanti was only 23 years old when he fell asleep at the wheel and his sport utility vehicle flipped while he was driving from the University of Michigan in Ann Arbor to Kalamazoo on I-94. I had taken that same route several times to drive home from U of M. I had just seen Shanti a month earlier when he came to Tampa for spring training and visited me. We had been roommates at

Joe Torre vacationed in Maui, Hawaii, last January, far away from baseball and far away from the Yankees. Or so Torre thought. Torre met Tiger Woods on the golf course while he was there, and the more the manager of the Yankees talked to the best golfer in the world, the more he thought about baseball and Derek Jeter.

"I looked into Tiger's eyes and I could see it was Jeter," says Torre. " 'I know I'm good, I think only about winning, and I'll be surprised if I lose, even though I'll respect the person that beats me.' "

Torre ticked off the similarities between the two young athletes, from the extreme confidence, to the endless passion for winning, to the incredible presence that both have. The manager was 5,000 miles away from the Yankee dugout, but he could have touched his nose and brushed his hand across his chest to signal for Tiger, doubling as Jeter, to hit and run on the next pitch.

"Tiger's eyes told me that he was just like Jeter. His presence, that comfort level with people, and that confidence. The thing is that winning once isn't enough. That fire keeps burning. He and Jeter are a lot alike in those areas, too."

Soon after Torre started managing Jeter in 1996, he became aware of the confidence, the honesty, and the accountability that the rookie had. When

Michigan, we had teamed up for a talent show in the fourth grade in which the two of us and Tyrone Bennett danced to Michael Jackson's "Pretty Young Thing." We had been friends, true friends. And now this? I put the phone down and wept like a baby.

I decided to compose a letter about Shanti that I wanted

Jeter was caught stealing third base with Cecil Fielder batting for the third out of the inning in an important game in September, Torre was ticked. It was a silly move. Torre planned to discuss it with Jeter the next day. Instead, Jeter sat beside him in the dugout, awaiting a lecture.

"A lot of guys would do something wrong and wait to be told that they've done something wrong. They'll pretend that they didn't do anything wrong. He's not like that."

Jeter is different from anyone Torre has managed. Just 26 years old, he has found the delicate balance between having more fun than any Little Leaguer while still wanting to win more than any major leaguer. And Jeter manages to do this in New York, where the attention continues to escalate and he continues to thrive.

"It's a natural thing for him, he lights up a room. Derek Jeter, at a very young age, is a legitimate superstar. It's not that he did one thing. Joe Namath won a Super Bowl and he did things style-wise to get noticed. Derek Jeter has become this superstar because he does his job very well and blue-collar-wise. There's nothing flashy about him. It's hard work. I know the people of New York appreciate that. When they look at Derek Jeter and he's single, good-looking, and he plays for the Yankees the way that he does, I think, not only the young women, but their parents, too, are proud to have their daughters feel that way about him because of his image."

Sharlee to read at the funeral. Since we were in the midst of our regular season, I couldn't go to the funeral. Yes, baseball is a business and the off days are rare. I would have loved to attend the services to offer support to the Lal family. I know how important a support system is when things are going smoothly in life. But, when a tragedy happens, it becomes even more paramount to be there for friends. I couldn't be there, but I wrote a speech about how Shanti and I had been friends since the fourth grade, about how much I respected him, and about how much I was going to miss him. I know Mrs. Lal still has the speech and I hope that it gave her a little comfort to know how much her son meant to me. I still miss him.

Never Take Friends for Granted

Some of the people who become our friends and part of our supporting cast wind up getting there out of pure good luck on our part. We can sit down and map out who we want to hang out with and who we want to be our friends, like we're ordering Chinese food off a menu, but some really good friends fall into our lives. That is what happened with me and Gerald Williams in 1993.

I was at major-league spring training with the Yankees in Fort Lauderdale in February of that year, hoping that I tied my shoelaces properly each day and didn't accidentally hit Don Mattingly with an errant throw. I really didn't know anyone, and the only reason I was even there was because I had been drafted in the first round the year before. I was 18 years old and weighed around 160 pounds, so I probably looked like a batboy. Actually, some of the batboys were bigger than I was.

There was an older infielder in the organization that spring who decided that he was going to haze me. I didn't know what this player was doing or why he was doing it, but he made sure to try to assert himself over me. That was bogus considering I was still a teenager and didn't know what was going on. I barely whispered a word to anyone, so I wasn't about to get in someone's face.

During batting practice, the pitcher will use a large bucket of baseballs for a group of hitters. When he runs out of the four dozen or so balls, it is everyone's job to collect the balls and put them back in the bucket so practice can continue. You learn that routine in the minor leagues. Everyone knows that it is everyone's job to pick up the balls. It's fair, it's faster, and it's a team game so everyone should contribute.

But when we'd finish the bucket that spring, this genius would order the other players not to pick them up and would say, "Let him do it." To this day, I don't know what this guy's problem was. I don't think I'd even spoken to him at that point, but he obviously wanted to behave like a tough guy in front of the other players, so I wound up scooping up all of the balls. As much as I wanted to defend myself and as much as I'd advise other people to defend themselves, this situation was a losing battle. He wanted a reaction. I wouldn't give one. I was the new kid so I took my medicine.

That's where Gerald Williams saved me. He asked me if I wanted to go to dinner one night and I was relieved to have someone to go out with. I felt like I had been the last kid on the playground waiting to be picked for a game, and finally someone had selected me.

From that first meal, I knew that Gerald was someone whom I would befriend. He speaks softly and thoughtfully and is more like a philosopher than a baseball player. You could sit down next to Gerald on a plane, take a three-hour flight, talk the whole time, and never, ever guess that he played baseball. Gerald would talk to you about politics, religion, health care, the judicial system, anything. He is a person who thrives on life. He always finds positives and has told me that he doesn't think he could ever overuse the word *positive*. If I had to make a model out of the type of person to have as a friend, a person you can lean on or joke with, it would be Gerald. He is a wise man, a candid man, a positive man. If you have friends with those traits, consider yourself lucky.

I'm 99 percent sure that Gerald said something to my hazing friend, because the nonsense ceased soon after we had dinner. That's the type of thing a friend like Gerald does. He helped me without my even knowing it, although I figured it out because the antics stopped.

But Gerald also put a positive spin on the incident. We were standing at Fort Lauderdale Stadium days after we met when Gerald quietly said to me, "As soon as you're ready to play up here, that guy is gone. You know that. Don't you?" That made sense to me, a lot of sense. It probably explained the player's animosity toward me, too. It was positive, motivational advice. Gerald told me to think about where I was going to be in three years and think about where this player was going to be in three years and then see who could act like the tough guy. Three years later, I was on the World Series Champions. My ex-teammate, the one who wanted to watch a teenager fetch baseballs for an extra 90 seconds, was not.

That experience taught me a lot about patience and perseverance. It would have been natural and easy for me to bicker with this other player and create a hostile scene. I was tempted. I'm sure you've had incidents where someone tried to dominate you in a similar way. It took a lot of restraint to let the situation evolve, as I did, and not get too unnerved by what was going on. There's not always going to be someone like Gerald to help smooth out matters, but, even without Gerald's help, I wouldn't have let that nonsense deter me from reaching my goals.

One of the things that you must remember about friendships is that you have to nurture them, too. Don't take your friends for granted. Your actions will remind them of their importance to you. I was disappointed when the Yankees traded Gerald to the Milwaukee Brewers in 1996. I told everyone that trades were a part of the sport, but I knew that I'd miss Gerald terribly. We had done everything together. We ate together, we sat next to each other on buses and airplanes, and we looked out for each other. My life changed after Gerald left.

But Gerald and I actually grew closer after he was traded. Gerald lives in Tampa and plays for the Tampa Bay Devil Rays, so we go to dinner almost every night during the off-season. We've worked at staying close because being there for each other means so much to us. If we haven't talked for an hour or for a week, we'll start a conversation by sarcastically saying, "Where have you been?" Then we'll both laugh. It's our signal that we've got some things to discuss. I know I've got some listening and learning to do, too.

Family Knows Best

Whenever you think about your most loyal friends and the people who are a major part of your support system, don't underestimate the importance of your siblings. You might have only one sibling, like me, or you might have 13, like my mother. But they are usually the people who know you the best and they are people whom you can trust from the cradle to the grave.

I remember a song called "Everybody's Free to Wear Sunscreen" that was popular in 1999. It was adapted from a mock graduation speech in Mary Schmich's column in the *Chicago Tribune* and turned into a song by Baz Luhrmann. The song is a series of snippets about life, some funny and some serious. But the words really make you think. One of the lines was "Be nice to your siblings. They're your best link to your past and the people most likely to stick with you in the future." When I heard that line, it made me think about what I have experienced with Sharlee. Exasperation and exhilaration, triumphs and tribulations, absence and togetherness, happiness and more happiness.

Now that I'm 26 and she's 20, we're probably closer than we've ever been in our lives. She's probably my best friend and sometimes I'll talk to her several times a day. Just to see how she's doing. Just to ask her questions. Just to ask her if she needs my credit card. Only kidding, I think.

I've tried real hard to be there for Sharlee because I know it was and is difficult to grow up as Derek Jeter's sister. By the time I was in my first full year with the Yankees, she was only a junior in high school. She was constantly compared to me by teachers and by coaches, which is so unfair. People used to ask her about me

I am so proud of my sister, Sharlee. I am hugging her here after a speech she gave at Kalamazoo Central in 1996, when I came back for Derek Jeter Day. I know Sharlee and I are going to be best friends the rest of our lives.

before they inquired about her. The typical conversation would be someone rushing up to her after I got a couple of hits for the Yankees the night before and say, "So, how is Derek doing?" Sharlee got so tired of hearing it that she would snap and say, "I'm doing fine. OK?"

Unwittingly, I might have made things worse for her by telling reporters in 1996 that she was the best shortstop in the family. Sharlee could really field her position and I wanted to compliment her. But the plan backfired because my words just put more pressure on her.

She could get three hits in a game for Kalamazoo Central and the article in the newspaper would say, "Sharlee Jeter, the younger sister of Yankee shortstop Derek Jeter, had three hits yesterday as Kalamazoo Central won, 8–7." Even when she performed well, she couldn't escape me. I wish I could have been there for her, although I don't know what I could have changed. Phone calls and letters don't have the same impact as being there for one of your siblings or your friends. Sharlee used to love to brag about me, but when I became successful and other people in Kalamazoo started talking about me like I was their own, she didn't want to brag anymore. It was like other people were taking a piece of me away from her.

Like me, Sharlee had a dream. It was to play softball for Michigan and then to make the United States Olympic team. I implored her to go for it because she really was the best natural athlete in the family. I had to work for several hours a day to get where I am today. Sharlee barely had to practice and she was still an excellent high school player.

But Sharlee abandoned her dreams in part because she was tired of being compared to me. It wasn't worth it. She had to face constant comparisons on the field and in the classroom, too. I was a solid student. I had a 3.8 out of 4.0 grade-point average and

I graduated in the top 10 percent of my class, but I wasn't perfect. Once I left and had so much success playing baseball, I think I took on a mythic status in some ways. Teachers forgot that I liked to talk in class, that I liked to joke around when the lessons got boring, and that I had faults, too. Sharlee heard how I had done no wrong, and if she missed a homework assignment, my name would be invoked. That's never fair because everyone is an individual. In order to have her own identity, Sharlee said that she sometimes tried to do the exact opposite of what I'd done and that meant rebelling.

It bothers me that Sharlee gave up her dreams to continue in sports beyond high school. As a protective older brother and as part of her supporting cast, I wish there was a way she could have pursued her dream of playing sports without feeling the type of burden that I never felt. I set the bar high—and Sharlee was judged more critically for her imperfections than I was or anyone else was at her age.

"He didn't have that shadow over him," Sharlee has said. "I had it every day of my life."

Sharlee used to tell my parents that girls were different from boys when they would enforce rules with her. I know that she rebelled against my parents as a teenager. Let me get this straight here. It wasn't like she did drugs or drank beer. No, we weren't raised that way. Leading a healthy lifestyle was important in our household. As a six-year-old, Sharlee actually got my father to quit smoking. Every morning when my Dad would drive us to school, Sharlee would sit in the backseat and scream, "Dad, I can't breathe. Open the windows. Stop smoking." I think he got tired of hearing her, and, thankfully, he got tired of straining for a breath and quit.

But Sharlee liked to push my parents in a way I never did. If her curfew was at midnight, she'd purposely stroll in at 12:05 just to see what my parents would do. If she was supposed to do homework when she got home from school, she would watch TV until they reprimanded her. If she was grounded for cutting a class, she would talk so much that my parents were tempted to let her go outside. Sharlee is tough and doesn't take grief from anyone.

Even today, Sharlee has admitted to me that it's hard for anyone to get too close to her. She has a few select friends who are part of her inner circle because she thinks there are only certain people she can trust, the people who won't care that I'm her brother. I praise her for that. I think it's shrewder to have three friends you can trust than 10 who just want to be around you because of who you are, whom you might know, and what you can do for them.

I guess it really hit me how much trouble Sharlee had trying to be Sharlee after the 1996 World Series. We had won the title, we had a ticker tape parade, and I was named the Rookie of the Year. There was a whirlwind of events and I couldn't walk the streets of Manhattan without someone stopping me every 10 feet to congratulate me. It was a wild time, a real special time.

Kalamazoo Central wanted to honor me after the World Series and I thought that would be a blast. I thought some of my teachers and some of my old friends would be there, maybe 100 people. But 3,000 people squeezed into the gymnasium to see me. I was shocked. Four years earlier, I had been scooping up grounders off the hardwood floor during indoor practices and now I was back as a member of the World Series Champions. It was a memorable day, for many reasons.

Sharlee was one of the speakers and I told her not to make me cry. I said it as a joke, not thinking that she'd make my eyes moist. But she did. Sharlee began talking about how the feelings our family had experienced during the 1996 season were indescribable. She mentioned how I deserved everything that I had accomplished because I had worked hard for it. Then she turned the speech into a deeply personal message from a younger sister to an older brother. Here is what she said:

"I am not a big fan of Derek's because of his many successes in baseball, but because of his personality and the role he plays as my big brother. He tells me right from wrong, he recognizes my successes, and, best of all, he is honest with me. Derek supports me in everything I do and takes time from a busy schedule to talk to me about things that may not even be very important.

"I believe that the bond between a brother and sister is very important. Sometimes, people take God's gift of having a sibling for granted. You don't know how much you're missing until it's gone. I've gone through almost four years in high school and I can count on two hands how many times I've had a chance to sit face to face with Derek and tell him what's been going on in school and sports. I've had to accept the fact that Derek will never see me play high school softball, something that my teammates may take for granted.

"There are days when I wish I had a brother to argue with because I've had a bad day. There are all the things I have not had for almost five years. But one thing I have had is someone who loves me for me, someone who made me realize that hard work does pay off and someone who has made me extremely proud.

"Derek, thank you for being my big brother and thank you for giving me my identity. To you, I am Sharlee, not Derek Jeter's sister. You have helped mold me into the person I am today and now it is my turn to make you proud and I promise I will. I love you. And, remember, you are my hero, not because of your baseball ability, but because of your support and love and making me proud to say that you are my brother."

I still get choked up when I hear that speech. I've got it framed and in my office at home, a constant reminder of how important Sharlee is and how much of a friend she is. Sharlee will earn her

What a great Christmas present—Sharlee framed the speech she gave at Kalamazoo Central for me.

bachelor's degree before me in mathematics from Spelman College in Atlanta. She has a new dream of going on to graduate school and pursuing a career in the business world. I'm proud of her for being strong, for being smart, and for being a terrific sister. She did what friends should do on that day in the gym. She told me exactly how she felt.

You don't have to be inside a gym with 3,000 other people to tell your sister, brother, or friend how you feel about them. You can do it in an empty room with no one else around. Surround yourself with good people and then hang on to them. When you have good, solid friends, people who care for you, you can assure yourself that you'll never be alone and that they will be there for you for the rest of your life.

7

Be Serious, but Have Fun

hanksgiving is about two weeks away and everyone in Florida is talking about football—pro football, college football, and high school football. There is no escaping the discussions about the Tampa Bay Buccaneers, about Florida or Florida State, and even about Chamberlain High School because it's that time of the year and this is a football-crazy state. I hear it on the radio, I hear it when I go out to eat, I hear it all around town. The World Series has been over for about two weeks, spring training is three months away, and it is quiet

and calm around the Yankees' minor-league complex on North
Himes Avenue.

That's when I'm here. That's when I love being here. I start
working out in the middle of November, no matter how far the
Yankees go in the playoffs. I think it's important to have a desire
to keep improving. I don't like bragging, but I don't know too
many people who work 50 weeks a year. I'm fortunate enough to
play for the Yankees and I know my career won't last forever, so
that's why I am so relentless. I want to keep getting better while
I can. I'll go on vacations when my career is over.

It's pretty empty here in November. There might be some players who are rehabbing from injuries and others who occasionally
work out, but I basically have the complex to myself. I won't
throw a ball or swing a bat until January, but I stretch, lift, run,
and try to get stronger. I always lose weight during the season, no
matter how many meals I eat, so I try to add pounds every year.

When the Yankees signed me, I was 6 foot 2 inches and 156.
I went into the 2000 season at 6–3 and 205. So I'm virtually the
same body with 49 extra pounds, and that didn't happen because
of eight straight years of hamburgers and shakes. I've specifically
worked to increase my strength in my legs, my arms, my middle
body, and my upper body, and to increase my flexibility. I'm not
trying to look like Mark McGwire's brother, but I want to get
stronger while remaining flexible.

After my third year in the minor leagues, I decided to move to
Tampa full-time to take advantage of the facilities that are available 12 months out of the year. I must admit I do take weekends
and Christmas off. But I think one of the reasons the Yankees are
so successful is because the facilities and the coaches are available
year-round. I might be alone in November, but by January there
will be about 50 players working out here. Most of them are

minor leaguers, but some major leaguers join me about a month before spring training starts.

If your school or your company offered this awesome chance to get better, wouldn't you take it? For me, it's a no-brainer. I see this as an invitation to improve. I'm one of only 750 major-league players. I want to take advantage of the time I have after the season to get better and stay in that elite class as one of the 750 men fortunate enough to have a job as a baseball player. There's no way I would ever pass up a chance like this.

This is really about being able to challenge yourself. When the season is over, I'm tired. I'm worn out, mentally and physically. We all know that feeling of wanting to dive into bed and sleep for three straight days. But, as important as it is to get enough rest, you have to be keenly aware of when you have a chance to make yourself better, too.

Some young people love the summer months because they don't have to deal with going to classes. I used to love the summer, too, but just because you're off from school doesn't mean your learning should stop. In fact, that could be the time you use to continue learning. You could take classes in a subject that interests you, or you could work an internship or take up a sport or travel or read all those books you've never had a chance to read.

If you love to paint, paint all summer. If you love to write, write all summer. For many of you, that's your off-season. Look at what I do in my off-season and know that's why I'm so confident playing baseball from April until October. When I'm hitting in a taut situation in August, I'm confident because I've been preparing for that moment all winter. Well, all my life, really.

My parents thought that moving to Tampa in 1994 was one of the smartest things I ever did. I know I'm established with the Yankees now, even though I also realize this could all evaporate tomorrow from an injury, a trade, or who knows what. But I'm aware that moving to Tampa sent a positive message to the organization that I was dedicated enough to work out at the facility every day, though I'm not obligated to be anywhere near here.

Say you're a Class AA player and there's some doubt about sending you to Class AAA next year because you and another player have similar abilities and only one of you can be promoted. Don't you think being in Tampa and working out every day works in your favor? I felt that way about my future. I might be the starting shortstop now and this type of logic might seem like it's irrelevant for me, but it wasn't then and I still feel that it's relevant today.

I've had Yankee officials like Mark Newman and Gary Denbo, men I respect, tell me how much it means to some of the younger players to see a major-league All-Star working alongside them during the off-season. I'm not doing it for that reason, but, if it teaches someone the importance of hard work and persistence, that's a bonus for me and for the Yankees.

"The Yankees have always had a long line of great models, some of them mythical and some of them actual," Newman told a reporter. "Derek is a model. He's here every day in the flesh."

One thing that always bothers me is when someone talks about my first four years in the major leagues and refers to me as an "overnight sensation." Huh? I never felt like an overnight sensation. People who say that don't know about my throwing the ball against a cement patch on the side of my house to strengthen my arm. They don't see me crying every night in the minor leagues. They don't see all the hard work I do during the off-season. People don't know all of the behind-the-scenes stuff, and if they did, I don't think anyone would call me an overnight sensation. I'm about two decades in the making and I'm still adding to the design.

```
DEREK S JETER
2415 CUMBERLAND
KALAMAZOO MI 49007




CONGRATULATIONS ON YOUR SELECTION BY THE NEW YORK YANKEES.   WE LOOK
FORWARD TO YOU BECOMING A MEMBER OF THE YANKEE FAMILY.

JOSEPH A. MOLLOY
NEW YORK YANKEES

21:54 EST

MGMCOMP
```

I see fans when I visit New York in December and January and they'll act like the off-season is one huge party. If they see me at a Knicks game or some other event, some will joke about how I must be enjoying a fun winter. I usually am, but it's not a non-stop party. They don't understand that I only visit New York a few days at a time after the season because there's really no off-season in baseball. If you want to keep up with your competitors, you have to treat it that way.

There was a new sign plastered outside our clubhouse at Legends Field this spring that read, "Unless you're the lead dog, the view never changes," which is a saying Chili Davis used to have on his T-shirt. When I saw it, I knew exactly who had this motivational saying put there: George Steinbrenner. That's the way Mr. Steinbrenner feels about everything, especially the Yankees. He wants us to win. Second place is not an option. I like that. I have the same attitude.

It's intriguing when Mr. Steinbrenner shows up at the minor-league complex on North Himes, which he does quite often. As soon as he wheels into the parking lot into the spot marked "GMS," a security guard announces "10–97" over the walkie-talkies, which tells everyone that Steinbrenner has arrived. They'll follow that with "The Eagle has landed," another ode to Steinbrenner, and everyone stands straighter and looks busier. If there's a scrap of paper on the floor, employees would sooner chew it than let the Boss see it. If a player's practice jersey is not tucked in, which I rarely see anyway, he tucks it in. Everything is neat, efficient, professional, the staples of a winning organization.

I don't get nervous when Mr. Steinbrenner is around. I mean I never have, not even when I was 18 years old. Why should I? I like to call him the Boss Man and he'll joke with me. I think it started with the Ohio State–Michigan rivalry in the Big Ten Conference. The Boss grew up in Cleveland and is a big fan of the Buckeyes, and I attended Michigan for a semester and love the Wolverines, so we'll jab each other about college football and college basketball scores.

I have a lot of respect for Mr. Steinbrenner because he wants to be successful and he expects everyone in the organization to be as dedicated and focused as he is. This is something you learn the first day you sign with the Yankees. That's the feeling from top to bottom. You see all the signs in the minor-league camp about winners and winning. He wants that Yankee tradition instilled in you and drills it in over and over. Even in the minors, we learned how to be Yankees, including hating the Red Sox.

Mr. Steinbrenner is a hands-on owner. There are some owners you might never see, but he's in New York all the time and I remember him being at my minor-league games in the Gulf Coast League and the Florida State League. I liked it when he would be there, just sitting with the fans. I liked it when any people were there, so having the owner there was much better. The first time I met the Boss, he told me, "Nice to meet you. Young man, we've got high hopes for you." I thought that was a cool thing to say. I thought it was even cooler that he knew who I was.

You could tell when he was around because certain people got panicky. I'm not one of them. The thing about Mr. Steinbrenner is he knows that I have respect for him, but I'm not intimidated. I think he understands that. I think that's why we have a good relationship. I don't treat him any differently than I treat Chuck Knoblauch, Bernie Williams, or Jorge Posada. I think he likes the fact that I treat him the same as my teammates. He signs the checks, so obviously he's the Boss. But if you play hard for him, he'll do anything for you. He's the type of owner who always takes care of players. He's very loyal to current and former players, and he has shown that with someone like Darryl Strawberry. There are always former Yankees working as spring-training instructors, so it's obvious that Mr. Steinbrenner wants to help them and wants to help us, because their guidance and presence is invaluable.

I like teasing Mr. Steinbrenner. I hope I get the chance to go for the hat trick in October of 2000 with him. I've poured champagne on the Boss's head and messed up his perfectly coiffed silver hair for the last two years after we won the World Series. If we win three straight titles, he had better bring a shower cap because I'll be coming after him again.

When we won the Series in San Diego in 1998, Mr. Steinbrenner was in the middle of our cramped and wet clubhouse, smiling and crying and rejoicing. He was wearing a blue blazer, a white turtleneck, and a black "World Champions" cap as he hugged players and told reporters that we were "the greatest team ever."

Mr. Torre embraced him and teasingly asked him for a kiss. I knew that the Boss was feeling pretty emotional so I picked that time to pounce. I sneaked up behind him as he was doing an interview and I think I said, "Someone's dry in here," and unleashed half a bottle of bubbly on his head and down his back. I've never seen him laugh so hard.

Fast-forward a year, and the scene was Yankee Stadium. Mr. Steinbrenner was standing about 30 feet from Mr. Torre's office in another chaotic clubhouse. Once again, he was wearing the ever-present white turtleneck and blue blazer, but this time he also had on a blue sweater and a tan "World Champions" baseball cap. I maneuvered past a gaggle of reporters who were interviewing him and blasted his head with another gusher of champagne. He looked up, knew that it had to be me again and announced, "That's the end of the interview, gang. I gotta get a towel. Jeter's in deep trouble." Then Mr. Steinbrenner quickly added, "No, no, no," so no one took his threats seriously. With the Boss, you never know.

I've been joking around with him for a while and I've included him in our champagne showers because he's a major part of the championships. We always have one of the highest payrolls in baseball, everything about the organization is first-class, and he'll add players and salaries for the postseason push if we need it. The Boss is also the man who hired Mr. Torre.

I wish I could advise you to pour champagne on your boss's head, but I don't want to be responsible for anyone losing his or her job. Remember, now, I did wait until we won the World Series before I did it. It's not like I did it after a ho-hum victory in June. You've got to keep your perspective, you know? If I'm going to mess up the Boss's hair and soak one of his blue blazers, I make sure that it's the World Series.

I always look forward to playing baseball in October, but even though I've played in the postseason four straight years, I know that could change in one second. Every year is not going to be an

All-Star year. Every year is not going to be a perfect year, although we're going to keep trying like heck to make them as perfect as possible.

I don't want anyone to talk about me as a player, whether it's an opposing manager or a guy sitting on a park bench, and say I didn't work hard. I think it would be almost impossible for someone to say that about me, and I'm as proud of that as anything anybody says about me. I love baseball, I love getting better, and I've never been averse to working hard at it while having fun. That started from the first time I threw a ball to my father as a toddler.

You've got to like what you're doing. One of the reasons I can work out so fervently in the off-season is because I like the process. I like getting myself in better shape and doing the things that are going to make me a better player. If I hated lifting weights or doing flexibility training, it wouldn't be so easy to do this. I admit that. That's why you have to find something you love doing and then be willing to devote yourself to it. If you really love it, it will show in your effort. Someone who wants to be a chef should not have any trouble spending hours and hours cooking. You have to want to be better. I know I do.

It would have presumably been easy to sleep in and ignore the alarm at 8:00 A.M. on a cool morning last November. Especially after we won the World Series in 1999 and I had an All-Star season with a .349 average, 24 homers, 102 runs batted in, and 134 runs scored. I guess it would have been just as easy to ignore the alarm after the 1998 season, when we won an unprecedented 125 games on our way to a Championship and I finished third in the American League's MVP balloting.

But who knows if 1998 or 1999 would have been so successful for me and for the team if I wasn't working out every day? I don't think it would have been, at least not for me. I can't speak for the entire team. But it's all about getting better and I find different areas to improve each year. I don't care who you are and I don't care how many times you've hit .300 or driven in 100 runs or won 20 games, you can always find areas that need improvement.

I think we have to continually motivate ourselves to get better. If you got a 100 on a test, you should think about the way you studied for that test, figure out if there's anything that needs refining, and try to get 100 again. If you won an award for being the best history student one year, you should want to win the history and the science award the next year. Look at Michael Jordan when he was playing. Look at Tiger Woods now. Michael could have decided that two NBA titles were enough. Tiger could say the same about winning the Masters. But what makes them true champions is that they never settle for being less than the best. You can study their passion for being successful and learn from it. I'd like to believe I'm the same way because I find my flaws, I try to erase them, and I'm never satisfied. Why should three World Series titles be enough? Who made that rule? We all make our own goals, so we all devise our own ceilings, too. If you feel that something is attainable, it is.

There's Always Room for Improvement

Since we lived behind Kalamazoo Central, I was always the first player to the field for games or, at worst, the second. All I had to do was hang out in my backyard and wait until one of my teammates showed up and then I'd hop the fence in my maroon-and-white uniform, the one I had tried on the night before, and go play high school baseball. It was a common occurrence for one of my parents to throw me batting practice with Wiffle balls before my high school games. Trying to hit my father's funky pitches minutes before I was going to be analyzed by two dozen scouts in a real game helped me understand there was a time for fun and a time to be serious, too.

I asked my parents to buy me an indoor hitting contraption when I was in high school so I could still practice when it got cold. I think it was called a solo hitter. It was a steel cage with a ball dangling down and you hit the ball into the netting of the cage, waited for it to flop back into place, and then hit it again. My parents reminded me that I couldn't just let this equipment gather dust if they purchased it. That wasn't a problem.

We set the solo hitter up in our one-car garage, which became my personal hitting area, and I probably used it every day of the year, whether the weather was cold or warm. I was so dedicated that I'd sometimes take one thousand swings a day. I was so dedicated that I would leave school during my free sixth period in my

Dad was the coach of our Westwood Little League team the year I was 12. He's in the back with the striped shirt, and I'm in the middle, holding a bat.

senior year and walk home to practice my swing for 45 minutes. Now, I could have hung out in the cafeteria or taken my car for a joyride, but I was more interested in honing my swing.

My closest friends, like Marisa, Doug, and Shanti, knew that preparing for the baseball season was as important to me as having food and water. I remember numerous times in which Doug would come over and I'd still be busy working on my swing, so I'd tell him to go watch television or make himself a sandwich until I was done. I was only 16 years old, but I was dedicated. After a while, Doug knew better than to even interrupt me. He'd see or hear me taking my daily swings in the garage and he would go into my house, plop down on the couch, and wait until I was done.

Was I different from other teenagers? Would most kids have stopped when their friend showed up? Maybe. But, if you're devoted to something and devoted to getting better, I don't think you can let anything interfere with it. A good friend like Doug knew that. He would have been angry with me if I had stopped.

Hal Newhouser, a scout for the Houston Astros and a former two-time MVP as a pitcher with the Detroit Tigers in the 1940s, visited me before my senior year to talk about the alternatives of college and pro baseball. I developed a close bond with him and actually thought the Astros might pick me first in the draft. Newhouser told them they should choose me first and then quit as a scout when they didn't and chose Phil Nevin, a college player.

But Newhouser sent me a letter with some advice after his earlier visit, and one of his tips was to swing a bat as often as I possibly could because it would toughen up my hands when I wasn't playing. "Al Kaline bought a tee and a ball and swung at it all winter," Newhouser wrote. "Look where it got him, the Hall of Fame." That was enough for me to hear. I knew who Al Kaline was and I obviously know what the Hall of Fame is, so the words influenced me.

I played junior varsity and varsity in my freshman year and felt pretty good about what I had accomplished. I pleaded with my parents to send me to the Nine-Star Baseball Camp in Mount Morris, Michigan, telling them I could get better and be seen by college coaches and major-league scouts. Although my father was still attending graduate school at Western Michigan and our family budget was modest, they agreed. I was thrilled, but there was a lesson attached to this gift.

My father spotted me playing tennis with a bunch of girls at Kalamazoo Central not long after that, and he was disappointed. I really wasn't playing tennis. I might have had a tennis racket in my hands, but I was there because that's where some cute girls were hanging out. Tennis was the way to meet the girls, nothing more. I had no aspirations to play tennis.

When I got home that night, my parents asked me to sit down at the kitchen table and asked me if my goal to be a baseball player had changed. I told them no. They asked me if I was still serious about baseball. I said I was. They told me there were lots of teams I could play on in Kalamazoo and they didn't want to pressure me. But, if I was serious about baseball and if they were going to pay $175 for a camp, I had to work at it every day. They were right, and I think they approached it in the proper way. If I wanted to play tennis, that was fine with them. But they weren't going to support me going to baseball camp, especially to the financial detriment of the rest of the family, if I wasn't serious about it. I couldn't tell you the next time I picked up a tennis racket. Maybe while I was killing time in a sporting goods store or something. I got the message.

So when my alarm clock buzzed at 7:15 one morning last January, I was tempted to punch the snooze button. I was working on about five hours of sleep on this day because I had gone to the Tampa Bay Lightning hockey game the night before and some of my friends returned to my house afterward, and stayed until 2:30 A.M. But a lesson like that tennis debacle will creep into my head. I got up. This is what I do.

I was leaving for New York that afternoon to attend a sports award dinner, so I wouldn't be able to work out for the next two days, making this morning even more important. It happened to be the day after I agreed to a $10 million contract for the 2000 season, and someone asked me if I thought about taking the day off to celebrate. That never crossed my mind. In fact, I think that gave me more reasons to work out and keep doing what has helped get me to this point. Besides, as much as people don't want to believe this and as much as I know it's hard to hear it from pro athletes, I'm not motivated by the money. To me, that money is Monopoly money. It's out there and it's mine, but it doesn't rule my world.

The motivation is to be the best player I can be, and if that means some people want to call me one of the best in baseball, that's up to them. I don't sit here every day and think about what I accomplished in the past and how I've got it made now. I'm always focusing on what I can do to improve in the future. What can I do to make myself better tomorrow? I know people don't care what I did last year. Seriously, last year is over with. My teammates and my coaches want to see what I can do this year. More important, I want to see it.

I think it's sensible for everyone to try to focus on making themselves better for the present and the future. Don't dwell in the past. Don't feel that you've achieved something and now you can relax. It's great to reach goals and feel proud of what you've done. But life evolves. What you thought was fabulous on Monday might be surpassed by one of your colleagues on Tuesday. Keep yourself motivated to do better and surpass him on Wednesday.

Once I arrive at the complex during the off-season, I'm pretty energized. There's always some autograph seekers lined up outside the parking lot. I don't mind signing, especially for kids. But one of my pet peeves is when I see the same faces over and over again. I realize these aren't true fans but dealers who show up to get autographs to sell. If I see 10 people and I recognize several of them from the day before, I'm apt to drive past them. I know that's unfair to the one or two people who might be there for the first time, but it's not fair to me to sign for dealers, either. It's really sad that these dealers ruin it for the real fans. I hate to pass people by, but I can't condone what some memorabilia dealers do in stockpiling and selling autographs.

Tino Martinez and I were the only major leaguers working out on this day in January. After we loosened up, we went to the batting cages. There are four cages right behind one of the entrances to the facility, aligned in sets of two and sitting back to back between two fields. There's AstroTurf across the floor and blue netting enclosing the cages to keep balls from squirting out onto the fields. I start out by simply hitting balls off a tee, which is just a plank of wood with a rubber post jutting out from the center. Denbo takes the balls out of a white bucket, places them on the tee one at a time, and I whack line drives into the netting.

It's monotonous, but it's important, too. Repetition breeds familiarity. Familiarity breeds comfort. Comfort breeds relaxation, and the best environment for achieving success is when you're relaxed. So, as Denbo puts balls on the tee and tells me to hit toward the right side, I imagine it's Pedro Martinez or Mike Mussina as I swing fluidly through the zone. Then I'll hit to right center, to center, to left center, and to left.

It's like preparing for any other job. If a public speaker wants to get better with his presentations, he practices his speeches over and over. I don't think you can ever get enough practice.

Sometimes you need a mental break. But there's no substitute for doing something again and again; doing it so much that you feel comfortable doing it in your sleep. It's like Michael Jordan draining a series of 20-footers at the beginning of a practice session and then schooling everyone on the court. I wonder how many thousands of times he did that.

As I mentioned before, the Yankees devise an individual development plan for a player after they sign him. They observe you for 30 days and then decide which adjustments you need to make. They won't touch a guy for at least 30 days because they don't want a player who has had success to come to the organization and be told that everything he has been doing is wrong. I liked that. I think it helped me. Besides, if they were to tinker with a player and he failed after the changes were made, what would he think then? I'm terrible? It's smart to wait.

Back in 1992, the Yankees watched me in the Rookie League and determined that as a hitter I needed to maintain my balance, I needed to keep my torso from tipping over the plate, and I needed to have better pitch selection. It was a pretty thorough analysis and I still work on these same possible problem areas today.

With the help of Denbo, who is the organization's hitting coordinator and who knows my swing better than anyone, we developed a series of swinging drills eight years ago that I still use in my daily workouts. These drills consist of about three dozen different swings I take, which are designed to help me combat the problems that the Yankees were sharp enough to detect after my first month.

After hitting to different parts of the imaginary field on the batting tee, I'll hit some soft-toss pitching. Denbo will stand behind a 6 × 6 screen and lob balls to me underhanded. Again, I'm trying to keep my body erect and drive the balls to different

Here I am hitting a home run against the White Sox.

My good friend, shortstop Alex Rodriguez of the Seattle Mariners, makes a vertical leap as I try to break up a double play at second.

Chuck Solomon/Sports Illustrated

This is a good way to stretch your muscles—I'm glad every catch I make doesn't require this much effort!

V. J. Lovero/Sports Illustrated

I was thrilled to be a part of the All-Star Game in Boston, July 1999, even though Nomar Garciaparra narrowly beat me in the fan vote. You can tell I was having a good time as we warmed up that day.

Chuck Solomon/Sports Illustrated

I work hard to stay in shape during the off-season so that I don't have to worry about making running catches during the season. All the workouts I do in January and February make me a little more agile and fast in August and September when it really counts.

It's so important to support your teammates. My dad taught me this when I was a kid, and I've carried the lesson with me my whole life. Here I am cheering on the Yankees with Darryl Strawberry.

Bernie Williams is a classy, talented ballplayer. I've learned a lot by watching the way he handles himself, on the field and off.

I am able to find role models everywhere I look, from Mr. Torre to my parents to Alex Rodriguez. Though he's my age, I still can find things to learn from him whenever I watch him play.

People compare me and fellow shortstop Nomar Garciaparra of the Boston Red Sox all the time. I'm proud to be compared to him—he's a great ballplayer and a worthy opponent on the field.

That's the smile of someone who can't believe he's realized the life he imagined. All I've ever wanted to do is play for the Yankees—and I'm doing it! I am living proof that with hard work you can make your dreams happen.

parts of the imaginary field, and even if it looks strange to see a major leaguer hitting underhanded pitches, this is a helpful routine. I use two different bats during the soft-toss, my regular 32-ounce bat and a 29-inch bat called a "short bat."

The short bat gives me a better feel for swinging with my top hand, first because I can swing one-handed if I want to. I can do the same if I'm focusing on my bottom hand, and I also use it when I'm swinging with both hands. This bat helps me to improve my swing by increasing the amount of time that I keep the bat in the hitting zone.

Denbo is a superb teacher, and he explained that one of the problems many hitters encounter is a tendency to not keep the bat in the hitting zone long enough. One thing that all of the great hitters—guys like Wade Boggs and Tony Gwynn—have in common is that they keep the barrel or the thick part of the bat in position to make contact for a longer period of time. The longer you keep the bat in the hitting zone, the better chance you have to make solid contact.

Whenever I use the short bat, it magnifies my mistakes. If I have trouble with a pitch while using the 29-inch bat, I'm either going to swing and miss or I'm going to hit the ball off the end of the bat. That happens when I don't keep the bat in the hitting zone. It's an excellent tool because it forces me to be extremely conscious of my timing on every swing and I carry that over into the games.

I won the Rookie of the Year award in 1996 after I batted .314 with 10 homers and 78 runs batted in. As happy as I was about the award and about our winning the World Series, I felt I struck out too often (102 times) and I didn't steal enough bases (14). Using the short bat is supposed to help you make more contact and, presumably, decrease the number of strikeouts, so I work with that during the off-season.

A Little League at bat—my swing has been a work in progress since I was young, though my basic style is still the same.

You know what? I didn't reduce my strikeouts. I struck out 125 times in 1997, but that's going to happen with me because I'm aggressive. Besides, I felt as if I made better contact when it mattered and I still do. I'll strike out, but usually not when the situation cries out for some contact. One indication of that is that I hit .254 when I had two strikes on me last year, which is 56 points better than the American League average. Even Mr. Torre said, "I thought there was a glaring deficiency in that he strikes out a lot. But then you recognize that Derek does strike out, but, when he shouldn't strike out, he doesn't. When he needs to put the ball in play, he puts the ball in play."

Still, 1997 was a frustrating season. My average dropped to .291, but what frustrated me the most is that I think we were the best team in baseball and we faltered in the Division Series. We were four outs away from beating the Indians in the American League Championship Series, but Sandy Alomar, Jr., homered off of Mariano Rivera and we lost Game 4. Then we lost Game 5 and I was shocked. I don't know if I was more depressed or more shocked after I got home, but it was an awful winter.

I had to attend the second game of the World Series between the Indians and the Marlins in Miami for an endorsement commitment, but I didn't even stay for the entire game. I couldn't watch it. I felt like we should have been there playing, so I couldn't watch any other teams. I left, but I used that season as motivation to improve. I didn't want to experience that feeling ever again, a feeling where I thought we were better and we lost.

Have you ever felt that way? Have you ever felt that someone picked the wrong student to play the lead in the play or the wrong person for that sweet summer job? It should have been you, right? While I moped about our loss for a few months, I didn't let the loss turn me into a couch potato. You can't let those setbacks ruin your enthusiasm. I went into 1998 fresh and ready.

Everyone knows we had an amazing season in 1998. Everything we did that season worked, from phenomenal pitching to timely hitting to reliable defense. Some observers have called us the best team in baseball history, and I'll say this: no other team ever did what we did. By going 125–50, we put ourselves into a spot in baseball history where we're all alone.

I did something dumb that year, which taught me a valuable lesson about trying to be who you're not. I'd never hit more than five homers in the minors, and I had had 10 in each of my first two years with the Yankees. So when I hit my 19th homer in our 143d game, I was pumped to hit my 20th, a milestone. But I stopped swinging to spray the ball all over the field and let homers happen, and tried to hit balls out of the park. It messed

You can see my stance here in high school—we were playing at Riverfront Stadium in Cincinnati.

up my swing for the last 19 games of the season and I went 18 for 72 with no homers and 18 strikeouts. My average plummeted from .334 to .324, and after chasing Bernie Williams for the batting title all summer, I wound up lagging 15 points behind him.

I learned a lot from that period. I learned that I should always try hard and set my goals high, but I shouldn't change the formula that had gotten me to that point. If you're having a great weekend skiing the intermediate trail, you might want to stay there and keep getting better at it. Don't ski down the most treacherous hill to try and be something you're not.

Still, even though I carelessly pushed myself to hit that 20th homer in 1998 and never did, the talk about my power remained a hot subject. I went to arbitration with the Yankees before the

1999 season because I had asked for a salary of $5 million and they offered $3.2 million. During the hearing, their lawyers criticized me for not hitting enough homers. I thought that was comical considering that my 19 homers were the most ever by a shortstop in club history.

I found that experience disconcerting. I think that arbitration cases can be a pain for the player and the team. I work hard to be a dependable player and then I had to listen to my employers criticize me. That stinks. The arbitration process is part of being a major leaguer, but I hated it.

Still, the Yankees probably did me a favor because they gave me one more thing to motivate me for the 1999 season. The day after that hearing, I went to work out and I told Denbo, "Gotta hit more bombs." He looked at me, didn't need an explanation, and said, "We can do that." We started working on it right after that. Sometimes, your sources for motivation come from weird places. This time it came from my employers. Even though I won the $5 million salary and proved I was right in this argument, their comments motivated me.

I've always been able to hit pitches the opposite way to right field. It's one of my strengths as a hitter, and I've been doing it since high school. I used to take batting practice in high school and I'd purposely work on taking outside pitches to right field. Some players were intent on pulling every pitch because that's what felt most comfortable, but I always liked to hit the ball the other way. I'd also fight off inside pitches with an inside-out swing that allowed me to drop balls in right and right center for hits, something that has been one of my trademarks in the majors. In 1998, I blasted an opposite-field homer into the right-field upper deck at Yankee Stadium, not an easy thing to do for a right-handed batter.

David Cone
ON DEREK JETER

David Cone will be relaxing on the Yankees' team bus, ready to leave for another road trip, when he hears that sound. It's a combination of shrieking and squealing and it tells Cone that Derek Jeter has emerged and is strolling to the bus.

"Derek obviously attracts enormous attention," says Cone. "It grows every year and it's amazing how he's handled it in such a short period of time. We go from town to town and there are girls crying and screaming and he doesn't let it affect him."

Jeter is baseball's version of the Backstreet Boys, the one-man Backstreet Boy who plays for the Yankees. Everyone wants an autograph or wants to get close to Jeter. Cone has played with superstars on the Mets, the Blue Jays, the Royals, and the Yankees and had not always handled the pressure of being a major leaguer so smoothly himself. But he has never seen a superstar as comfortable as Jeter.

"The thing that impressed me early on with him is the way he acted around people. Not just with fans, but with his teammates, too. He showed the right deference and he was always asking questions. He wanted advice."

Cone was surprised when Jeter asked him in 1996 where he should position himself for certain hitters on certain counts. Jeter had noticed that Cone was likely to toss Roberto Alomar a backdoor slider on an 0–2 count, so he

Major-league pitchers know I like hitting the other way, so they would try to jam me on the inside corner and prevent me from extending my arms to hit the ball. I started working on driving inside pitches more before the 1998 season. Gary explained that I needed to be able to handle the inside pitches because I could generate more power and hit more homers that way.

asked Cone if he should take an extra step toward the shortstop hole. He was a 22-year-old rookie who sounded like a 42-year-old baseball lifer.

"I've never had an infielder come to me with that kind of insight. It almost floored me. To read patterns and hitters and adjust from pitch to pitch is amazing. He didn't just do this on his own. He went up and asked the pitcher, too."

When Jeter gets on the bus or on an airplane, he'll sometimes call Cone, who is 11 years older, "Mr. Cone." Jeter has probably done it a hundred times, but it makes Cone laugh. Cone is not sure why. Maybe because it's Jeter.

"He has this universal charisma that's infectious. I don't want to sound like I'm overinflating my opinion of him. Nobody is perfect, but Derek has this universal appeal. He's got an even-keeled personality that has a calming influence on the team."

Jealousy exists in major-league clubhouses, and players who make the most money and receive the most attention can be targets. But Cone insisted that no Yankees resent Jeter, who is the best player on the team, who smoothly handles the attention, and who, most important, works to make himself even better.

"He'll come into the dugout and say that he stinks because he didn't get a hit. He's never satisfied. He's on his way to 200 hits and he's not happy. I think that's part Don Mattingly, part Paul O'Neill, part Tino Martinez. Derek has gotten it and he still gets it."

What I needed to do was stay more upright in the batter's box and use a refined top-hand swing. I'm eager at the plate, and, as the Yankees told me when I was only 18, I have a tendency to let my torso tip forward and not maintain my balance. If I was going to hit these inside pitches, I would need to remain a little more rigid at the plate. In addition, a top-hand approach would level off my swing to create more backspin when I hit the ball and cause flyballs to carry deeper.

"Strength is an issue," said Denbo. "He [Jeter] sees A. Rod and Nomar and they're bigger and stronger. That motivated him. More strength means added confidence. With that added strength and because he's standing upright, he can wait longer to recognize what a pitch is."

The changes worked well in 1999 as I drove pitches to left field like I never had before and had my finest all-around season. I worked on my top-hand swing for the 2000 season, trying to continue to drive inside pitches. When I was a rookie, the Yankees saw me as having the potential to hit 15 homers in a season. Now there's talk about me hitting 35 or more.

To do that, to keep up with players like Alex, who has hit as many as 42 in one season, and Nomar, whose high is 35, I've got to keep getting stronger. That's why I went to the International Performance Institute in Bradenton, Florida, an athletic training center, during the off-season and had a training program designed to increase the strength in my legs and my core or middle body without getting too bulky. I wanted to stay flexible.

This is a place where Nomar goes, and Casey Close, my agent, had implored me to go there, too. I had never lifted weights for my legs before, so they taught me routine exercises like squats, and I also did unusual exercises like putting a 30-pound sandbag around my neck and then running left, right, backward, and forward. That drill was designed to increase my explosiveness. I also wanted to get stronger in my core, the middle of the body that connects the torso to the hips. We worked with something called a physioball, which looks a lot like a medicine ball. I'd lean against the ball with weights in both hands and would have to use my middle body to keep my balance, strengthening that area. I feel I got much stronger and I gained about 20 pounds, but I'm still lean and loose.

I could feel a difference in my body when I was working out before spring training. I was driving balls deeper than I had in previous springs. It's a nice feeling when the work you've been doing provides results right before your eyes. You should use those kinds of accomplishments to motivate yourself. I know I do. If the hard work shows it's working, then work even harder.

My stance is not something you'll see in a textbook. I like to lift the bat high above my shoulders and wiggle it while my body shifts slightly. I'll bend my right knee and lift my left foot a little and then I'll torque my body when I lean forward and finally whip the bat through the strike zone.

**Something from Mom's scrapbook—
line scores from my first
Little League All-Star game.**

LITTLE LEAGUE

**Baseball
Little League District 2 Tournament
Major Baseball**

Westwood   020 020 — 4   4   1
Milwood   220 001 — 5   5   1
   Chris Humphrey and Joel Wierda; Damaine Spearman and Matt Berner.
   Westwood hits: Derek Jeter (home run), Chris Humphrey, Don Schroeder, Luke Chadwick.
   Milwood hits: Mark Pownell, Jim Boer, Damaine Spearman, Josh Smith, Jarrrod Boer.

South Portage   230 020 — 7   6   0
Northwood   000 200 — 2   4   5
   Matt VanderVeen and Andy Boersma; Eric Tattro and Matt Hazelhoff.
   South Portage hits: Leo Cherette 2, Matt Vander-Veen 2, Derek Haines (home run), Andy Baker.
   Northwood hits: Aaron Colwell (double), Andy Weaver (double), Eric Tatro, Ray McCarty.

Schoolcraft   100 011 — 3   2   4
Portage NE   301 10x — 5   3   4
   Todd Wright and David Kauffman; Alan Barnum and Don Keegan.
   Schoolcraft hits: Geoffrey Coats (double), Brian Crissman (triple).
   Portage NE hits: Darrick Brown, Don Keegan (double), Steve Carlton.

Alamo-Gobles   120 003 — 6   3   9
Oakwood   054 27x — 18   5   2
   Todd Kroes, Tony Lobrello (5) and John Holmes, Cris Coash (4); Robert Terrell and Jason Battles.
   Alamo-Gobles hits: John Holmes 2, Chris Rockafellow.
   Oakwood hits: Andy Cavanaugh, Casey Wade, Mike Johnson

Parchment   004 201 — 7   12   4
Eastwood   001 52x — 8   5   4
   Robbie Alban, Lee Putnam (4) and J.J. Markee; Trevor Mortord and Tony Patterson.
   Parchment hits: Robbie Alban 4, Mike Dunbar, Brady Rouech 2, J.J. Markee 2 (double), Kevin Pratt, Matt Corliss, Brodie Nelson (double).
   Eastwood hits: Matt Waits 2 (double), Trevor Morford, Mike Sims, Tony Patterson.

Coldwater   010 010 — 2   4   1
West Portage   020 001 — 3   3   0
   Tobey Elliot and Joel Rzepka; Randy Smith and Kevin Stewart.
   Coldwater hits: Tony Landis, J.J. Combs 2 (triple), Joel Rzepka.
   West Portage hits: Kevin Stewart, Mike Carr (triple), Randy Smith (double).

Vicksburg   131 104 — 10   7   0
Mattawan   010 001 — 2   4   2
   Bougher and Neils; Kruzich and Mausen.
   Vicksburg hits: Batton, Dinzik, Hildebrand 2, Myers, Nunter 2.
   Mattawan hits: Kruzich, Berchiatti, Marr 2.

I have a scrapbook that I started keeping when I was a kid because my father had one and used to tell me how, someday, I could get one if I ever got my name in the newspaper. My father's was rather thin, with a few articles, but he loved showing it to me and he loved showing me the clipping about the one collegiate homer he hit while he was at Fisk University. You would have thought he had hit 71 in a season, he showed it to me so often.

Since my mother was especially diligent at clipping articles and saving school awards, my scrapbook grew to be bigger than the Manhattan Yellow Pages. There's a picture on the cover of me as a three-year-old wearing a blue cap and a white baseball uniform and smiling, maybe nervously. Again, my Mom's touch. I always teased my father about how much bigger my scrapbook is and lamented to him that they must not have had too many newspapers covering baseball back in his days as a player.

Anyway, there are pictures of me in Little League and high school in this book, and my stance then didn't look too much different than it is now. There's one picture where I'm crowding the plate, another where I'm wiggling the bat above my head. These are some of the things I still do today. My mother has told me she looks out at me and still thinks I'm in Little League, too.

The Yankees had a scouting meeting in January of 2000 and Newman told me that they showed videotapes of me hitting in rookie ball in 1992 and videotapes of me from the 1999 season. He said it was real helpful to them because of the way they try to project players. You could see the changes the Yankees had made with me over the eight years, but you could also see the same essential model. There were things I did at the plate then that I still do now, idiosyncrasies that have probably been part of my routine since I was a tyke.

I also have pictures of me playing defense, where I'm staying low to field grounders. Defense is something I don't think enough young players work on. We all love to hit and hammer pitches all over the park, but my early problems in the minors reinforced how critical it is to be a strong defensive player.

If I hadn't worked on my defense religiously in the Instructional League in 1993 and the years since then, there's no guarantee I would have made it to the Yankees as a shortstop. I turned myself into an above-average defensive player. There might be a part of your job that you find less enjoyable, but that doesn't mean you should ignore it. You should work just as hard at it as at the parts you enjoy. At least then you'll feel optimistic when you have to attack that aspect of the job.

I finish my off-season workouts by playing defense, which I know can get tedious for some players. So I work to make these sessions fun. I stand on the edge of the infield grass, sweeping my glove across the grass to remind me to keep it low, as a minor-league coach whistles grounders at me. I try to field every ball the same way. I'll work on making backhanded plays and darting to my left and I'll holler at the coach to smack the groundballs even harder and make the workout competitive.

I feel like a goalie out there. Keep them coming. I turn my glove, I catch another one, and I throw it to first. It's a fun experience. The more grounders I field, the more comfortable I get and the better I feel. I made only nine errors in 1998, which is a long way from the confused kid who made 56 in his first full minor-league season and a long away from crying 56 times on the phone.

One of the rules that I have for myself when I work out is that I'm always going to be the last player off the field. If I've been taking grounders for 2 minutes or 20 minutes and another player comes out to join me, I'll stay on the field and continue working until he's done. It's not a superstition. It's about being devoted to working and getting better.

If that takes 20 more minutes or two more hours, I'll keep on scooping up grounders right next to him. If someone else can be out there working, why can't I? That's a work ethic that applies to everyone. Make yourself better. I always want to be the last guy working every day, the last one to pick up the baseballs and decide that it's time to go home. Until tomorrow comes and I start all over again.

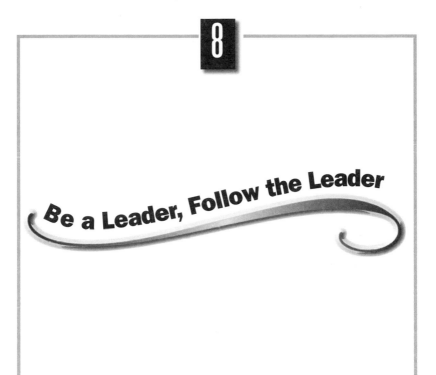

8

Be a Leader, Follow the Leader

 t was the most gratifying $12 pizza I've ever eaten because it was the night I told my father that I wanted to start a charitable foundation. We were sitting in my room in the Ritz-Carlton in Dearborn, Michigan, on September 9, 1996, munching on a few slices. I didn't want to traipse out for dinner because it was the first time I'd seen my father in a while and we wanted to be alone. The Yankees were playing the Detroit Tigers at Tiger Stadium the next night, a homecoming for me, so my father drove in from Kalamazoo a day early to see me.

It was an amazing time for my family and me because I was having a solid rookie year and the Yankees were about to qualify for the postseason, where we would eventually win a World Series. Everything was going smoothly. I had no reasons to make any adjustments. But, between bites of pizza, I told my father something that changed his life, changed my life, and has changed thousands of other lives for the better.

I always wanted to start a foundation once I made it to the major leagues. Even though I hadn't finished one season in the majors, it turned out to be the perfect time to begin a dialogue with my dad. I don't remember why I chose that night to do it. I didn't have it planned. Like I said, things were terrific. If someone had offered me one free wish to change anything that night, I wouldn't have wished for anything. I was content, perfectly content.

But there was something relaxing about sitting in a quiet hotel room with my dad. It reminded me of being a kid, just me and Dad hanging out, discussing the season, my future, our expectations. I always wanted my parents to be proud of me, and one of my greatest fears to this day is that I'll ever let them down. I knew my father would be proud when I told him how I wanted to do something for kids. Like a three-year-old holding up a finger painting and seeking some acceptance, I blurted out, "I want to start my own foundation."

My parents have always been giving in the ways they dealt with others so that's part of the reason I wanted to do the same. My father coached my Little League teams; my mother started one of the first mentoring programs for public school students in Kalamazoo; they were active in the PTA; and they both were constant supporters at any school function Sharlee or I participated in. Even if neither of us was in the school play and even though we didn't play in the band, my parents would be there to support the kids who were.

They have always lectured me about helping others. My mother used to say, "If you have a little, you give a little back. If you have a lot, you give a lot back." I was only 22 years old, but I already felt like I had a lot to give back. I was making $130,000, not the $10 million I'll earn in 2000, but my baseball dreams were unfolding as I'd always hoped they would, and I wanted to share what I had with other people, especially with kids.

You see, I've always had a great relationship with my parents and I know not everyone is fortunate enough to have that. Some people aren't even fortunate enough to have both of their parents active in their lives. That was the biggest factor that motivated me

Founding Turn 2 has been one of the most satisfying things I've ever done. Here I am at a dinner we had in New York with my grandfather, Sonny Connors.

to start the Turn 2 Foundation. The whole basis for it was for me to use my experiences to guide kids in the right direction by telling them why they shouldn't use drugs or alcohol. I'm always trying to help out kids as much as possible. I admired Dave Winfield as a player because of what he did on the field, but also because he was the first active player to have his own foundation and he has helped thousands of kids. He inspired me to do the same.

That's always been important to me. I tutored other students when I was in high school and I've always had an affinity for helping underdogs. We should all give back. Look around. No matter how bad you think you might have it, there is always going to be someone who has it worse. Whether you can give time, money, or hope, you should give something. It's easy to ignore other people and not think it's your job to volunteer, but that's a selfish attitude. If you or someone in your family ever needed help, you would pray that others didn't have that kind of attitude, so you shouldn't have it, either. Someday, you'll need help, too.

I've always liked being a leader who leads by example. Don't talk about doing something to help people. Just do it. We all have the ability to do things for others. Sometimes, you might not even realize you're helping another person. Someone might idolize you because of the way you act, and that person might learn from you without your even knowing it. Since I play with the Yankees and millions of people watch our games, I've had that happen to me. I have to tell you that it's incredibly satisfying to know that you've helped someone by being yourself, by simply enjoying life and being a decent person.

I get lots of fan mail, hundreds of letters a week. The majority of them contain baseball cards and self-addressed stamped envelopes so that I can sign them and return them. It can get monotonous. Open, read, sign, and send. But I received a letter from Barb Calabrese of Otego, New York, earlier this year in which she wrote about her 14-year-old grandson, Cody, and it was a lot different from the rest. There was no baseball card to sign. It was a one-page letter about a special boy, and I was transfixed by it.

She explained how Cody is a little slow and his comprehension and intelligence will never advance beyond that of a 10-year-old. Barb wrote about how difficult it can be for him in school. Cody likes watching cartoons and he also likes watching NASCAR racing with his younger brother and father. He picks the driver he hopes will win each week and calls him "his man," but unfortunately, Cody's driver routinely loses and he gets upset and doesn't know what to do.

Barb said that one weekend she grew weary of watching cartoons with Cody, so she put on a Yankees game. The grandmother was trying to teach Cody nine words for a test and he also had to answer the question, "Who is one person who has been influential in your life? Describe what this person has done for you." Cody cried because he didn't understand the question. I was moved reading these words on Barb's salmon-colored paper and hearing about the troubles Cody experiences, troubles most of us never even think of in our daily life. But, happily, Barb's letter turned positive.

"That's where you come in, Mr. Jeter," she wrote. "After watching three or four Yankees games, Cody was sensitive enough to pick up the fact that you enjoy the game. You smile even when you strike out, you are the first one out of the dugout when another player does good, and no balls get past Cody's man.

"Cody wrote his essay, on his own idea and merit, about 'his man,' Derek Jeter," she continued to write. "I thought, even in a special class, he would be made fun of. He called me and was so proud. He got 100 percent. It was the first time he answered any question like it. He even does the Jeter cheer. Two fists up, crouches down, and then wiggles his butt. I was so happy I promised to take him to Yankee Stadium this year. So Cody and I want to thank you for making such a positive influence on such a special boy. We're both saving up to see you play in person."

That letter meant a lot to me. If there's ever a day where I might not be feeling totally motivated, all I have to do is think about someone like Cody and realize there are fans I don't even know who are counting on me, and my motivation instantly returns.

You know what? I bet you we all have a Cody in our lives at some point. Think about it. I'm sure there's a person who was an underdog whom you had the chance to help. Maybe you gave up a seat on the subway, or maybe like me you didn't even realize you had helped somebody by setting a good example. But that means so much. I'll tell you what. I slept well the night I got that letter. I was pretty happy that Cody found someone to be "his man," and I was even happier that he selected me. To me, that's being a leader by example.

Find a Leadership Style

There are different ways to be a leader. You can be a calm leader whose soothing approach makes it easier for those around you to relax. That's the way Joe Torre is with our Yankees team. I've rarely seen his expression change. You could take a picture of Mr. Torre with us leading 10–1 or us behind 10–1 and you wouldn't be able to tell what the score was. We look at Mr. Torre and we feel everything is fine, even if there are some days when it isn't. He never looks panicky. I like that. We can all learn from that approach because panicking doesn't help anyone accomplish anything.

If someone gave me a pencil and paper and asked me to describe the perfect manager, I'd put two words on the paper: Joe Torre. The thing that makes him so much fun to play for is that everyone knows you're going to make mistakes in this game and he understands it and accepts it. He played and he struggled at times like the rest of us have, so Mr. Torre knows that the results are not going to be there every night. But I know Mr. Torre has the same amount of confidence in me whether I've had four hits or I've struck out four times.

I think his demeanor is great, especially for young players. Sometimes a young player can be intimidated when he makes it to the major leagues. That can become exacerbated if you have a manager who is always telling you that you did this wrong or you did that wrong. Mentally, that could really damage a player.

Mr. Torre will let you know when he thinks you have done something wrong, but he's very understanding about it. That's great for a young player because he's usually just trying to prove that he can play in the majors. Don't let Mr. Torre's stone face fool you, though. He doesn't show

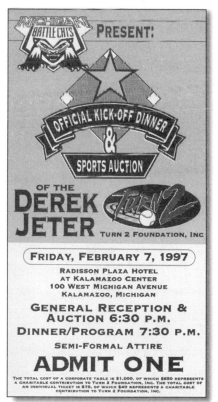

This is an invitation to Turn 2's first dinner.

much emotion, but he'll tell you when you make a mistake. He just does it in a way that's not embarrassing to you.

I like Mr. Torre's style of leadership. I think most people would prefer having a boss who treated them the way Mr. Torre treats us. The work environment is healthy if you know your boss has faith in you and is not going to embarrass you if you make a mistake. Mr. Torre's management style could work for any boss, not just in the baseball world. Don't panic. Trust your employees to do the job, until they show you they can't be trusted. If that ever happens, gently reprimand them, remind them of the expectations, and trust them all over again, like Mr. Torre does.

I guess I've always viewed Mr. Torre as a strong leader because I started calling him "Mr. Torre" from the first time I met him before the 1996 season. We were at the Yankees Fan Festival in Manhattan, and I just naturally called him that out of respect. That just seemed appropriate to me then and it still seems like the right thing to call him now. I've never called another manager Mister.

Heck, I don't even call Mr. Steinbrenner that all the time, but I think he likes being called the "Boss" or "Bossman" better than "Mr. Steinbrenner" anyway. But I'm sure I'll call our manager "Mr. Torre" for as long as he manages and even beyond that. People have asked me about this habit, but it really comes down to having a deep respect for Mr. Torre and I don't see that changing.

Leaders can also be boisterous. They can be someone like Tim Raines, who could make me laugh with one word, one smirk, or one of his famous cackles. I've never been around a player who had as positive an influence on other players as Raines did. He would make fun of our names by screeching "Ohhhhhh-Neeiilll" to Paul O'Neill and by calling Bernie Williams "Big Bernie." He would imitate the way we made an error or he would tease us about a haircut. Raines was the David Letterman of the Yankees. Anything for a laugh and to break the tension.

Rock would make people laugh and he'd get away with it because of all that he had achieved and because we all knew what he was doing. He was just trying to keep everyone loose. For example, O'Neill is the most intense player I've ever played with because he really expects to be successful all the time. When O'Neill comes back to the dugout after a strikeout, sometimes he throws bats, he spikes helmets, and he knocks over water coolers because he's so intense. Sometimes, you want to have shin guards on to protect yourself. But Rock could mumble something to make O'Neill go from seething to smiling. That's hard to do.

Then there are those kinds of leaders who lead by example—they do such a great job that you feel compelled to follow their lead. Everywhere I looked, there were players with tremendous work ethics. I saw Bernie doing situps like a punished Marine after we won a postseason game. I watched Joe Girardi catch an extra-inning game and then go lift weights to get stronger for the next extra-inning game. I saw John Wetteland buzzing around on Rollerblades with a hockey stick, strengthening his legs.

We have that same type of hardworking group today, and I think that has a lot to do with why we've won three of the last four World Series. Roger Clemens knows he is going to the Hall of Fame and I don't think anyone runs more, lifts more, or thinks more about getting better than he does. It's hard to even find Rocket by his locker because he's always doing something in preparation for the next time he has to pitch. Chuck Knoblauch's frame is so chiseled from working out and eating properly that he looks like a body builder. Tino Martinez and I push each other every day during our off-season workouts. Who is going to miss that first grounder? Who is going to hit that first homer?

I think I'm a mixture of leading by example and leading by tweaking guys, which I learned a lot about while listening to Raines for three years. If Mr. Torre comes out to make a pitching change, I'm always enthused and always confident that we'll get out of that perilous situation, and I bring that attitude to the meeting on the mound. That's my personality. I'll never change and I hope it calms others down and helps our team. You can do a lot for friends and colleagues by always being positive and optimistic. If you have a massive report due and one of the people you're working on it with is confident about its getting completed, then you're bound to be more confident, too. So take that approach and be a confident leader the next time you're worried about a deadline. It should help.

I love to instigate harmless flare-ups between teammates and try to get them arguing over something foolish. If Mariano Rivera asks Ramiro Mendoza to grab him a bottle of water out of our lounge and Mendoza forgets, I'll pounce on that situation. I'll ask Mendoza how he could treat his loyal friend like that. I'll ask Mo how he could accept that from a younger player he's helped so much. I do it to keep things loose. We spend seven months together, so there's got to be camaraderie that goes beyond baseball. I think I know when to push the right buttons with different players because I watch my teammates and know how far guys will let you go. I'm always playful, never too personal.

Well, there was one time when things got personal with a teammate, and that happened on the field with David Wells during the 1998 season. Boomer is a solid pitcher and he can be a fun guy. He says what he wants and he does what he wants so he gets a lot of attention for being a motorcycle-driving, Metallica-loving, steak-eating rebel. But, I'll tell you what, Boomer is also one of the toughest left-handers in baseball. He's got pinpoint control and I think his arm is made out of rubber.

But there was one September night in Baltimore when I felt (and I know a lot of my teammates felt) that Boomer didn't show the proper respect to a few of us. So I made sure I told him about it. Boomer was pitching against the Orioles when a pop fly dropped in short left field, between me, left fielder Ricky Ledee, and center fielder Chad Curtis. It might have been a catchable ball, but none of us got to it and it fell in. I admit it looked bad, but that wasn't the point. The point is what Boomer did in front of 48,113 fans and our team.

Boomer was not thrilled with us and he didn't disguise his body language. He lifted his arms to his side as he peered into the dugout, basically asking, "What the heck happened out there?" without having to move his mouth. I didn't think it was funny and I didn't appreciate his showing us up.

As soon as I returned to the infield, I strode toward the mound and told Boomer in a forceful manner, "We don't do that stuff here. That's not right and you know it. We don't do that if you give up a run. We're all out here trying. That was baloney."

Boomer just looked at me. He listened to what I said, looked right at me, and then didn't say anything. I think he knew right then that he had made a mistake or he would have kept the dialogue going. That's Boomer. He's not flustered for words too often. He apologized the next day.

I wasn't trying to make a big deal out of it. People know that I'm easy to get along with, so when I say something like that to a teammate, they know I'm serious. I wanted Boomer to know how I felt. I wasn't thinking that I had to be a team leader and chastise him, but I reacted the way a leader would by saying what I felt was right. It didn't matter to me that Boomer has been in the major leagues longer or is 11 years older than me. I said what needed to be said. We didn't discuss it again, nothing like that ever happened again, and Boomer and I celebrated together when we won the World Series the next month.

That's part of being on a winning team. We all have to work together toward common goals. I think there are ways to do that. Once the game starts, how I feel about another player doesn't matter. Similarly, if you're working at a fast-food restaurant with some people who are not your greatest friends, you have to focus on doing the best job and getting the orders finished. No one says that you have to hang out after your work is done. But you do have to work hard and try to be successful.

No matter how much success I have on or off the field, it's important to me to just be one of the guys. I work hard to maintain that. I often get more attention than a lot of my teammates, but I don't think they resent me because I still work extremely hard and I'm not pursuing this attention. It comes and I deal with it, but I don't stand in front of my locker campaigning for myself and talking about how great I am. I'll praise the team, not myself. It means a lot to me when my teammates, someone like David Cone, notice that.

"I don't think I've ever been around a young player that didn't need some sort of grounding or some sort of hazing to keep them in line or to teach them some sort of lesson," Cone has said. "Derek never needed it because of the way he handled himself and continues to handle himself. I never once thought that the veterans better sit him down and talk to him about a certain issue. I can't recall being around a young player that didn't need that."

If I wanted to, I could live in New York during the off-season and make millions doing appearances and endorsements. But I choose to reside in Tampa, which doesn't exactly have New York's nightlife, because I want to be able to work on improving all-year-round. To me, that's part of being a leader, too. I think we all can get better at what we do and we can all be leaders. It might be as simple as making one extra call to help out a colleague, but there are ways to show that you understand you are part of a team and that you can be trusted to be a leader.

Find a Way to Give Back

After I told my father about my hopes for starting a foundation on that fateful evening in Dearborn, he stopped eating his pizza and we talked. Dad is serious and direct when he asks questions,

Turn 2 allows me to help out kids who need help the most. Promoting healthy lifestyles is one of our main goals.

but he can get animated and say "yes, yes, yes" or "all right, all right" if something excites him.

At first, he questioned me like a friendly prosecutor about the idea of a foundation. He asked my motives for starting it then and he wondered how serious I planned to be about this endeavor. You're talking about a significant step, he reminded me. You don't want to start a foundation, be lazy with it, and then embarrass yourself and disappoint people if it fails. Who are you going to trust to run something with your name emblazoned on it?

The answer to that was simple. I think he knew that. I wanted my parents to be heavily involved in my foundation, especially my father. As a social worker who had counseled patients about substance abuse for more than 10 years, I thought my father would be invaluable. I trusted my parents more than anybody in the world and I thought my father's expertise in drug and alcohol abuse counseling was essential to making this foundation a success.

Dad told me that he didn't want to be involved in something that I was going to treat casually. If I wasn't genuine about this, my father asked me to tell him so. Instead, I told him I planned to take this endeavor as seriously as I take training for a new baseball season. Then he knew I was serious.

I wanted a foundation that would allow me to give back to communities in western Michigan and New York City while interacting with kids and instructing them about the dangers of drugs and alcohol. It has been a rewarding experience for me and my family. In less than four years, we have raised over $1.5 million and easily impacted thousands of kids. We have even started an endowment account so that the foundation can continue after I'm done playing.

I wanted to put together programs that would help as many kids as possible by advising them on the way to lead their lives. I didn't want to send donations to different schools or charities and hope the money was used properly. I wanted to establish programs that would have a lasting impact, and we're doing that.

We have leadership programs for strong students. We help pay for college scholarships for model students. We have renewal programs for children who have encountered problems in school or with drugs and alcohol. We have preventative programs for pre-teens so they stay away from those problems. We have baseball clinics in every borough in New York, but we also provide an antidrug and antialcohol message mixed in with our lectures about hitting and fielding.

We had almost 1,000 kids at our Funfest clinic in Queens in the summer of 1999. Imagine that. One thousand kids. It was an excellent opportunity to tell them face to face about why they shouldn't get involved in drugs or alcohol. I can tell when a kid I've been talking to is listening and gets the message. That's the most gratifying experience for me. When a kid thanks me for running the clinics and says that some of his friends use drugs and he's not going to do that because of what he's heard us say, that's when you know you're having an impact. You hope that kid will stay strong and be able to bring that message to his friends, too.

I didn't know it when we started Turn 2, but I had made a decision that would bring me a lot closer to my parents and would allow my father to achieve one of his own dreams. My father had his own private practice, but he saw Turn 2 as the way for him to help thousands of children. These were his new patients, kids that he could get to before they became ensnared in the problems that my dad's old patients blamed for their afflictions.

My father was 49 years old at the time, comfortable in his job, and about 15 years from retirement. He could have told me that it was a noble idea and that I should hire someone else to coordinate it. He didn't have to uproot his life, but he surmised that everything he had learned in his years as a therapist could be utilized in the foundation. It would give him the chance to impact more people while he was doing the same type of work.

Since my father was involved in every aspect of my career, he figured it made sense for him do this, too. Your relationship with your parents changes as you get older, and this was a good way for my father and me to strengthen ours. I think it's made us a lot closer. We laugh about it, but from 8 A.M. to 5 P.M., I'm the president of Turn 2 and he's the executive director, so I can tell him what to do. But, any time before or after those working hours, he's the father and he's in charge. On a September night in 1996, my father and I finished a pizza and we started a foundation.

"We have impacted thousands of kids," my father has said. "Sometimes, it's hard for me to envision the impact Derek has on young kids. When we're at these events and Derek interacts with the kids, I sense there are a lot of positives going on. The kids feel good about being around him. He relates to them and he gives a positive message. That's what I'm most proud of."

Just like in baseball, I had big dreams for my foundation. But it doesn't have to be something as grandiose as a foundation that inspires you. It could be volunteering a few hours a week at a soup kitchen. You could deliver daily meals to elderly people. You could go to the hospital and hold crack babies who don't have a stable set of parents. Regardless of what you choose, I'll guarantee that it'll make you feel better after you do it. I know I get more out of seeing kids benefit from my foundation than people could ever imagine.

I first latched on to this idea because of Winfield's foundation. I loved watching Winfield play for the Yankees. He was a tremendous athlete, all 6 feet 6 inches of him hustling around the bases, swinging from his heels with a bat that looked like a toothpick in his hands, and loping through the outfield.

I liked Winfield so much because he reminded me of my father. My father isn't 6–6 (more like 6–1) but when I was younger he was the biggest person in the world to me. I always wanted to be like my dad, who was a college shortstop. I watched every move Winfield made when I watched Yankees games, just like I had always watched my father. To me, it was impossible to watch a Yankees game, on television or in person, without gazing at Winfield first.

Anyway, I read Winfield's autobiography in 1988, which is one of the few sports books that I've ever read, and I was intrigued with his Winfield Foundation. I thought it was commendable that Winfield's foundation helped to send thousands of kids to games

The whole family is involved with Turn 2. Here I am with my mom, on the left, and a group of my aunts.

in his Winfield Pavilions, financed scholarships, conducted health fairs, and provided substance abuse awareness clinics and AIDS awareness clinics. Winfield was the pioneer in this area. When he was making $15,000 a year, he was donating a grand of it to charity. There weren't many athletes doing that 25 years ago, and that idea stayed with me. It became part of my dream.

I used to always go to see the Yankees play when they came to Tiger Stadium, and I was more enamored than ever in early June of 1988. I had read Winfield's book, and as we walked along Michigan Avenue, past the T-shirt vendors, past the cab drivers, and past hundreds of fans, I once again reminded my parents that they were going to come here to watch me play with the Yankees someday. How could I know it would happen less than a decade later?

I also told them in the whiney voice of a kid who would turn 14 in a week that I had to get Winfield's autograph that day. I wasn't obsessed with autographs like so many people are today, but I was obsessed with getting Winfield's.

My sister, my parents, and I found out where the visiting players left after games and we stationed ourselves there with dozens of other people and hoped. There was a white stretch limousine parked outside the door and someone told us it was for Winfield. That made sense. He was one of the biggest stars in baseball and the Yankees were the type of team that attracted big crowds on the road, with Don Mattingly, Rickey Henderson, Willie Randolph, Ken Griffey, and Ron Guidry on the roster. That hasn't changed. The Yankees still draw more fans than any other team away from the stadium, a league-best of 2.68 million in 1999.

I didn't know how much of a chance we'd have to get the autograph, since we were stuck behind a wall of people and wooden barricades. When Winfield finally appeared, he was dressed in a suit and tie and looked like he could have been going to a wedding. I stared at him. I inched forward but got swallowed up by people and couldn't even see him after a few seconds. But my mother imitated Barry Sanders and wriggled, twisted, and slipped past security guards and under the barricades to get to Winfield.

Guards were grabbing at her and people were screaming at her for getting ahead of them, but just as Winfield was about to disappear into the limo she held up a ball and begged him to sign it for me. She might have mumbled how I had just read his book. I think he was both stunned and impressed that she had made it that far, so Winfield signed it and then zoomed away. Sometimes, when I see a stack of mail in front of my locker, knowing the majority of the letters include autograph requests, I cringe. But then I think back to chasing Winfield and I break out my pen and start signing.

When Winfield was one of our guests at our third Turn 2 event in New York, my mother told him how she had climbed over and around people to get his autograph in 1988. Dave's long face broke into a smile and he laughed. He didn't recall the incident, but that didn't matter.

Dave told me that he always likes it when people talk to him about what he has accomplished off the field. Winfield's statistics are all there: 3,110 hits, 465 homers, a World Series ring, a 22-year career. He'll go to the Hall of Fame, but he likes hearing tales like my mother's as opposed to tales about him drilling a two-run homer. Dave knows the statistics he's accumulated so he wants to hear about the people he has impacted.

To me, being responsible and recognizing those obligations is a part of being a leader. I'm in an unusual position because I have the chance to impact kids whom I don't even know. If they hear me say it's important to go to school, obey their parents, and stay away from drugs and alcohol, I hope it resonates with them.

Even if I meet someone for only one minute while I'm leav-

Dave Winfield
ON DEREK JETER

Dave Winfield wanted to play major-league baseball and he wanted to help kids and he did both for more than two decades. When Derek Jeter was searching for role models, he naturally chose Winfield because he loved the way Winfield played and he loved the fact that a major-league player cared enough to have a charitable foundation for kids. Jeter wanted to be just like Winfield.

Winfield doesn't remember exactly when he heard that Jeter considered him a role model, but he remembers being asked about it while he was working as an announcer for Fox Television during the 1996 postseason. Jeter was on his way to winning a World Series ring with the Yankees and had just begun discussions with his father to start his own foundation. Every time Jeter expressed a desire to help kids, he mentioned Winfield's influence on him.

"It felt pretty good to know that this exciting young shortstop thought I was a role model," says Winfield. "I was really pleased to hear that. There were different images that people who didn't know me had of me as a player during my career. It was important to hear that I had affected him in the right way."

When Jeter's Turn 2 Foundation invited Winfield to a dinner in 1997, a glossy invitation was sent out to the former Yankee. But Winfield, still trying to teach and still trying to get to know this young man who idolized him, called

ing a restaurant, I try to be cordial. That minute probably isn't too memorable for me, but those 60 seconds might mean everything to a fan. Five or ten years from that meeting, that person might still be talking about that because they love baseball or the Yankees. So I don't think it takes much to be polite. Sometimes it can be a pain if people interrupt you when you're relaxing with friends or if they're overly aggressive, but I try to be gracious. If back and said that he wanted Jeter to call him. It was a small test from one player to another.

"He called. I wanted to hear it from him. I wanted him to call me. We had fun and we raised a lot of money that night."

Winfield dressed beside Jeter's locker for the 1999 Old Timers' Game at Yankee Stadium, the first time he had been back for the event since he retired in 1995. While Winfield didn't want to lecture Jeter, he did talk to him about having a relentless approach each day because the season can be so draining. As Winfield could tell Jeter already had this grinding mentality.

"He's clean-cut, he plays hard, he communicates well, and he achieves out there. Once you get on the field, you can influence people in lots of different ways. Whether it's up close or long distance, you can affect their lives. I think Derek realizes that."

Dave Winfield, Jr., is five years old and is falling in love with the game his father played for 22 years. Since Winfield, Sr., is an astute judge of talent and character, he wants his son to admire certain types of players. That is why Winfield smiled when little Dave approached him earlier this year with a piece of pertinent information.

"You know what he told me? He told me that Derek Jeter is his favorite player. I told him that was great and that he should watch all the things Derek does on and off the field. That was perfect."

I can be polite when I get stopped so often, I think other people can do it, too. It doesn't cost extra to be polite.

You Never Know Who's Watching

As much as my parents taught me to be a leader and to give something back to others, they also implored me to watch people I respect and learn from their actions. You don't have to be a follower who never makes his own decisions, but you should study others and learn as much as you can by watching them. I often think the smartest person in the room is the person who isn't saying a word. He listens to everything, soaks it in, and gets smarter while everybody else is too busy listening to themselves speak.

I know I followed this advice whenever I attended spring training and saw someone like Don Mattingly, a nine-time Gold Glove winner who worked like he was a 21-year-old rookie trying to hang around the major leagues. Mattingly fielded grounders until the sweat was glistening on his forehead and then he fine-tuned his swing in the cages. He worked with a medicine ball to strengthen his back and his abdominal muscles. Every time I saw Donnie, he was doing something different to improve himself. I felt like taking notes. In my mind, I did.

Mattingly's last year was 1995, which was also the Yankees' 34th and final year of spring training in Fort Lauderdale, Florida. Fort Lauderdale Stadium was a cozy, aging ballpark where the fans sat in blue seats that were so close to the field that they could breathe on you. There were advertising signs crowding the outfield fences and an asphalt path behind first base where players could stand and watch games if they weren't playing that day. The public address announcer read a license plate number during every game and said that the driver had left his lights on and the car running. That joke got laughs every time.

Fans lined up outside the parking lot for autographs and departing players couldn't avoid the gauntlet, unless they miraculously left by helicopter. In many ways, it was the best of what spring training could be for fans. They could actually be within a few feet of a player like Mattingly and say something that he could hear. After the Yankees left Fort Lauderdale to hold spring training in Steinbrenner's hometown of Tampa at the brand-new Legends Field, the Baltimore Orioles moved into Fort Lauderdale.

There was one main field at Fort Lauderdale Stadium where the exhibition games were played and where hundreds of fans studied the Yankees in batting practice. It seemed like the sun was always a little brighter and the sky was always a little bluer on the main field. All Mattingly or Bernie Williams had to do was crack a ball off the fence and they were cheered like they had just won a game against the Red Sox in September. Most of these fans would get one glimpse of the Yankees all season and that was before one meaningful pitch would be thrown. Seven weeks to leave an impression. No Yankees ever got booed at Fort Lauderdale Stadium.

Then there were the back fields—the two fields behind the main field where the younger players worked out. It was quiet there, with no fans watching. There was no accessibility, except through a gate in the left-field corner of the main field. The only sounds came from balls hitting bats, instructors barking out directions, and the hum of propeller planes landing on the airstrip behind the field. We used to joke that the planes were Steinbrenner's and he was watching us.

On these back fields I learned so much by just working and watching. I remember one sticky morning where I had completed the normal routine of hitting, fielding, and running wind sprints. The Yankees had already left for a road game, but some of the veterans, like Mattingly, didn't make the trip and worked out with us.

I was impressed that Mattingly, a former MVP and the captain of the team, wasn't just hitting in the cage and then heading for the pool. Showalter and his staff were gone. Mattingly, a lifetime .307 hitter, worked hard in February and March to make sure that he would be successful in August. I liked that. It's what I do now. It's a logical approach. I work even harder when I don't have to and I know it produces results. That's easy for anyone to do. We all know when we have down time. We all know what we could be doing instead of hanging out, too.

I loved watching Mattingly work. He leaned back in his crouched stance and then whipped the bat through the zone so quickly. It was so compact, yet his whole body, arms, chest, legs, seemed to be jumping at the ball in unison when he swung. And you could see in Donnie's eyes, above the lampblack he applied, when he thought he had pulverized a ball.

I finished my wind sprints the same time as Mattingly that day. We were both sweating and exhaling as we scooped up our gloves and started back to the clubhouse. When we got to the chain-link fence that separated the main field from the back fields, Fort Lauderdale Stadium was a picture of tranquillity, a perfect postcard. There were no players or coaches on the field, and the fans had bolted. I've been in churches that were noisier. But Mattingly did not let the emptiness change what he was about.

"Let's run in," Mattingly told me. "You never know who is watching."

So we ran. Side by side, stride for stride, across the green grass of the outfield, to the dirt of the infield, past the grass around the pitcher's mound, and through another fence that led to the clubhouse. Our spikes clicked across the asphalt path as we finally stopped running. It took us about 30 seconds, but that brief experience meant a lot to me. If Mattingly was so intent on galloping across a barren field with no one watching, what should a 20-year-old like me be doing? Sprinting? Or carrying him on my shoulders? Or sprinting while carrying him on my shoulders?

It only took a few minutes for me to figure out what Mattingly was doing. There's a saying that the true character of a man is revealed by what he does when no one is watching. So, even if the stadium looked empty and even if Steinbrenner wasn't in Florida, Mattingly did what was proper. The right thing was to hustle across the field, not stroll. We get paid to play baseball and to behave like baseball players. If you're Mattingly, you run across the field. I appreciated the lesson. I run from field to field now, even if the stadium is empty, like I'm trying out for the track team.

I never really had the chance to talk to Mattingly about that jog, but I know reporters have asked him about it. He speaks rather matter-of-factly about how it was the right thing to do. But one reporter told me that Mattingly said that he was very pleased I remembered it and took something from it. Donnie said he knew that his 14-year career was nearing completion in the spring of 1995 and it became more important for him to influence younger players.

"I didn't want anybody to ever see me walking on the field," Mattingly has said. "There could always be people watching, anyone from top to bottom, whether it's the kids in the stands or the owner. You want them all to see you hustling. That whole thing stems from me not wanting people to see me walking. I'm glad that Derek even remembers it."

That was a memorable moment for me. I already thought I was a hard worker, but that incident remained with me. We can all benefit from having that kind of dedication. Whether it is at work, at school, or at home, the kind of dedication Mattingly displayed that day is rare. I don't know of too many players who would have done that or who would do it today. I don't know of enough people who work so diligently every day, but we all can. It's in those private moments that you prove what kind of leader you are.

Going to the Show

It was May 28, 1995, later that year, when I got the phone call that made me shake. The Yankees were recalling me from Class AAA Columbus. Tony Fernandez had strained his rib cage muscle a few days earlier and the Yankees needed me to join them in Seattle and play shortstop every day. I had done it. I was about to realize the dream that had consumed me my entire life.

I called home. Man, this was different from the hundreds of calls I'd made crying, complaining, whining, and hoping that I would get to the majors. Sharlee answered the phone. I told her what had happened and she quickly gave the phone to my father. "I'm out of here," I shouted to my dad, the giddiness apparent in my voice. "I'm going to the Big Leagues."

Everything happened fast after that. My father got up at 3 A.M. to fly to Seattle to watch me, while my mother remained in Kalamazoo because Sharlee had an important softball game. That's the way my parents did things. Even my major-league debut with the Yankees wasn't going to detract from the importance of Sharlee's game. We have two parents, so one would be with each child.

I didn't get a hit that first night. I've seen the videotape of my father at that game and he was more nervous than I was. He looked like he was talking to himself while I was hitting, but I guess he was offering me advice. After I went 0 for 5 in my debut, Dad and I closed out the night in style. We had dinner at McDonald's. It was the only place we could find that was open. I got my first hit off Tim Belcher in my second game, and my father leaped out of his seat at the Kingdome. He's told me that the whole experience never really sank in with him until a year later. He had watched me taking grounders with Mattingly, but it didn't seem possible that I'd actually play in a game.

There have been so many great baseball players who have played for the Yankees at the stadium—I'm proud to be part of the tradition. There have been some great shortstops, too, like Hall of Famer Phil "Scooter" Rizutto, whom I'm walking with in this picture.

Once I joined the Yankees, I was trying not to make any mistakes. I wanted to learn, I wanted to be respectful, and I wanted to stay. There was a rain delay during one game after I got there and I noticed that Mattingly elected to sit in the dugout. I figured that was the right place for me, too. We sat in silence as the rain bounced off the dugout roof and off the tarpaulin covering the infield in front of us.

Without any warning, Mattingly stood up, approached me, and started talking about the way I had been making plays at shortstop. He told me that every play I made, whether it was a routine grounder right at me with a slow runner or a shot up the middle with a quicker runner, was a "bang bang" play at first.

Mattingly meant that my throws were barely beating the runners to the base, and he grinned and told me that I was making a veteran first baseman nervous by the bag. Donnie had an easy way about him, almost fatherly. He spoke firmly yet softly to me, using his hands or scrunching his face for emphasis. I viewed him as a peer at that point and that felt nice.

I soaked up the information, listening intently. He told me that it looked as if I was taking an extra step before unleashing the ball. Mattingly mentioned how shortstops like Cal Ripken, Jr. and Alan Trammell seemed prepared to throw to first almost before they caught the ball. It was just a fluid motion. Get in position to field the grounder, catch it, and—zoom—throw. There was no need or time to catch, set yourself, and throw. You've got to get rid of the ball in the majors, Donnie told me.

Mattingly not only went out of his way to help me, but he did it in a way that wasn't condescending. He didn't force his advice on me, but instead said this is how he had seen other shortstops do it. I have adopted that approach when I'm offering advice to players. You can't force your thoughts on someone, because everyone has pride and everyone has a way that they feel comfortable doing things. When I offer tips to other players, they're tips. They're not demands.

I immediately started to incorporate Donnie's advice into my routine. Practicing in front of my hotel room mirror, I visualized how to field a grounder and start my throwing motion before I even had it. I worked on it in fielding practice. I started fielding the ball in front of me and throwing it. Mattingly didn't mention it again, but he'd nod toward me after I made a play because the plays weren't "bang bang" anymore.

"Two days after we talked about it," Mattingly has said, "he was doing it the exact way I'd talked about."

You bet I was. I felt more and more comfortable. I was in the big leagues. I was trying to watch how other people acted, people like Mattingly, and just do what I had always done. I didn't want to leave. I didn't think about Fernandez's injury healing or my getting sent down. I was a Yankee. This is where I planned to stay forever.

But I found out that dreams get interrupted. I hurried into the clubhouse at Yankee Stadium after we beat Seattle 10–7 on June 11 because I couldn't wait to get on the plane for our next trip. The Yankees were going to Tiger Stadium for a three-game series, and my parents told me that over 100 people were planning to travel from the Kalamazoo area to Detroit to see me. I was 20 years old. I felt like a war hero.

Unfortunately, a few minutes after the game ended, my dream took a quick detour. I went from being able to float to Tiger Stadium to being deflated near my locker at Yankee Stadium. The Yankees informed me that I was being sent back to Class AAA, and I felt like I was in Class A again.

It was a difficult message to receive because it was the first time in my career that I had been demoted. I guess I should have expected it, but I didn't. I have extreme confidence in myself and I thought the Yankees would keep me in the majors, and there had been speculation about moving Fernandez to second. I called my dad and told him what happened. I had the same feelings I used to get in the minor leagues and got a little choked up. He kept telling me that I would be back with the Yankees. Be patient.

I passed Mattingly on my way out the door and limply said,

"I'll see you." He looked up from his corner locker and said, "Where are you going?" I told him the Yankees were sending me back to Columbus, and Donnie said, "Don't worry about it. You've shown them what you can do. You'll be back."

It was spoken with the authority of a leader. I listened. I knew he was right.

9

Think Before You Act

 t was a short telephone call, a call I wish I never had to make. I dialed up Darryl Strawberry the day after he was suspended from baseball for a year for testing positive for cocaine. It was the third time Straw had been suspended for violating baseball's substance abuse policy and it pained me to see a friend put his life in jeopardy by using drugs. I hated having to call Darryl last February because that meant he had faltered again.

I called Straw because I wanted him to know how I felt about him. Everyone had been speculating on how a one-year suspension would impact Darryl's baseball career. Would he ever be able to return at the age of 38½ and with more than a year out of the game? Would the Yankees still be interested in him? I didn't care about that. I cared about Straw's future, but not his baseball future. It didn't matter to me if baseball was a part of his life and it shouldn't matter to him, either.

When I spoke to Darryl, I barely even mentioned baseball. I told him that I loved him like a brother and that I would always be there for him whether he was playing baseball or not. I told Straw that if he ever needed me, to call me. Then I hung up. Darryl knew that he had made a mistake, and I hope he also knew that he needed to get away from baseball and focus on restoring some normalcy, if that's still possible, to his life. He has a wife and five kids, so he should forget baseball and remember how to live his life without threatening it.

Darryl's situation reminded me of some of the lessons I had been taught to follow as a teenager: Think before you act. Remember that you have a lot to lose. Don't put yourself in a position to make mistakes. I took these lessons to heart growing up and follow them even more strictly now.

Since I've achieved success in baseball and have become pretty well known, there are often people who try to get close to me and masquerade as my friends. They usually want to do something for me. We can get this for you, they will say. Do you want us to do this for you? I'm always skeptical when someone offers me something for nothing and I think a long time about these decisions. I refuse to lose perspective and I know I must continue to make smart decisions. That's something we all can do, whether you're famous (I hate that word) or not.

I do this every day of my life. I always try to think how something will look before I do it, because I don't want to later regret my decisions. Sometimes I'll confer with my parents or my friends before I do something. If I don't have the time to do that, I'll ask myself how my parents would feel if they knew that I was doing this. That will always give me a gauge as to whether or not I should do it. I would never want to do anything that's going to embarrass my parents. I'm 26 and I'll be thinking that way forever. Not making immature choices is my way of thanking them for all they've done.

Do you really want to sneak out to a party on a night when you're supposed to study? Do you really want to tell a coach that your Uncle Bob, who doesn't exist, had a heart attack and that's why you missed a game? Do you really want to make fun of someone who can't defend himself? Think about how you will feel when you fail the test, or if your coach finds out you lied, or when the person you've made fun of gets so upset he or she goes to the principal. Is this how you want the world to see you?

Now I could have asked much more graphic questions, like questions about drugs and alcohol. I used these tamer questions to show that it should be easy for you to decide between right and wrong. So, when the decisions become even more serious, your responses should become easier, not tougher. I know it's not simple to avoid pitfalls, but you should try to make it as easy on yourself as possible. Do what's right. Stop and think about the consequences. It's your life. Just like Darryl's life is his life and my life is mine. We soar or stumble with our own decisions.

We all have to face peer pressure. There is always going to be someone in a group who wants you to do something that you don't want to do. I know that's a dicey situation because I've experienced it, but you have to be firm about your decisions and focus on what is important to you.

Don't think that every difficult decision you have to make has to be an automatic no or yes, either. If you can delay a decision, that gives you more time to think about it, or the right answer might become clearer, or the question might solve itself. Tell someone you're not sure if you want to be involved in using bogus driver's licenses and they might turn to someone else to help them. Again, this is a tame example. I know there's a real world out there with much stickier decisions than whether you should use a fake ID.

I went to parties in high school and some of my classmates drank alcohol, but that never appealed to me so I wouldn't stay too long. I was so focused on what I wanted to do with my life that I never got caught up in those things. I'm not saying it was a breeze. I'm not saying I didn't want to have the kind of fun

I managed to have a good time in high school without going overboard. You can have fun without causing trouble. Here I am as part of the homecoming court at Kalamazoo Central.

other people seemed like they were having. It would have been a kick to hang out at the beach all night or stay at a party until 2 A.M., but I wanted to do those other things a lot more. I had more fun working out and playing baseball than I would have had if I'd done the riskier stuff anyway.

I know we all like to have fun and go to parties. But if you have a vocation, if you're passionately interested in something the way I am about baseball, then you will better be able to resist peer pressure or anything that keeps you from doing what you love.

Would you rather disappoint that so-called friend or disappoint yourself or your parents? When you crawl under the blanket at night, the person you have to answer to is yourself. Don't let someone else force you to make choices you don't want to make. You can help yourself avoid these problem areas by thinking before you act. That logic applies to teenagers as well as to a man like Straw. He knew what he was doing to himself and he still did it. That's the power of the addiction, but it also shows the importance of not even being in a position where you have to resist the temptations.

Even before I started playing for the Yankees, I was doing this. We all know the difference between right and wrong. We all should realize when we are doing harm to our bodies or harm to others. We have to be confident and secure enough to make the proper choices, regardless of what the people around us are doing.

As I've said, I never drank or smoked in high school because it scared the heck out of me. I didn't want to try a beer or marijuana, because I knew it was wrong and I was worried about how it would affect me. Some adults drank when in high school and are responsible people now, and that's fine for them. I chose to refrain. And even today, long before I ever walk into a club, I've thought about how I'd like my night to unravel and it always ends with me leaving sober.

Don't Go Find Trouble

Thinking before you act is an attitude. Sometimes, I'm so used to doing this that it keeps me away from situations that could be ticklish. The friends I go out with know what I will and won't do, so they won't even ask me to do some potentially risky things. They know that I won't go to certain places and that I don't want to go somewhere where I don't feel in total control. On at least one memorable occasion, thinking ahead of time rescued me from being near a possible fiasco.

I was eating dinner with Sean Twitty and two other friends in Manhattan last December 26th, trying to decide what we wanted to do when we were done. Should we go out? Should we go back to my apartment and watch TV? We debated this burning question and none of us immediately came up with anything we felt like doing on this chilly Sunday night. That should have been an ominous sign to me to simply go home.

Then one of my friends mentioned a club I hadn't been to before. I thought about it for a few minutes. I didn't know if the place would be crowded and didn't know if I felt like being out late. Twitt shrugged and wasn't sure what he wanted to do, either, so I finally told everyone, "I'm going home. Staying out of trouble tonight." They all laughed at my joke because I've been pretty good at staying out of trouble since I've been in New York. We paid the check and we all went home.

The next day, my joking words sounded prophetic. There had been a shootout at this club. What? I said to myself. That's the place we were talking about going to. We could have been there. We could have been in a place where shots were fired. Man, just the thought of that made me nervous.

You never know what might happen. That's why you not only have to think before you act, but you have to think about not putting yourself in a position where you could get in trouble. I could have gone out that night and been in that club when those people pulled guns. If that happened, I would have unintentionally put myself in a perilous position. And, let's face it, even though I would have had nothing to do with the situation, my name would have been in the newspapers, just for being there.

It makes sense to always be aware of your surroundings. You can behave more appropriately if you're aware of what is going on around you. If I had gone out that night, it probably wouldn't have been my fault if my name was associated with what happened. But whether it was fate, dumb luck, or my habits about wanting to stay low-key that helped me, I stayed out of trouble.

That sort of incident works in two ways for me. I'm happy that I wasn't there that night and it's made me think long and hard before I'll go to some place that I don't know too well. We all can learn from incidents like that. If you don't know much about some place, ask questions before you get there. If you don't like what you hear from even one person, don't go. There are plenty of other places to go and other things to do. Why go some place that is going to make you feel nervous?

If you make a glaring mistake, you're going to pay for it, even if it is related to a health problem like addiction. Look what happened to Darryl's life. He was supposed to be the left-handed designated hitter for the Yankees this season and probably would have gotten 400 at bats, and if he was healthy, I think he could have hit 30 homers. I've never seen a better home-run hitter than Straw. I've never seen a better swing. Straw looks like he's flicking his wrists and he wallops baseballs over 400 feet. He worked out with me in January and February and he looked awesome.

This was the first time the Yankees had ever depended on him as a starter going into the season. I'm not contradicting what I said earlier about how baseball shouldn't be everything for Straw. I don't think it should be. But he did have a lot riding on this season, besides the most important thing—staying clean and sober. Unfortunately, he failed. I know baseball is important to him and that makes all of his troubles painful. But he's got to get beyond baseball and make his life and his family the priority.

The frustrating thing about Darryl is, he cares so much about others. I was in the clubhouse at Yankee Stadium three years ago when I heard someone holler, "Hey, Jeet." I turned to see Darryl motioning me to his corner locker. He asked me to sit down next to him, and, without any prompting, he lectured me about what I could anticipate as a young athlete who was gaining fame in New York. We spoke for what seemed like two hours. Actually, he spoke and I listened.

I felt a kinship with Straw because he had also been a first-round pick out of high school by the New York Mets in 1980 and there were expectations for him, just like me. But the expectations for Darryl were much higher because he was the first pick overall in the draft and because people were already calling this skinny kid out of Compton a black Ted Williams. If you're getting compared to Ted Williams when you're 18, yeah, I'd say that's pressure. Straw is one of the few players I could talk to who had been through what I was going through, and then some.

Straw told me that the second year was going to be a lot tougher for me. People know you now, he said, both on and off the field. Be wary, be careful, be smart. I'll never forget that conversation because Straw was serious. He sounded like a preacher and got close to my face, like he was trying to protect me from what he had experienced. "Don't do what I did" appeared to be the message he passed along without actually saying the words. At that time, Straw had been suspended from baseball three times, had drug problems, marriage problems, and tax problems, too.

He was like a big brother who was telling his little brother not to make those same mistakes. I've thought about that conversation ever since Straw tested positive before the 2000 season and I wish there could have been a magical switch that he could have flipped to help him heed his own advice. From what I've heard from my father and other drug counselors, I know Straw's battle is very difficult. I know that Straw's battle has to be fought every day of his life for him to be successful and drug free.

Some people have asked me if anything Straw told me lost its power because he hasn't been able to stay clean of drugs and alcohol himself. I think it's the exact opposite. The advice I got from Straw makes it even stronger now that he's failed. He'll be the first one to tell you that he's had a rough life. He hasn't made all the right decisions. We can all learn from his mistakes.

But how many people have lived such exemplary lives that they would want every move they've made since they were 18 years old available for the world to see? If you're a professional athlete, all your mistakes are written about and are on TV, especially if you're Darryl Strawberry. There are doctors, lawyers, and teachers who are addicted to drugs, but the world doesn't know about it or when they relapse. I'm not making excuses for Darryl. I'm just stating it like it is. He has had his trials and tribulations.

Straw's life is proof to all of us, athletes or not, about the perils of addiction and not acting on a daily basis to deal with that addiction. He told me that I should stay away from drugs, and when I see what drugs have done to his life, I know he's right. He may sound as if he's contradicting himself, but he's a strong individual. He's battled back from colon cancer and now he needs to come back from this and get his life organized because his family needs him.

It's not easy to admit your mistakes, but I think Straw is doing that. He knew what he was doing when he used cocaine. He knew that he was risking his career, his financial means, and more important, his life. But he still did it. That shows you how powerful that addiction is. He didn't sit down one night and say, "Let's have some fun and see if I can get caught." The thing that bothered me is that too many people were focused on the suspension. Who cares about the one-year suspension? He needs to worry about his life outside of baseball.

There was speculation that Commissioner Bud Selig might give Strawberry a chance to return after 120 days if he continued to stay clean and participated in counseling. Some people wanted him to have the chance to come back after two months because of good behavior, but what then? Go back to using drugs? I don't think that would have been a good idea for him. The way it is now he knows he can't play baseball for a year so he can't worry about baseball. He's got to worry about his life, which is how it should be. Straw is getting older in terms of his baseball life, but he's young, real young, in terms of his whole life. As a friend, I'd like to see him enjoy that part of his life.

You know, it's weird because I remember watching Straw in the 1986 World Series. I wasn't a Mets fan, but I liked Straw and Doc Gooden. I had two pins, with Doc's face on one and Straw's face on the other, and they lit up when you clicked them. So, whenever Straw came to the plate, I'd click that pin on for good luck. When Straw homered off Boston's Al Nipper in Game 7 of that series, I truly believed it was because I had clicked my pin on. I was real innocent then, which we're all supposed to be when we're 12 years old. I'm still a big fan of Straw's. I'm just not that innocent anymore.

Don't Assume the Worst

No matter what type of situation you're faced with, you can help yourself by taking an extra moment to ponder how you should react to it. Sometimes we're forced to be spontaneous and act instantaneously. Sometimes we do something in a flash and then wonder if it was the right decision. But whenever you can take the time to review what you're about to do, you'll feel better about yourself and your decision.

If you're driving and you're not sure whether you are taking the proper exit, see if you can pull over to the side of the road and figure out where you are. If someone pushes you as you're trying to retrieve your luggage at the airport, think about whether it's worth it to confront a person you might never see again for the rest of your life. If you get charged for something you didn't order at dinner, ask for an explanation before you start berating the waiter or waitress. It might be an honest mistake. You might save yourself some angst.

This kind of measured approach involves not making unwarranted assumptions before you do something. You shouldn't walk into a room, notice that people have started to whisper, and assume that they are talking about you. Unless you have evidence or bionic hearing, that's a foolish approach. When you assume without knowing all of the details, you can put yourself in confusing situations. I had an encounter with a teammate last year in which he assumed something about me, something that wasn't true, and that created problems for both of us.

On August 6, 1999, we were playing the Seattle Mariners—a team that we don't like and a team that doesn't like us. It's a fierce rivalry, a fun rivalry, and one that I'm sure goes back to the epic Division Series we played against them in 1995. I had been plunked with a pitch the night before, so I wasn't even in the starting lineup on that Friday night last August.

Yogi Berra
ON DEREK JETER

Yogi Berra was standing beside David Cone's locker in the Yankee clubhouse last April, talking with players and waiting to talk with Joe Torre. Suddenly, a voice rang out from the other side of the spacious room.

"Hey, Yogi," bellowed Derek Jeter, a smile already beginning to crease his face. "Come on over here."

Berra stopped talking and began shuffling across the clubhouse, his arms pumping and his eyes staring straight ahead as he approached Jeter. While Jeter was obviously readying a sassy remark for Yogi, Berra had a serious expression by the time he reached Jeter. But there was nothing serious about this meeting.

"When are you going to get me some chocolate chips? " Jeter asked Yogi, straining to keep a puzzled look on his face.

Berra, who does a television commercial for chocolate chips, said, "You want some?"

Jeter told Berra that he would love some free chocolate chips and listed all of the cookies he loves to eat. Berra nodded, agreeing with the selections. Both of them settled on chocolate chips as one of their favorites.

"I'll get you some," Berra promised Jeter. "They're really good."

This discussion could have taken place between two coworkers comparing what they had in their lunch pails or between two grade-school kids doing the same with their lunch boxes.

Well, after Alex Rodriguez clubbed a three-run homer in the eighth inning of a game that we eventually won, 11–8, Jason Grimsley fired a fastball over Mariner Edgar Martinez's head. Grimsley's next pitch drilled Martinez in the side and he was ejected from the game. Jason swore that he was not intentionally

But it was Derek and Yogi, two Yankees who are identifiable by their first names only and who have a combined 13 World Series rings, chatting like a prankster grandson and a knowing grandfather, talking like a couple of regular guys.

"I tease him all the time," says the 75-year-old Berra. "He's asked me where I keep all my World Series rings. I told him it's tough to get 10. He's got seven to go. It's going to be hard."

Berra loves watching Jeter because he's a great competitor and he cares first and foremost about winning, which is how Berra's team used to be and how the Yankees have been while winning three of the last four World Series. Since Berra played with the likes of Joe DiMaggio and Mickey Mantle, he is a perfect authority for forecasting where Jeter could fit in Yankee history someday.

"I think he's got a great chance to be one of the all-time great Yankees. I really do. He doesn't need any advice from me. He's just got to keep doing what he's doing."

More than a half century ago, Berra joined the Yankees as a 22-year-old, trying to survive in New York. Obviously, Berra did more than that in a career where he slugged 358 homers and won three M.V.P. Awards. Jeter became a Yankee regular by the time he was 21 and Berra admitted there are glaring differences.

"I was only 22 when I first came up, but I didn't have to go through what he goes through. I didn't have all those girls screaming at me all the time. I wasn't as good-looking as him."

trying to hit Martinez, but it didn't matter. We expected the Mariners to retaliate.

Mariner pitcher Frankie Rodriguez plunked Chuck Knoblauch in the ninth, which everyone at Safeco Field expected. But we also expected the umpire to toss Rodriguez, just like he had done with

Grimsley. When Rodriguez wasn't booted, our players yelled at the umpire. Rodriguez must have figured we were squawking at him because he dropped his glove and basically challenged our entire team to confront him.

From there, it got ugly. Joe Girardi told Rodriguez that if he wanted to come after someone then he should go get them. Rodriguez did and clocked Girardi twice, vicious shots that knocked him to the ground. Joe is a religious man who is more at home being a peacemaker than a fighter, so he didn't even take a swing at Rodriguez. Girardi later admitted that he'd never been in a fight in his whole life.

After things had settled down and the players were returning to the dugouts, I wound up next to Alex. We weren't going to throw any punches. Most of the players on the periphery had been talking, keeping each other away from the middle of the field. This had been a prolonged brawl, with Bernie Williams belting Dan Wilson to the ground, Chili Davis wrapping his hand around the neck of Steve Smith, one of Seattle's coaches, and Rodriguez punching Jim Leyritz. But, like most brawls, there were a lot of people who were bystanders, like Alex and me.

Alex told me it was ironic that Grimsley hit Martinez after Alex's homer and I told him that it wasn't intentional and that's how Grimsley pitches. His fastball jumps around a lot. I told Alex that's exactly what Jose Paniagua did the day before when he came in tight on Knoblauch and then hit me. I wish Joe Torre or one of our coaches had been wearing a microphone, like they sometimes do for nationally televised games, because that's precisely what we said.

As we were heading back to our dugouts, Alex told me, "If we fight again, I'm coming after you." I might have smirked or smiled at that comment. I'm not sure. But, as I got near our dugout, Chad Curtis confronted me a couple of feet in front of it.

I just looked at Curtis. I didn't think I had done anything wrong and I definitely didn't want to discuss it on the field. Chad tried to continue his one-man debate in the clubhouse after the game, with about a dozen reporters observing, and I walked away again. That was the second time he tried to talk about something in the wrong place, something he didn't understand.

"You're a good player, but you don't know how to play the game," he had said to me in the clubhouse, but that statement wasn't called for. Curtis had assumed that he knew what happened between me and Alex and he was wrong. I told him that he didn't know what he was talking about—and, plainly and simply, he didn't. Chad knows that, too. Whether he's willing to admit it is another thing, but he knows that he messed up. He didn't think before coming to a conclusion that I was being disloyal to the team, and he spoke out when he should have just kept quiet.

"We agreed to disagree on the issue, but I apologized in the manner I went about it," Curtis told a reporter a week later. "You've got to take into context what was going on, the brawl and the adrenaline flowing and the way I approached him wasn't the way I should have went about it. We still disagree, probably, on the issue but it's not that big of an issue."

You can have your own opinions, but I think it was bad form for Chad to criticize me in public. It's not smart. We all might get irritated with each other at some point during a long season, but we need to think before we lash out with accusations. Chad didn't do that and that ticked me off. I asked David Cone, one of our clubhouse leaders, about my actions the next day. I asked him if I did anything wrong. He told me I wasn't wrong. He said Curtis was wrong for saying it and then he was wrong for wanting to fight me over it in the clubhouse with reporters around. Why would I risk fighting someone who was so easily swayed by the emotions of the moment and couldn't understand what was going on beyond the brawl? Sure, Chad apologized two days after the incident, but he apologized for how he approached me, not for his critique of me.

Believe me, I'm not looking for defenders for my behavior, but Cone and Rodriguez are among the many people who have said to me privately that they thought Chad was wrong, and have spoken out to reporters about how Curtis shouldn't have gotten in my face about something he didn't understand.

"I just thought it was unfair criticism for him to be knocking Derek, who is the ultimate team player and the ultimate professional, in any way, shape, or form," Rodriguez told a reporter. "For a platoon player to start talking about Derek, I thought that was very ironic."

Coney said, "There was no need to get on Derek. I thought he handled that situation well. He was verbally attacked in public and he walked away. He wasn't going to let that situation with Chad escalate, especially in public."

I learned that people are always going to pass judgment on you. I know that some people thought Curtis was right and I shouldn't be out there talking with an opposing player during a nasty brawl. People ask me why we were joking around. But, the truth is, we weren't joking. No one enjoys being involved in a brawl, whether you're in the middle of it or you're running out of the bullpen to get into the skirmish, but, believe me, I didn't take that brawl lightly.

That incident reiterated to me that people are going to draw their own conclusions, even though they don't know the specifics. I've told many people that Alex and I were talking about the two pitchers, not swapping jokes. More than ever, though, the incident reminded me that I have to be clear and careful about everything I do.

It bothered me that some people had this perception about me not showing enough respect after Girardi had been hit and not being involved with what was going on with my teammates. There's nothing I can do about what people think. I gave my side of the story. It's over with. But I didn't have to deal with Chad anymore. That's the way I dealt with the situation. Even last year, I was done with him after that happened. He was my teammate and I wanted him to do well for the team, but I wasn't going to talk to the guy or go out to dinner with him. No way, not after what he did.

That's not the best story, but thinking about your actions involves contemplating whether you want to deal with a person's attitude. I didn't want to be bothered with Chad. You might have a person who lives next door to you whom you can't stand and it behooves both of you not to have a relationship. You can coexist, but you're not inviting him over for a pool party. So don't push the issue if it's unnecessary. We're not going to get along with everyone, and that's what I decided I'd do with Curtis. I would be civil toward him and be his teammate, but the less said between us after August 6, 1999, the better off we would be. (As it turned out, the matter was settled for both of us when Curtis was traded to the Texas Rangers on December 13, 1999.)

You know, the assumptions continued two days after the incident, but this time it wasn't Curtis making them. It was a radio reporter. Chad hit a homer as we beat Seattle, 9–3, and I wasn't the first player out of the dugout to congratulate him. Ever since I was in Little League, I've tried to be the first player out to shake hands with teammates after they score. We're all trying to win, so I'm always showing my support by bursting out of the dugout quicker than the batboy.

That enthusiasm goes back to a lesson my father taught me when I was 10. The Little League team I was on had just gotten destroyed. I don't remember the game's score, but I know that we made a lot of errors and it was a frustrating afternoon. When my teammates left our bench after the loss to shake hands with our opponents, I stayed behind, sat, and sulked. I didn't want to join my teammates because I was upset with all the mistakes we'd made. I blamed everyone except myself.

My father wasn't coaching my team yet, but he was at the game. When he saw me sitting there alone, he was incredulous. I remember that disappointed look he gave me and I remember him telling me that I had embarrassed myself by refusing to congratulate the other team. My father gave me a brief but stern lecture that day. He told me if I didn't think I could be enough of a sportsman to gracefully win or lose as a team then I should take

My parents have always been enthusiastic about life and sports and have taught me to be the same as well. Dad played with me in a father-son softball game when I was 16, shown here.

up an individual sport like golf. Then, I would always be able to blame myself or praise myself. I didn't like the sound of that because I loved baseball too much. My father was right about winning and losing as a team. I had to remember that I was part of a team, and I've been very diligent about supporting others ever since that day I sulked.

It's a nice way to act in life. We all need support so we all should give support. When you're trying to complete an arduous task, it helps to have others reminding you that you can do it. So we should all realize the importance of showing support the next time we see someone struggling with a chore. It might only take one encouraging sentence to give a person an emotional lift, and you'll feel better about yourself for doing it, too.

Anyway, I wasn't the first one to congratulate Chad 48 hours after our public dispute and a reporter asked me how thick the bad blood was between us. He reminded me that I was always the first one out of the dugout and I wasn't with Curtis. "Actually," I told him, "I was kind of busy in the bathroom at the time." The reporter didn't know what to say. Again, that situation just told me that people are always watching to see what you're doing, so you had better think about how you're going to act. Even if you're in the bathroom at the time.

Stay Alert

I always have a plan that I know I'm going to follow. That's why I can think about things before I do them because I've already braced myself for different situations. I was with Casey Close, my agent, when the car service dropped us off at the wrong entrance to Fenway Park for the 1999 All-Star Game. It was a gorgeous, sunny day and I was at the park early for a television interview.

When I got out of the car, I was thinking about my parents

because they were attending my Aunt Catherine's funeral service. I was hoping they would get through this traumatic day, but I was also trying to focus on enjoying the All-Star Game. Maybe I'd sign a few autographs on my way into Fenway, and say hello to the fans.

Forget about that. As soon as the Red Sox fans near Yawkey Way saw me, I was Derek Jeter, the despised Yankee, the anti-Nomar, the villain, and I got walloped with verbal abuse. Nomar Garciaparra had narrowly beat me out to win the starting short-stop spot for the American League, and I'm sure some of the fans figured I didn't even belong on the ballot with him. I heard a ton of profanities, words you couldn't print in a family newspaper.

So I quickly walked past this gauntlet of fans, hearing the abuse but not really listening to it. I could have said something or I could have been angry. But I wasn't. I wouldn't allow myself to be. When we got safely inside, I looked at Casey and said, "They really hate me here, huh?" That is why a thick skin is a pre-requisite for being a baseball player. For me, it's especially impor-tant to have a thick skin in Boston. For Nomar, I'm sure it's the same in New York.

One of the best things that happened that night was meeting Hank Aaron. After Ted Williams was driven in from the center-field warning track in a green golf cart to throw out the first pitch, it was an emotional scene because all of the All-Stars and the All-Century players slowly inched toward him. It was like a bunch of five-year-olds getting closer to Santa Claus.

Even though I was about 50 feet away, I could hear Williams talking to Ken Griffey, Jr., Mark McGwire, Tony Gwynn, and Cal Ripken, Jr. Williams kept chatting, we kept listening. Williams was wearing a white baseball cap and was chewing gum and he had tears in his eyes as the greatest players of this era and previous eras bowed and saluted him. No one wanted the game to start because we were fixated on Williams. It was a rare experience, a moment that you savor and bottle up inside your mind.

The public address announcer implored us to return to our dugouts so the game could start. Still, we lingered. When we finally started to disperse, I saw Aaron ambling over toward me. He shook my hand and told me that he wanted to meet me because he enjoyed watching me. Hank Aaron liked watching me? I was shocked. I was probably 6 feet 9 inches tall instead of 6 feet 3 at that moment, because I had to be six inches off the ground.

That was a real special moment to have the all-time home run king seek me out and give me a compliment. The closest I had ever gotten to Hank Aaron before that was in my imagination, when I tried to shatter his record back at the Mount Royal Townhouse Complex in Kalamazoo. I didn't have time to tell him that. Not sure I would have anyway. But when you have a Hall of Famer like Hank Aaron give you a compliment, that's something to call on whenever you need inspiration.

"You want to let someone like Derek Jeter know you appreciate the way he plays," Aaron later told a reporter. "He does things the right way and I like him. I watch him all the time."

I went from several special moments to a surreal moment after the game. I was with Sean Twitty and went out to a club on Newbury Street after the American League beat the National League, 4–1. The place was crowded. They couldn't have jammed another person in there for a million dollars. It's the kind of situation where I'm careful and I'm glad to have someone smart and burly like Sean with me.

We left the club and it was pretty late, close to 3 A.M. Twitt and I tried to flag a cab to go back to the hotel and a woman rushed over to me and stopped just short of tackling me. I didn't know her so I was jolted. I stopped for one second, told her we were leaving, and kept walking toward Twitt. She followed me, which was rather disconcerting. Twitt got the cab and I had to tell this woman a second time that I was calling it a night and I had to go. She followed me right to the cab door, showing persistence and also scaring me. I was relieved when we got the door closed and the cabbie whisked us away.

You see, you don't have total control over whom you're going to meet or whom you're going to be with. I work as hard as anyone on this planet to keep myself insulated and I'm still occasionally faced with perplexing situations. I always think these situations out, but things can happen anywhere and they can happen when you're trying to do absolutely nothing.

I was at a club in Manhattan with Jorge Posada a few years ago. I'm not going to mention the name of the place, but we went there after a game to hang out and unwind a little. I need to distance myself from baseball after games and I can't do it by staring at the walls in my apartment.

Jorge and I were trying to be as inconspicuous as possible. Suddenly, a guy squeezed past a bunch of other people and said, "Hey, Derek Jeter." Now I'm always wary of loud or pushy people because there are some of them you just don't want to deal with. My approach with people who seem to be too obsessed with getting to me is to sign their autograph or shake their hand and let them move on. I turned and I nodded to him. He told me that he thought it was me, that he was real glad to meet me. He said, "I got something for you," and I couldn't understand the rest of what he uttered, but it sounded like something with an x in it.

I immediately backed away from him, shook my head, and said, "No, no, no." That was a very awkward situation. I didn't know

I am always talking to kids about not doing drugs or drinking—it's such an important message, and kids need to learn it young, like I did. Here I am with some students at Derek Jeter Day in Kalamazoo.

who the guy was. I didn't know if he was offering me Ecstasy or aspirin, but I knew I had to get away from him. If someone only caught a glimpse of that and saw the guy holding the pills out to me, that situation could be read in the wrong manner. You never know who is watching you. What if I took one and held it up as a joke? What if I nervously smiled and someone construed that as a happy smile, as in, I was happy to accept these pills? That's the type of situation I don't want to be anywhere near and the type I've been able to avoid throughout my life. I wasn't offered drugs in high school, so this was really the first time someone had done this to me and I was uncomfortable.

When this guy realized I wasn't interested, he backed away and bumped into a few people as he tried apologizing. "I'm sorry, I'm sorry, I didn't know." I was spooked by the whole incident. I know Jorge was, too. And what did the guy mean when he said that he didn't know? Did he just assume all pro athletes must use drugs once in a while? Had someone dared him to do it? We were out of that place in about 30 seconds and we haven't been back since.

"There are people like that out there," Posada has said. "You don't always know what people want or what they're going to do. I know it took us a long time to go out again after that. That shakes you up a little."

That's why it's so important to be secure in whom you are with and where you are going. And don't ever be afraid to hurt someone's feelings. Obviously, we didn't know this guy. But if that guy had been a friend of a friend and he offered us pills, I wouldn't have laughed and I would have left the place just as quickly. Remember, you've got to answer to yourself and do what is natural for you. Using pills might be normal for some and they might insist that it's not a big deal. My advice is not to become one of those people, because it is a big deal.

Unfortunately, I found myself in a similar situation when Tino Martinez and I went out in Baltimore not too long ago. Even though I didn't fully comprehend it at the time, this was another instance when I had to be acutely aware of my surroundings so I wouldn't do anything foolish.

We were in the middle of a crowded club sipping drinks when a man came up to Tino and me and asked Tino if we had any candy. Tino said no. We were thinking to ourselves that it was a strange question. He shook his head, muttered something and seemed disappointed. He hung around so I was much more wary of him, sort of watching him as he watched us.

Then he leaned back into our conversation. Like I said, I don't try to mess with people who get real close to me. You never know whom you're dealing with, so I try to be polite and then move on. I asked Tino if he had any gum or mints to give this guy and

Tino, just as befuddled as me, said that he didn't. The guy stomped off.

It wasn't until he left and we had thought about it that we realized the guy was probably referring to cocaine, which is also called nose candy. He must have thought we were uninterested or clueless, which is fine with me because both of us *are* uninterested in coke and clueless about it. And if being clueless means I'm a nerd for not knowing that he was talking about cocaine when he mentioned candy, I'll be a nerd the rest of my life.

Once again, I guess this guy figured that he saw two professional athletes and might be able to interest us in coke or at least find some for himself. I didn't stay in that place long enough to count to 60 after that, either. You've got to be comfortable about where you are, and that place felt strange after that incident.

Tino and I tease each other about that night. I'll ask him if he has any candy and he'll tell me he'll try to get me some gum. We're joking about the bizarre nature of the situation, not the actual situation. That was not a position I wanted to be in. That was serious. In fact, it was dangerous.

But I think part of the reason Tino and I bring it up is just to remind ourselves about staying alert. We can all do that and should do that. It's not hard. Our parents told us from the time we were toddlers not to accept anything from strangers, and, as these stories illustrate in a revealing fashion, that adage is always true. I don't even accept a drink if someone offers it to me in a club. I have to be careful with that.

I've always felt that way. In my position, I don't want to take something from someone because then they might feel like I owe them something. I think that's a logical approach. It's nice for someone to try to give you a gift, and most of the time I'm sure people are genuine.

But, for the times when someone isn't sincere and is hoping that gesture will enable them to move closer to me and extract something from me, that's not worth the complications. It's sad that I have to act that way because there are dedicated fans who just want to show their appreciation, but I've thought this out before these situations ever occur and that's the way I have to deal with it.

All you have to do is lose your senses one time and it could be damaging. All I would have had to do is scoop up the pills from that first guy or tell the second guy that I wanted candy and I could have disrupted all that I've worked for since I was a kid. But I thought about what was going on before I acted, and I made the rational decisions. Then I left both places. I didn't put myself in a position to be near drugs or people who are dabbling with them. You can do the same. It's up to you to think about what you're about to do. Make the shrewd choice and then act.

Life Is a Daily Challenge

know that I live in a fantasy world. I'll make $10 million this year to play baseball. Ten million dollars to play a sport I've always loved playing. I know I have a wonderful job. I have someone who pays my bills, invests my money, and pays my taxes, so I never even see my paychecks. I don't even know what that much money looks like. I actually prefer it that way. It's less of a temptation, less of a distraction.

I don't live in the real world. I understand that and I think the quicker that professional athletes understand that, the better off we are. Our lives are not normal. The best way for me to view my status is to consider all of the off-the-field stuff fake and not take it seriously.

I don't think that because I play for the Yankees and make millions that I'm better than someone who carries my suitcase onto an airplane or someone who picks up my dry cleaning. That's a weak attitude for anyone to have. If you ever feel that way, you need to reevaluate yourself and your priorities.

You can't let career or monetary success spoil you, whether you're making a million or you're making $50,000. You can't let the size of your salary change you. I try to be the same person I was before people started recognizing me. I'd still act the same way if I never played another game for the Yankees. I might be able to be more adventurous in public because no one would care about what I did. The sight of me hanging out in a bar with a few friends wouldn't be newsworthy if I wasn't a Yankee. Unless I did something amazingly stupid—and I wouldn't let that happen, even if I wasn't a major leaguer. I'd be me, this me.

Every day is another challenge, no matter who you are and no matter how successful you are. Each day we are faced with different obstacles and questions and we define ourselves as people by how we make those decisions. Believe me, if I was a doctor instead of a Yankee, I'd still be very cautious in the way that I lead my life. I'd still be careful whom I surrounded myself with, I'd still try to stay out of trouble, and I'd still have good morals. The protective wall that I build around me might be slightly thinner, but it would still be in place.

My father's mother was a smart and caring woman from Alabama who used to clean houses and work in school cafeterias for modest pay. She had a saying she would use with my father all the time: "If things are going so good for you that you think it's too good to be true, you better start running." My grandma meant that if everything was so perfect that you couldn't believe your good fortune, you'd better study the situation closely and not get too comfortable with where you were, because the smooth ride could turn into a bumpy ride before you could spell the word *pothole.*

My father repeated those words to me so much as a kid and still says them often enough to me today that I can enunciate them before he does. I know he says it to keep me grounded, and I respect that and expect it.

Be careful. Be smart. Don't take things for granted. You know what? That still makes sense for me, and I think it makes sense for everyone. Regardless of whether you're an architect or an actuary, I think this message is valuable for anyone to continue to grow as a person and not get blinded by their own success.

I've thought a lot about what my grandmother meant by this saying, and I've interpreted it to mean that you have to be prepared for anything. Don't shut yourself out and rest on your laurels because you did well on one test. Remember that an excellent score on a test guarantees you nothing on the next test. Don't hesitate to continue putting money on a stock if you're making money, but remember that your best day in the market could be followed by your worst day. Be prepared to react to any kind of development, good or bad.

With all of the phenomenal experiences I've enjoyed since the Yankees drafted me in 1992, and having things as good as I do, if I followed my grandma's words, I'd be halfway around the world now, running from my too-good-to-be-true life. In fact, I'd be running seven days a week. Maybe I'm due for some negatives. Seriously, I don't think that way. I love being a positive person, so, although I stay focused and don't take things for granted, I don't sit around waiting for something bad to happen. That's unhealthy. I think you have to accept the fact that there are going to be new challenges for you every day and then go into that day believing that you can overcome them. It works both ways. Bad days can follow good days—and vice versa. If you falter on Monday, have the attitude that you'll thrive on Tuesday.

I think we can all learn something from my grandma's simple message. You should think about your life and where you are going every day. Maybe one day you'll feel that your life is perfect. You're in love or you received a major raise or you won a pivotal game. That's great. You deserve to feel good about what you've done—but don't live in those moments or take them for granted.

Conversely, if things aren't going well in your life, that doesn't mean that you should give up and believe that the next day is going to be just as gloomy. If I had taken that defeatist attitude when I was struggling in Rookie League, who knows whether I'd be here now? You have to stay consistent in your approach to life. I'm not saying that you should be afraid to take chances, because taking calculated risks can be one of the most rewarding parts of life. I'm just saying don't get too giddy when life is going well and don't get too depressed when your life is not going as well as you'd like it to. Like my grandmother used to imply to my father, and he to me, be suspicious if everything seems too perfect, and be prepared. The challenges that life provides never fade away.

Now this doesn't mean that you should stifle yourself and refuse to enjoy your success. Absolutely not. When we win World Series titles, I drink champagne with everyone from Joe Torre to Jorge Posada to the fans, I go out in New York and celebrate with my teammates, and I soak up the entire experience. I could still describe how it felt after each World Series we've won. It's like I have those awesome feelings on permanent recall, available whenever I need a mental boost. They'll always be there.

But don't let your past achievements, no matter how significant they may be, obscure the visions and goals you still have. There is always more that you can achieve in life. I don't think I'll ever get too comfortable with my existence. No matter how high my batting average is or how many awards I win or how many times the Yankees win the World Series, I won't put my life on cruise control. I won't ever forget what it took to get to this point, and, just as important, what it takes to stay here. I've never been a person who allows himself to get too comfortable. We have to inspire ourselves and we have to want to be better people, better friends, and better workers. You've only got one life, so you should be proud of what you do.

Look, Listen, and Learn

A lot of people I've met think my life is a breeze. I've had people tell me that I've got a perfect life, something that I know obviously isn't true. By no stretch of the imagination is my life perfect. I know there are people who don't know me who think that my biggest decision of the day is where I'm going to eat dinner, which woman I'm going to ask on a date, and which new bat I'm going to hit with. I'm telling you that no one's life is that easy, including mine.

People ask me what I worry about. Do you worry about hitting .300? Do you worry about making errors? Do you worry about getting hurt? I don't worry about any of those things. I worry about whom I'm going to marry. I'm serious. I'm sure there are people who think this is laughable because I've dated Mariah Carey and other beautiful women and I hang out in Manhattan and could meet a lot of women when I choose to, but I'm serious about this concern.

I do worry about whom I'm going to spend the rest of my life with, whom I'm going to have kids with, and who is going to become the most important person in my life. I haven't found that person yet, and to be honest I think it's natural to be worried.

I do know that the woman I eventually decide to spend the rest of my life with is going to have to be independent. It's a long base-ball season and I'd want her to have her own interests so that she's more than Mrs. Derek Jeter. When will I find that person? I don't know, but that's ample evidence that my life isn't perfect. I see how happy Mom and Dad have made each other and I know they wouldn't be the same without each other, so I don't think my life will be complete until I get married.

I know it irritates my parents when someone talks about my being perfect and having this perfect life. They think that anyone who says I have a perfect life is undermining what I've done to succeed in life.

"When I hear the word 'perfect,' it's like that fame has just been laid out for him and it happened," my father has said. "It's like he stumbled into this perfect life. He got on *Who Wants to Be*

Baseball meant so much to me as a teenager, and it still does now. I know how fortunate I am to be living my dream, and I won't do anything stupid to make it all fall apart.

a Millionaire and he won a million. When people say he's perfect, they don't understand the trials and tribulations Derek had growing up in a biracial family. Some of the rejection he felt from people who weren't willing to give him a chance, not being accepted on certain levels when he was younger, and the struggling with his career early on. People don't realize it's not like Derek just walked off the plane and was part of a championship team."

I also know that most people forget or don't realize that I'm eight and a half years removed from being a 17-year-old with a severely sprained ankle who wondered if his dream of being a major leaguer had ended. Wondered if it had ended before his senior year in baseball was two weeks old.

We were playing Portage Central on a damp and snowy day at the beginning of the 1992 season. It was a typical April day in Michigan, the kind of day where the cold seeps underneath your uniform to chill you and where your hands feel like giant toothaches when your bat makes contact with the ball. Despite that, we were squeezing in two games. There were 40 scouts there on that day because Portage's Ryan Topham was another prospect, so there's no way these games would be postponed. I think we would have played through a blizzard.

I tapped a slow roller during the second game and hustled down the soggy baseline, trying to beat it out for an infield hit. I touched the slippery base off center and rolled my ankle. I immediately felt a stabbing pain and started hopping up and down. I didn't have control of my foot because of the slick base and my ankle felt awful.

I was afraid to touch my ankle or look at it because I was scared that it might be broken. I draped my arm around my father's shoulders as he helped me to the car. All the fans were quiet, which scared me some more. Everybody knew that I was in excruciating

I was lucky I never hurt myself skiing—I hated missing baseball games for any reason. Here I am in my Yankees jacket on the slopes at age 12.

pain. My friend, Doug Biro, had just arrived at the game as I got hurt, and I remember him rushing over to me and asking me what he could do to help. I stared at him and couldn't even muster an answer.

"I looked at Derek and he was in a state of shock," Doug said later. "Everyone there was in a state of shock."

I had already ripped three homers in my first nine at bats of the season and there was speculation I would be the top high school player drafted, so the timing was terrible. Plus, it happened in front of 40 scouts. After I found that the ankle wasn't broken, I was still concerned because doctors told me I'd probably miss between six and eight weeks of play. That's most of the season. I knew I'd make it back sooner. I had to come back sooner, I told myself.

I returned as a designated hitter after missing just three games. I wore an ankle brace and high-top cleats, but I was convinced I had to play. I was worried about dropping in the draft, and I wanted scouts to be able to see me back on the field. In retrospect, I shouldn't have returned so quickly. It was dangerous. Besides, most teams had been scouting me since my junior year and knew my skill level.

Still, I missed playing and I was worried about my future. I hobbled for most of the rest of the season, but I wound up hitting .508. I only managed one homer in my next 50 at bats, and I didn't have much speed. But playing baseball again was an amazing relief after those initial days of uncertainty, no matter how much my ankle hurt.

That incident frightened me and taught me how quickly good things can end. You can have everything going for you—and then it's over. You never know what's going to happen.

We're not guaranteed tomorrow, so we had better enjoy today. I tell myself that constantly, and that attitude is appropriate for a 65-year-old engineer, a 38-year-old housewife, or a 15-year-old skateboarder. You should want to make something out of each day and take something out of each day.

I go into every day hoping that I'll learn something new. I'm not saying that I stumble out of bed and pick up *The New York Times* or flip on CNN and try to immediately get smarter. No, I have to eat some cereal first and open up my eyes. But as the day progresses I know there'll be situations I'll encounter where I can learn something. I'm not even specifically talking about baseball, although there are always things I can learn in baseball. I'm talking about life. You can learn so much if you want to. I love to listen to people because I think that's one of the best ways to learn about the world around you. You don't have to be a shortstop for the Yankees to be a good listener and an avid learner.

We should all want to continue learning, because no one knows all they need to know or all they should want to know about life. If you don't learn something every day, I don't think you have enough passion for life. You can learn from people you meet and you can learn from what people say. I've had people tell me they saw the polite way I treated an aggressive person in a restaurant and that taught them about patience. Someone might tell you they were impressed with the way you waited and held the door for an elderly person and it made them aware of doing that the next time they had a chance. Or maybe someone won't actually say anything, but that doesn't mean your actions failed to influence them, just like their actions can influence you.

You can learn so much from listening, watching, and asking questions. I still do that with people I've just met and friends I've known for years. Even if I'm dealing with a person whose opinions I disagree with, I'll look into his eyes and I'll never interrupt him when he's speaking. My parents taught me to do that when I started elementary school as a way of showing respect. I don't think enough people listen well or show enough respect. Listen better and display more respect for people, and see how much smarter and gracious you will become.

Think Positive

I flew from Tampa to New York with David Cone a few years ago, and I used those three hours to pick his brain. I wish I'd had a tape recorder to save some of his thoughts, because he is a player I respect, a player who is honest, and a player who has had a plethora of learning experiences in the big leagues. Coney won't sugarcoat any answers, not about himself, about me, or about anyone else.

There's no one like Coney. I mean, this guy is an ambassador for the game of baseball. He's a tremendous pitcher and competitor, he's intelligent, he's one of the most respected players in our clubhouse, and he's great in dealing with the news media. Coney thoroughly enjoys the give-and-take with reporters, and I know he does some of it to take the pressure off of the players who are not as comfortable as he is in talking to the media. Some of us owe him for that.

Coney is the only guy I know who could put shoe polish around the inside of a teammate's cap and act dumbfounded when the player's forehead turns black, and a few minutes later receive a telephone call from President Clinton and sound as eloquent as anyone. He can adjust to any situation, whether it's bawdy clubhouse humor or a serious speech at a formal dinner. I always joke around and tell him that he could be the next commissioner of baseball if he ever wanted to do it.

I remember I had one probing question for him during that flight we took. I asked him that if he could give me advice about one thing, whether it was on or off the field, what would it be? He told me that I should continue doing what I had been doing and to stay clean off the field. He told me to continue to be careful because my reputation as a rising player was being established, but all it would take is one incident, one stupid decision, for it to disintegrate.

Then Coney talked about some of the situations he had encountered while he was on the Mets in the late 1980s. They were a veteran team that liked to party and prided themselves on winning and returning to the hotel bar and taking over the place. There would be 15 Mets drinking, shouting, and bonding, like a bunch of overaged frat boys. This was a double-edged sword because, while those players were tight on and off the field, Coney conceded that there were several times when they made immature choices.

I listened to every word Coney said, pretty much hanging across my seat to hear him. When he gets churning, his green eyes bulge while he's making points. He's a player who loves playing in New York and has thrived on it, but he's had some good times and some bad times and he'll be the first to admit it. If I've got a question, he's the first player I'll go to. I trust him and I know he'll be candid.

When Coney talked about remaining careful, I admitted that it's tough to always be cautious. Everyone is human and we all want to have fun. I just know there are lines that I refuse to cross. Coney nodded when I told him that, the nod of a man who has been on both sides of that line.

"There's never a worry about Derek," Cone told a reporter. "Even though he's a young, famous player who lives in Manhattan and goes out on occasion, I've never seen him out of control. He handles himself so well in public."

I've been in situations where I've questioned myself for what I might have said or done around someone, and I've occasionally wondered if I'd put myself in a ticklish spot by being in a particular place. Thankfully, I haven't made any significant mistakes. Not to this point anyway, but I'm aware of how Darryl Strawberry and Dwight Gooden used drugs and nearly destroyed themselves when they were young and successful in New York, and that's another reason why I'm always on guard. I don't drink too often, so that helps me keep my wits. I would never go out and drink a lot because it clouds your thinking. I can't let that happen. I've come too far in my career to disrupt it.

I always have to know whom I'm surrounded by and what is happening around me. When you drink too much, you usually don't make rational decisions. I might do something that I would regret.

I don't think I've missed a whole lot by never being drunk in public. As much fun as you think you might have while you're drinking with your friends, you're also risking putting yourself and them in a bad situation. Our lives are about making important decisions every day, and you make sharper decisions when you're sober. There's nothing wrong with having fun, but I think there's something wrong with getting so incoherent that you're not true to yourself. I don't have a crystal ball, so I can't predict what I'll do on the field or how long I'll play, although I'd like to play another 10 or 15 years. I can't say that I won't make any mistakes, because everyone does. But I can unequivocally tell you that my morals and my values won't change in the next week or the next 20 years. That's something I control and something I know won't change.

I know that everyone is human and everyone likes to party. But, think back to the nights where you might have made choices that you regretted. How long did that bother you? Usually, the price for one night of fun isn't worth the damage it could cause later. That's one more thing I've learned by watching others and listening to them when they talk about hasty decisions. I know it's a challenge to leave a party in high school when everyone seems to be having fun, but I did that because I didn't want to mess myself up. I knew what my goals were and I knew what would help them and hinder them.

One of the best ways for dealing with any challenge is by always being positive. It might sound simple, but it's hard for some people to simply focus on positives. Too many people focus on negative things and what's gone wrong or what could go wrong. They worry more about what they don't have instead of focusing on what they do have.

People who are faced with obstacles should focus on the good things they can do and the positive way they can get around the obstacles. Don't focus on what the negatives might be and what you think the negatives could do to you, because you can always find a positive in any situation. If someone closes a door, work hard at finding another door.

I do that all the time with the Yankees. The second after we lose a game, I tell myself to forget about it. The circumstances could be dire, but I don't dwell in the past. We trailed the Cleveland Indians, 2–1, in the best four out of seven American League Championship Series in 1998, and there was a little bit of tension around our team for the first time in an incomparable season. We were expected to destroy opponents that October because we had won 114 regular-season games and now we were behind, two losses from seeing our season die.

Still, I was confident. This was fun. This was what we were supposed to be playing for, wasn't it? I spotted Mr. Torre sitting, stoically as always, in the first-base dugout at Jacobs Field a couple of hours before Game 4.

I walked up to him, stuck my finger in his chest, and said, "Mr. Torre, this is one of the biggest games you've ever managed in." His blank expression changed and his face opened into a wide smile. That was my way of showing that we were still playing the same game we had dominated all season and that we were still the better team. I was thinking positive, and of course we won that night and never lost again in that postseason. I'm not insinuating that my comment to Mr. Torre had anything to do with our winning. I am saying that I was relaxed because I was positive that we'd meet those challenges. And we did.

I learn a lot from watching what other people do. Everyone is going to make mistakes, but you can learn from those mistakes. You don't have to just learn from your own mistakes. You can learn from other people's mistakes. I try to do that often, even if some of the mistakes that we all can learn from do make me cringe.

Stay Out of Trouble

It would be refreshing if every sports story that was on television or in the newspapers simply dealt with the final score, the action on the field, and the different personalities. Of course, that would mean we were living in some kind of fairy tale, because that would happen only if all athletes walked a straight line and didn't make terrible choices. Unfortunately, that's not always the case.

I watch television all the time. It's always turned on when I'm home, even if it's just on as background noise. Most of the time I'll watch ESPN, because I want to get scores and I want to hear if anyone has been traded or injured. I'm not just talking about baseball. I played baseball, basketball, and soccer while I was growing up and I even briefly tried football and tennis, so I like to know what is going on in every sport. I'm a fan, too.

But, lately, it's hard to go more than a couple of days where there isn't a negative story about an athlete flashing across the TV screen or landing in the newspaper. Whenever one of these stories is on the news, my father will call to talk to me about it.

Anytime an athlete makes a serious mistake and my father reads about it or hears about it, he mentions it to me. It is a learning device my parents have used since I was in elementary school. If they felt there was a real-life situation that would benefit me, they would pounce on it and we would discuss it as a family. You can't offer kids better lessons than the real-life lessons that unravel in front of them.

When I was in the eighth grade, there was a very good basketball player at Kalamazoo Central, the school I so desperately wanted to attend, who was caught with marijuana and was suspended for the entire season. I remember how talented this player was, and I remember feeling upset that he had wasted his senior year. All because he wanted to smoke a joint. I'd go crazy if I couldn't play baseball for a month, never mind a whole year, and my parents knew that. By talking about the mistake this guy had made, my parents knew they were reinforcing to me how important it is to make intelligent choices.

I know when my father grabs on to the latest headlines he is reiterating everything we have discussed for years. My parents seize every chance to remind me about making good decisions, about surrounding myself with good people, and about taking care of myself. My father might preface his words by saying, "You can do with this what you want, but I want to let you know that I don't agree with you going there," or "You're an adult. Do what you want, but your mother and I feel you should do it this way." I always listen. Even if I have heard these words a billion times, I listen because it doesn't hurt to hear them again.

Athletes and celebrities—people who are making a lot of money and have what look to be great lives—can lose all of it in a minute by making poor choices. It's a daily challenge for all of us, celebrities or not, to stay out of trouble. If I make a mistake, it'll be on the news. If you make a mistake, it may or may not be reported on the news, but that doesn't make it any less serious. So be positive and make positive choices. It's the only way to deal with the daily challenge.

I think too many celebrities get caught up in this celebrity lifestyle, thinking that they are bigger than everyone and that they can do whatever they want. It's obvious that the coddling we get has an impact on the way a lot of celebrities behave. I know it's easy to lose your perspective and think you're infallible when you're making seven-figure salaries and people are begging to be around you. Hey, what can they do to me? That's what some people think. But, make the wrong choice and you'll see what could happen to you.

Sometimes, celebrities lose all sense of reality because our lives play out like fantasy worlds. We're on TV, we make millions, people are anxious to meet us. At times it's easy to think that if you're a celebrity, you're larger than life. There are ways that we are treated in society, preferentially treated, that make some of us think we can go out and do whatever we want and get away with it. But that's not true.

My parents always remind me there's a real world out there. Just because I'm an athlete, it doesn't mean I can do anything I want and not be accountable for my actions. Just because you reach a certain status in life doesn't mean the laws don't apply to you. I know they apply to me. It took me a long time to get to this point in my life and I know that if I do one stupid thing, it could all be gone. I'm no different from you. We all have to abide by laws.

It seems like more celebrities are messing up these days, getting in trouble with the law. I don't know why this happens, but it shouldn't. We should feel honored to be in the position we're in. This is such a rare opportunity and it doesn't last long. Sometimes, it's bleak when people treat their careers and other people the way they treat rental cars. It's sad when another arrest is treated like ho-hum.

These unfortunate examples make it more difficult for children to find role models. I believe in being a role model. I know I'm not immune to making mistakes and I'm sure I'll make my share of them in the future, but I do try to set a good example. I think anyone who says they're not a role model doesn't get it. If you play pro sports, you're automatically a role model. You can talk for hours about how kids should view their parents as role models and that's true. But, when you're in the public eye and you're on TV, you're going to be a role model. You're going to have kids looking up to you and trying to emulate you.

Once you admit you're in that position as a celebrity, you should try to have a positive impact on children. You can shy away from your responsibility as much as you want, but kids are going to look up to you. We shouldn't forget that young kids are impressionable and we can do so much for them by preaching about the importance of education and a healthy lifestyle. It's not only how we behave on the field that should impress kids, but off the field, too. That's more important.

I'll hear people say that because I'm earning $10 million a year, that enables me to have a great life. Obviously, it's comforting to know I can take care of my family financially, but it doesn't make me a better person. I make myself a better person. The money doesn't.

Every day, there are people who see you, who see the way you behave, and who know what kind of person you are. They don't stare at your bank statements to figure out whether or not you're a good person. That has nothing to do with it. That goes for me and for you. We're not defined by how much we make. We're defined by our actions, good and bad.

Everyone likes to be liked. A lot of times people have a certain perception of you before they even meet you and it's not accurate. Some people say I'm cocky. I don't understand that description. The people who say that don't know me. I don't like talking about myself and I don't do backflips around the bases. I smile. I have a good time when I'm playing. If people think I'm cocky because I'm smiling when I'm playing baseball, that's a faulty perception.

I've had hours of discussions with Alex Rodriguez about life and about getting better as a person and a player. There aren't too many people whom I can talk to who understand exactly what I'm going through, but Alex is one of them because he's going through the same experiences.

We talk about so many different topics that, half the time, we

I was the sixth pick overall in the baseball draft, just a 17-year-old high school shortstop who had to decide whether to go to college or try my best at making it to the major leagues.

First-round selections

No. Team	Name	Amateur team	Pos.
1. Houston	Phil Nevin	Fullerton State	3B
2. Cleveland	Paul Shuey	North Carolina	RHP
3. Montreal	B.J. Wallace	Mississippi State	LHP
4. Baltimore	Jeffrey Hammonds	Stanford	OF
5. Cincinnati	Chad Mattola	Central Florida	OF
6. N.Y. Yankees	Derek Jeter	Kalamazoo Central HS	SS
7. San Francisco	Calvin Murray	Texas	OF
8. California	Pete Janicki	UCLA	RHP
9. N.Y. Mets	Preston Wilson	Bamberg (S.C.) Ehrhardt HS	OF
10. Kansas City	Michael Tucker	Longwood (Va.) College	SS
11. Chi. Cubs	Derek Wallace	Pepperdine	RHP
12. Milwaukee	Kenny Felder	Florida State	OF
13. Philadelphia	Chad McConnell	Creighton	OF
14. Seattle	Ron Villone	Massachusetts	LHP
15. St. Louis	Sean Lowe	Arizona State	RHP
16. Detroit	Rick Greene	Louisiana State	RHP
17. Kansas City	Jim Pittsley	DuBois (Pa.) Area HS	RHP
18. N.Y. Mets	Christopher Roberts	Florida State	LHP
19. Toronto	Shannon Stewart	Southridge (Fla.) HS	OF
20. Oakland	Benji Grigsby	San Diego State	RHP
21. Atlanta	Jamie Arnold	Osceola (Fla.) HS	RHP
22. Texas	Rick Helling	Stanford	RHP
23. Pittsburgh	Jason Kendall	Torrance (Calif.) HS	C
24. Chi. White Sox	Eddie Pearson	Bishop State (Ala.) JC	1B
25. Toronto	Todd Steverson	Arizona State	CF
26. Minnesota	Daniel Serafini	Serra HS, San Mateo, Calif.	LHP
27. Colorado	John Burke	Florida	RHP
28. Florida	Charles Johnson	Miami	C

■ The Colorado Rockies made the popular choice by taking Burke, who is from suburban Denver, in the first round. They signed him five hours afterward. Sources said Burke's signing bonus was about $300,000.
■ Wallace received a signing bonus of about $500,000. He was 8-3 with a 3.03 ERA this season.

probably don't even know we're helping each other out. He'll answer one of my questions about being out in a city you're not too familiar with, and three weeks later what he said will be in the back of my mind: "Oh, yeah—Alex said to be careful if you ever run into that kind of problem." It's a great friendship because we can learn from each other every day.

We both remind each other about how our careers, though successful, are only snapshots right now. We want to make them into full-sized posters. I'm in my fifth season and Alex is in his sixth, which might wind up being only a third of our careers, so we have to keep focusing on getting better. I know that one of the challenges I have is to do what the Winfields and the Ripkens did or are doing. Go out there every day for another decade. My father has told me that it would mean a lot to him if someone watched me in 2010 and I still hustled to first base on a grounder back to the pitcher. That sends a message about being a consistently great player.

It's flattering when people talk about me, Alex, and Nomar Garciaparra as perhaps being the three best shortstops to play simultaneously, but I think it's a little premature. None of us has played more than five seasons yet. There are lots of players who have had four or five solid years—and then you never hear another word about them. I don't want to be one of those guys. I've seen on the scoreboard at Yankee Stadium that my .318 average is the fifth-highest in team history, but the players who are ahead of me are Babe Ruth (.349), Lou Gehrig (.340), Earle Combs (.325), and Joe DiMaggio (.325), and they all played a dozen or more years. I've got a lot more playing to do to belong in the same sentence with them.

You want people to respect you for what you do, and part of earning that respect is to keep doing it, on and off the field. I'm like anyone else. I like to be liked. Once you get to know me, if you don't like me, that's fine. I try not to judge anyone until I get a chance to know him. Sometimes, I might be the only player signing autographs, and the fans will tell me that I'm the only nice Yankee. I stop signing for a moment and offer them a lesson right there. I tell them not to say that because they don't know what the other players have to do at that moment. If I were still working on my fielding and couldn't sign that day, they'd be dogging me. So I tell them that they're not always aware of the situation with other players, so they shouldn't make hasty judgments. That's true for you, too. Don't always assume the worst about someone who you think should have done something for you. Remember, if you're asking for a favor or a service, everyone deserves the benefit of the doubt.

I had an experience with one so-called fan that tested me last year. I was leaving a restaurant in Manhattan with Sean Twitty, and we were late for our next appointment. I was signing autographs as I walked toward the exit, but it was obvious that I was in a hurry. I probably signed 30 sheets of paper by the time we reached the door. Once I got there, I was done. One more fan saw me and asked me to sign for him and I told him that I couldn't.

"You're an asshole," he said, very loudly and in front of a lot of surprised people.

I stared at him, shook my head, and left. But you know what? That irritated me. For whatever reason, I couldn't get those remarks out of my head. I think most people would have forgotten about it, but I couldn't. Twitt kept telling me it wasn't worth my time. I tried to forget it and I couldn't. Why would someone say that? Someone who didn't even know me? As much as I'd advise you to ignore an ignorant person, this time I couldn't.

As fate would have it, Twitt and I were at another restaurant about a week later and I saw the same guy. I couldn't resist this opportunity, so I confronted him. He was surprised to see me and surprised that I even remembered him.

I was very direct. I asked him if he had ever considered that I had signed 30 autographs before he saw me that night and that I was in a hurry. He answered no to both questions. I told him that he was being selfish because I had already accommodated 30 people and he called me an asshole because I didn't do something for *him.* He apologized, lifting that burden I'd been inexplicably lugging around for a week.

I shook hands with him and had started walking away when he said, "Hey, could you sign this?" What would he have done if I said no this time? I don't know. I just signed it, hoping my message to him made it home with my signature.

One of the challenges for me is keeping my cool when I meet someone like this person. If I have one complaint about being a celebrity, it's the constant verbal criticism I receive from people who, I guess, think they're being funny. At the ballpark, I expect it. People pay for tickets and they want to boo you. That's fine. I don't always understand it, but I can live with getting badgered when I'm in my Yankee uniform.

It's away from the games where I get testy. I have heard just about any insult you could dream up. Please, don't imagine any more because I might get a headache. I've been called a pretty boy and a cover boy. I've been told that I stink and told I stink using much more graphic language than the word *stink*.

I've been told that I'm not as good a hitter as Nomar and not as talented as Alex. And I hear Rey Ordóñez's name mentioned to me so much when I'm out in Manhattan that I should probably change my middle name from Sanderson to Rey Ordóñez so I'll know when to respond. I've been in restaurants with friends and family, and people have shouted profanities from the bar to our table, 10, 50, or 100 feet away. It's uncomfortable for me and it's uncomfortable for the people I'm with because I've got to tell them to ignore it, too.

"Hey, Derek Jeter," one person yelled in my face while I was trying to eat one night. "Rey Ordóñez! Rey Ordóñez!"

That's all he shouted at me, the name of the Mets shortstop. So I said, "Thanks" and kept eating. You know, I'm not Mike Tyson, but I would love to be able to react to that. I feel like doing something, but I can't do anything. That's what people who antagonize you want you to do. They would love it if I confronted them or tried to get into a fight with them, and then I'd obviously wind up in more trouble than them. But I'm not going to lie about the verbal abuse away from the ballpark. There are times when I'd love to be able to do something or say something and just see how bold someone is then. But I don't. Basically, I can't.

It's critical for me to show restraint. I get a lot of attention with the Yankees and, like the other players, have to accept the fact that there are always going to be people who will want to harass me, tweak me, and try to rattle me. We're public figures, and there's a price that comes with having your face on television and getting paid handsomely to pay baseball. It's a weird part of the price, but it exists.

You might run into these same types of people in your life. The person who cuts into the long line at the Department of Motor Vehicles, and the person who smokes in the nonsmoking section of a restaurant. My advice is to closely measure the situation and decide whether a confrontation is worth it. Most of the time, it's not. For me, 999 times out of 1000, it's not. But not everyone has to deal with George Steinbrenner if someone ever tries to punch you. I do. George has a lot invested in me.

I think it takes a bigger man to walk away from a problem than to stay and fight about it. What would you gain from fighting? It's nothing but trouble. If someone wants to be an idiot and wants to get into a fight with you, don't give him the satisfaction. Just let it go. You'll feel better because you will have made the savvier decision.

Seriously, I believe in standing up for my rights. But I also believe in being logical. I just wish I didn't have to deal with imbeciles who think it's humorous to antagonize me when I'm out with people. That's insensitive. Hey, you learn something from every situation. Even negative ones. I've learned to have a thick skin, to have ears that I turn off on cue, and to know the easiest way to bolt from places.

The Yankee Tradition

It's obvious that some of the more taxing challenges I face are actually away from my job. When I'm on the field trying to get better as a player, that's exhilarating and I don't consider it a chore. It's after I leave the field and have to deal with the unpredictable demands and lack of privacy when things get sticky. But, on the field, I wouldn't change a thing about being a Yankee or playing with this team at this time. It's a real special time to be a Yankee.

From the first day you play for the Yankees, it's impossible not to think about the tradition and the mystique that surrounds this team. Twenty-five World Series titles, 36 American League pennants, the Team of the Century, and come on, let's be honest, no other team was even close. Take a walk through Monument Park at Yankee Stadium and the legendary names jump out at you like kernels in a popcorn machine—Ruth, Gehrig, Mantle, DiMaggio, Berra, Ford. . . .

Throw a dart at a map of the world, fly to the city where the dart lands, ask the first person you meet in that city who the Yankees are, and they will know. That's one of the magical things about being a Yankee. Everyone knows who you are, and everyone either loves you or wants to beat you. I love knowing that our team creates such passionate feelings.

I love that tradition. I love our pinstriped uniforms. I love our stadium. I love the fact that I've seen Yogi Berra, Don Mattingly, Goose Gossage, Mickey Rivers, Graig Nettles, Reggie Jackson, and the late Catfish Hunter working as instructors or just visiting during different spring trainings. If you can't feel the tradition with these legends around, you're in a coma. Especially with Yogi.

I've talked to Yogi and I've listened to Yogi. (There's my listen and learn advice again.) I'm envious of him. I got three World Series rings in my first four full years, a great run, but Yogi won 10 in 18 years. Think about that. Ten World Series rings. That's amazing, and it's nice and neat, one for each finger. I've joked with Yogi that I want to do that, too. I want to look like Liberace with all those rings on my fingers. I don't need a calculator to know that the current Yankees need many memorable seasons to get anywhere close to what Yogi's clubs did from 1946 to 1963.

But it's motivating to think about it. The game has changed dramatically with free agency, and it's difficult to keep teams together for extended periods. I mean, we could win our third straight title in 2000 and four of the last five, and to me that's got to be a modern-day dynasty. No one has won three straight titles since the Oakland Athletics did in 1972–1974. I'm hoping it happens again when I'm 26, which I turned this year.

I'm not brash or cocky enough to say that we're chasing Yogi's standard. Not yet anyway. We've got to win a few more Championships before we can whisper that possibility. But check back in a few years. If the Boss can keep our young nucleus together and keep us infused with fresh talent, we might have a chance at keeping this going. Hey, that's one reason I play. I want to be on a team that has a chance to win a Championship every year. As much as getting to the majors was my dream, winning while I'm here is a significant part of continuing that dream.

Once I made it to the Yankees, my goals naturally increased. We've had a taste of winning, so now I want to win every year. I don't care if someone thinks it's impossible, because I don't. I treat every day like a smaller piece of my personal and individual goals. What can I do today to get better as a player and a person? I don't need these thoughts stamped on my forehead when I look in the mirror. It's a way of life. Do something today to make yourself better.

Someone asked me what I wanted to accomplish by writing this book, and I said that I wanted people to believe that I'm a normal guy who had extraordinary dreams. I want you to believe that, because that will help you understand that my pursuits aren't any different from you chasing your goals. We're all people

who have visions. Different people, different dreams, and different outcomes.

I'm a shining example of making dreams happen. Big dreams, huge dreams, extraordinary dreams. I'm the same skinny kid from Kalamazoo who bounced a ball off the side of my house and swung a bat every day in my garage. I eat at fast-food restaurants, wear the same two pairs of sneakers, and constantly watch sporting events. But I overcame challenges. I made it to the majors and made it as the shortstop for the Yankees. You have to make sure that you don't treat your dreams like they are only dreams. You have to feel that they can become realities, too, or you will never think it's possible to attain them.

Believe me, I'm thankful every day that my dreams have unfolded. I think about what I have to do to improve, about how long my career might last, about where I've been, and about where I should be going. I keep myself motivated that way. Now, grab hold of *your* life and take it seriously. Face the challenges and work hard to do everything you want to do. That's what I did and what I'm still doing. You can't treat your life like a soiled T-shirt, not for one day.

About the Authors

DEREK JETER is the starting shortstop for the New York Yankees and is the founder of the Turn 2 Foundation. He divides his time between Tampa, Florida, and New York City.

JACK CURRY is a baseball columnist and reporter for the *New York Times*. He lives with his wife in New Jersey.